The Writer's Job

ROBERT C. COSBEY

University of Saskatchewan

SCOTT, FORESMAN AND COMPANY

This book is for June,
who knows why.

Introduction

In this book I have analyzed and described the job of the writer of expository prose, hoping thereby to make his work more orderly and more effective. I have in mind writers on many levels of thought and skill, faced with many kinds of writing problems, including the college freshman struggling with an impromptu theme in his classroom, the sophomore in the library inundated with printed materials for a term paper, the graduate student about to startle the world with Chapter One of his dissertation, the businessman compiling a speech or jotting down his ideas on community development for a local newspaper, the sociologist writing a report.

All these writers face the job of communicating through prose. Writing, in this sense, is not just something one learns in Freshman English. The Freshman English student is going to be facing the same basic problems of exposition long after he has left that class behind. What he will always need is an understanding of what exposition is and how the job of the expository writer must be tackled.

This book is based on the assumptions that all writers of expository prose have a common task, that the task can be reduced to a set of necessary steps, and that a detailed examination of those steps will help writers of exposition to operate more efficiently. For a quarter of a century I have been teaching composition to college students, using this approach, and for the same period I have been, in a modest way, a professional writer. I offer here what has proven most helpful to my students and most natural in my own writing.

One of the key doctrines of this approach is that writing must be considered as *communication,* not self-expression. (All writing is both, of course, but as long as the writer is concerned with self-expression, he is not likely to solve the problems of exposition.) The writer of exposition must consider that his goal is not eloquence but *efficiency,* not beauty but *utility.* How to get ideas from one human head into another human head with as little distortion, loss, friction, or static as possible—that is the writer's problem.

If he is fortunate, beauty will follow, as it sometimes does follow function, but the designers of the Yankee clippers were not trying for beauty, and neither is our writer.

Another important principle that must be made clear from the start is that the reader is boss. We judge everything by how well it serves the reader. Not that we intend to coddle him, but if we make him labor and stretch his mind, it will be the *ideas* he labors over, not the *expression* of those ideas. "Easy writing," said R. B. Sheridan, "is curst hard reading." We must prevent that kind of hard reading. Our job is communication, which means that an essay on paper is not a finished process, any more than a written play is, or the score of a piece of music. The final test is not what the essay looks like to the writer on paper, but what it is like in the head of the reader.

Because our job is communication, we intend to keep what is commonly called *grammar* in its place. After all, if a garage mechanic sends me a penciled scrawl saying "You car are redy and should pick up," and if in the same mail a college professor sends me a printed report beginning "Consideration of child guidance center principles in the interest of total child welfare comprehension is desirable," we shall not hesitate to say which of the two is really communicating. If the point of writing is to befuddle naïve readers with a show of erudition, the second passage is better than the first; but if language is for getting an idea from one head into another, the first passage is far superior.

Correct usage is largely a matter of social status, not communication. The man who says "I have none" feels superior to the one who says "I ain't got none"; and college professors savor their scorn of deans and businessmen who say "Our task is to quickly and cooperatively move to a solution of our problems." If I were to point out the errors in English usage to the garage mechanic and the professor quoted above, the professor would only be annoyed, but the mechanic would be ashamed. All of which has nothing whatever to do with communication but only with what is socially approved or disapproved.

Not that we can afford to be prejudiced *against* grammar. We must use good grammar, just as men must wear neckties when they go downtown, and hold doors for women, and write thank-you notes to their hostesses. We must also concede that correct grammar is usually necessary for accurate and precise expression. But we must not kid ourselves that mechanical correctness in itself constitutes or guarantees communication.

Take a writer who has a strong urge to get something said, show him what the process of communication involves, and he will pick up grammar and usage quickly along the way, just as he picks up the rules of bridge or poker or the cleaning of paintbrushes or how to use a city transit system. On the other hand, make a student study by rote the routes of a transit system in a city he has never seen and does not anticipate visiting, and you will have a learning situation much like that in which instructors try to teach grammar to students who do not yet have an urge to write.

Because our job is communication, we are not concerned with propaganda, in the sense of language used to deceive. In our time, language is used a great deal to hide meaning rather than reveal it. Politicians trying to sound forceful but be noncommittal, advertisers trying to distract attention from the shortcomings of a product, exam-writing students cramming bluebooks with windy phrases to conceal the fact that they don't know the answers—none of these is welcome here.

This train don't carry no ramblers,
No bull-slingers, no word-crammers,
This train is bound for clarity, this train.

This book assumes a writer who really wants to say something to a reader who really wants to know.

My high endeavor is to be useful to college students (both in and out of English classes), men and women in the professions, and indeed anyone who has to write. Whoever you are, I hope this book will help you tackle the job of the writer systematically. If we are both lucky, it will help you *read* better, too; for if you are familiar with the problems of writers, you can see more clearly what any given writer is doing.

Indeed, my secretly cherished ambition is to make you such a good reader that you will always recognize *bad* writing, wherever you see it. But that motive we keep hidden. The only avowed purpose of this book is to help solve the basic and eternal problems of those who communicate in prose.

Table of Contents

The
Writer's
Job

CHAPTER ONE

Dividing the Big Job into Little Ones

In twenty-five years of teaching, it has frequently been my duty to assign impromptu themes, either as in-class essays or as parts of examinations. I am always curious, in such situations, to see how students will *begin* to write. Most of them tackle the job inefficiently. Some sit and stare at the blank paper, unable to begin at all, then chew their pencils, glance around the room, squirm in their seats, and finally, having wasted almost the whole period, jot down a few desperate thoughts and flee. Some write a couple of pages and then scratch them out or crumple them up and start over again, and hand in unfinished essays with notes at the end saying "Not enough time!!!" Others, despite the fact that they have just seen the assignment and cannot possibly have had time to think about it, rush into their essays headlong, like swimmers rushing into cold water at the beach.

The blocked, the false starter, and the headlong—I see them everywhere, not only in classrooms, for in fact most writers fall into one or another of these patterns. So for most of us the first rule has to be this: Consider the writer's work as a methodical, orderly process. Take time to think over each project as a problem in writing. Whether you are writing a formal report, a term paper, a business letter, or a five-minute answer to an examination question, think it over as a problem in how to express yourself to a reader. (Yes, even in examinations, for the less time you have in which to work, the more important it is to work methodically.) Always do any writing job in three steps: first *see it,* then *let it out,* then *revise it.*

An essay—and I use the word *essay* as a convenience, meaning any complete piece of expository writing—reaches the eyes of its reader in a linear flow of words set one after another in print upon a page, just as a piece of music reaches the ears of the listener in a series of notes one after another. Somehow, the reader must be àble, from this linear flow, to comprehend a whole, though he can no more see the whole essay at once than a listener can hear a whole sonata at once. We make it possible for the reader to make sense of these flowing words by *grouping* them, so that the reader takes in clumps rather than single words. The clumps are of varying size: phrases, clauses, sentences, groups of sentences, paragraphs, and groups of paragraphs.

Not every reader is conscious of this clumping process, and not every writer uses the process consciously to get his ideas across to the reader. Just as an ignorant or careless or naïve listener hears a formless flow of sound in which musical phrases occur, so the reader often takes in words as a formless flow, catching phrases or sentences but not larger clumps. We must not be content, as writers, with this kind of reading, for it makes impossible anything but the simplest or vaguest kind of communication. We must encourage the reader—even *force* the reader—to see the larger clumps of words so that he can get the point and follow the thought of our essays. When we are speaking, we ask, "Do you follow me?" and if the answer is no, we try again, but in writing there is no second chance to explain ourselves; we must *make* the reader follow us.

Before we can make the reader see the progression of our thoughts, we must see it ourselves; in fact, before we start writing we must see the finished work shining in the air before us, all parts in place in the perfect whole. Edgar Allan Poe once said, speaking of the writing of short stories, that the first sentence must know what the last sentence will be. This is more urgently true of expository writing.

It's easy to demonstrate that good writers see their essays before they start writing. Consider the structure of the first paragraph of "The Transition to Humanity," page 177.

dialectic

[1]The question of the relationship of man to the other animals has been a persisting one in the human sciences. [2]Since Darwin, it has hardly been doubted that there is such a relationship. [3]But concerning its nature, and particularly its closeness, there has been very much more debate, not all of it enlightening. [4]Some students, especially those in the biological sciences—zoölogy, palaeontology, anatomy and physiology—have tended to stress the kinship between man and what we are pleased to call the lower animals. [5]They see evolution as a relatively unbroken flow of biological process, and they tend to view man as but one of the more interesting forms life has taken, along with dinosaurs, white mice and dolphins. [6]What strikes them is continuity, the pervasive unity of the organic world, the unconditioned generality of the principles in terms of which it is formed. [7]However, students in the social sciences—psychologists, sociologists, political scientists—while not denying man's animal nature have tended to view him as unique, as being different, as they often put it, not just in "degree" but in "kind." [8]Man is the toolmaking, the talking, the symbolizing animal. [9]Only he laughs; only he knows that we will die; only he disdains to mate with his mother and sister; only he contrives those visions of other worlds to live in which Santayana called religions, or bakes those mudpies of the mind which Cyril Connolly called art. [10]He has, the argument continues, not just mentality but consciousness, not just needs but values, not just fears but conscience, not just a past but a history. [11]Only he, it concludes in grand summation, has culture.

Sentence 1 states the subject of the whole essay: *the relationship of man to the other animals.* Sentences 2 and 3 state the subject of the paragraph: *a debate over the nature of this relationship.* Sentences 4 through 6 present one side of the debate: *the idea of man as part of a larger biological whole.* Sentences 7 through 11 present the other side of the debate: *the idea of man as separate and distinct from other animals.*

Could such an ordered structure have come about accidentally? Hardly likely, is it? And when we come, as we shall later, to examine how the author has forced the reader to see that sentences 4 through 6 are one unit, and 7 through 11 another unit, we must conclude without any doubt that the structure is deliberate. The lesson here, for beginning writers, is that Clifford Geertz has planned this paragraph before writing it.

Now look at sentences 2 and 3 of that first paragraph, and compare them with sentence 1 of the second paragraph—"The reconciliation of these two points of view has not been easy, particularly in a field such as anthropology, which, in the United States at least, has always had a foot in both camps"—and you'll see that the two paragraphs themselves represent clear and deliberate steps in thought: paragraph 1: *two theories about man in relation to the other animals;* paragraph 2: *the attempts of anthropologists to reconcile these two theories.* Without going on to analyze the whole essay, we can already see that the writer has worked it out, as a composer might work out a sonata, into a series of steps and that he had to know what those steps were before he could write.

Well, you say, that's all very well for a formal essay such as this, but how can the same be true of informal writing? Consider the piece from the *New York Times* called "A Funny Thing Happened on the Way to Antigua," page 124. Here the writer seems to be simply talking without planning—that's the tone of the informal essay—but appearances are deceptive. After two brief paragraphs on what an unlucky fellow he is comes a careful introductory paragraph in three steps: (1) We decided to go to Antigua; (2) I knew we'd never make it; (3) our defeat began with smudges on the wall. Then follows a step-by-step account, from smudges to termites, ending with all hopes of Antigua dashed. Notice the careful reminder in paragraph six that Antigua is the goal, and then ponder this question: Is it not true that our delight in this brief informal essay comes in part from precisely our awareness of *form,* from the careful way we are led along a series of steps, from the feeling we get as we read "It all started with finger smudges" that the writer knows exactly where he's going, has seen it as a whole and planned it all out?

In these examples the writer presumably had plenty of time for planning, but, paradoxically enough, if one is writing under pressure, the need for planning is all the greater. If you find yourself in a final examination with exactly seven minutes to comment on the causes of the Civil War, or the differences between Shakespearean and Petrarchan sonnets, or the second law of thermodynamics, you had better take two minutes to plan your answer or you'll be at a disadvantage competing with the student who does. Or if, later in life, you find yourself dictating a fairly long letter into a tape-recorder, you will have to make up your mind first what you want to say or you'll waste your time and that of your secretary.

The whole subject of *how* to plan a piece of writing in advance is so important that it must have a chapter to itself, so I'll say no more about it here. It's time now to anticipate an objection: It's all very well to talk about these people planning their essays when they have something to say, but how about the poor student with an assigned subject and nothing in the world to say about it?

"I don't appreciate your subjects!" a student once told me sternly after an examination in which she was asked to select one from five subjects and write an essay.

Two things must be said. First, it is a corrupt situation when anyone writes without having anything to say, for writing is a method of getting something said. There is nothing more deadly or more surely calculated to produce bad writing than forcing a student to write about something when he has nothing to say about it — unless it is the voluntary attempt by a writer to handle a subject of which he is ignorant. Teachers of composition are constantly faced with an awkward problem in this matter of subjects, and various ways of dealing with it have been tried. One of the worst, I think, is to give the student a collection of essays on various subjects — democracy, education, racial tensions, automation, conservation — in an attempt to drum up enough interest to motivate him to write on these subjects himself. Half-baked ideas resulting from shallow acquaintance with a subject can be expected to produce dreadful essays, as indeed they do. If the teacher of a composition class will take my advice, he'll never assign *subjects* at all, but only *problems*. ("Explain to someone outside your major field one of the basic concepts of your field" is a problem. "Define *evolution*" sets a subject.)

But there is another side to this question of having something to say. The author of "A Funny Thing Happened on the Way to Antigua," I assume, wrote that essay just because he felt like it, but few writers enjoy that luxury. The student taking an examination, the businessman dictating a letter, the reporter covering a story, the professional writer preparing an article, the scientist explaining his theory, all write because they have to. Not one of them writes because he just happens to feel like it; writing is part of their jobs. Writing is, as a matter of fact, hard work. I know very few people who like to write, though I know many who like to get things said. Usually writing is done as a job, whether the writer is a college student or not. Corruption comes not from writing on demand, but from writing when one has nothing to say.

Most writers have to prepare themselves to have something to say. In one degree or another, they first make themselves knowledgeable about a subject and then communicate what they know or have thought out. It's perfectly reasonable to ask college students to do this. What is a student doing studying history, for example, if he does not thereby acquire something to say about history? He cannot make himself an expert on democracy, or education, by reading three essays on the subject, but he can find out enough about a limited subject to have something to say, if he can use a library at all. The first step, then, whether the writer chooses the subject or is given it, is to know something about the subject.

It is true that students often find themselves being asked to write *impromptu* — to write about a subject without having time to find out about it or let it develop as an idea in their minds. The best advice I can give a student about to write an impromptu essay is this: Don't be satisfied with generalities. Pick the subject about which you can think of the most details, examples, illustrations; remember that you don't really have a subject if you can't give details. General statements are necessary parts of an essay, but they can not constitute an essay all by themselves. (See Chapter 4.) Thinking of details is as close as you can come to gathering material for an impromptu essay.

The second step in writing is to decide what you want to say about your subject. That's not always easy, for it means picking out of a whole amorphous subject some coherent statement. But easy or not, it's one of the most important steps in writing. (I like to tell my students that the more work they do *before* they set down the first sentence, the better they are writing.)

This step cannot be reduced to any formula, but it helps to keep some principles in mind. The most important is that writing is communication. What you decide to write is what you decide to *tell someone.* For this reason, it is often helpful to talk the subject over with someone beforehand. Try *telling* someone about it, and notice what he needs to be told in order to get the point, to understand. You will clarify your own thoughts by being forced to express them to him, and you'll learn something of the particular problem of communication which is involved in explaining this subject. What background or introductory information does he need? What examples or illustrations does he need? To tell somebody, and note his reactions, makes a useful preliminary to telling the same thing in writing to your reader.

Another helpful procedure, especially if you work alone, is to jot down unrelated thoughts and ideas on a sheet of paper—a scratch sheet—just as they come to you, and then look them over and decide which are primary, which are illustrative, how they can be arranged into a logical sequence, which must be eliminated as irrelevant, what gaps must be filled with more notes. The scratch sheet can be a most useful preliminary, especially to *blocked* writers, for anyone can jot down unrelated thoughts and notes on a subject if he knows anything about it. And it is easier to arrange thoughts when they are spelled out before you.

Finally, a rule of thumb, to serve at least until we return to this subject in Chapter 2. If what you are writing is no more than a few pages long, you should be able to make a shrewd guess at the number of paragraphs you will use and what will go into each of them. When you know not only the *subject* but the *structure* of your essay that well, you are ready to write.

Letting It Out

An unskilled writer tries to do everything at once; a skillful one takes the job step by step. After the process of selecting and organizing the material comes the process — the *luxury,* I should say — of just letting it out. This is not only a luxury for the writer but a great advantage for the reader, for it results in the smoothness, the sparkle, the personality of the writer being caught in print.

All art is based on paradox. One paradox of good expository writing is that it *appears* perfectly natural but *is* perfectly artificial, or constructed. We must separate the steps which achieve these different ends. After the careful planning, there must come a time of carefree expression, to be followed by careful revision.

Set your outline or scratch sheet before you for a guide, and then just write. Don't stop to look up anything — neither spelling nor grammar nor punctuation nor factual details. When in doubt, put a mark in the margin to come back to, and keep on going. This is the time to be headlong, as a bobsled rider can safely go headlong after the track has been carefully prepared, though it would have been suicide to try it sooner. If you can manage it, don't stop for the telephone or the doorbell. While the writing is flowing well, don't even stop for lunch.

"In writing," said Henry Thoreau, "conversation should be folded many times thick." To catch the spontaneity of good conversation, to catch not only the tone, the flow, but the excitement, the happy inspiration, the exact metaphor or analogy or example, the loaded phrase, the exact word, which spring to us when we are animated with our subject, is one of the chief aims of the writer of good expository prose. It's true, as Thoreau says, that conversation must be "folded," or condensed. But first it must be there.

A later chapter takes up in detail the question of style. But the deepest truth about style must be stated here. "The style is the man himself," said Buffon. Let it be the man at his best, in all the excitement and interest of his subject, for this excitement is contagious. There is no better safeguard against leaden, laborious, pompous style than the spontaneity of a writer who knows his subject, who has seen his essay, who is simply but delightedly getting it said.

It is true that there is value in false starts at times. If you have to rewrite the first paragraph three times, ringing it like a coin to judge if it *sounds* right, before you catch just the right tone, that's fine. That's very different from rewriting because you can't make up your mind what to say. But once the tone rings right, you must be off to the races.

A tension may develop between your outline and your spontaneous writing. If you let the subject pour out, you may find that it wants to go in a different direction, include different points, even reach different conclusions, than your outline. If the difference is unimportant, such as the shifting of position of two points, let the outline go, for outlines should not be strait jackets. But if you find yourself really at war with the outline, you're in trouble.

This is the point at which a kind of heroism is demanded of you. The basic purpose of writing is to get a subject into the head of a reader. You must be true to the subject and to the reader, at whatever cost to your outline or your ego. If the outline, on second thought and in the midst of writing, is seen to be inadequate, you must stop and think the subject out all over again. If the rush of enthusiasm has carried you away from the subject and the outline is truer to the job at hand, you must sacrifice any beautiful writing whatsoever to get back on the track, for your enthusiasm must be in the service of the particular job. At any cost, you must choose the best way of telling the truth about the subject to the reader. Resolve the differences, and get back to letting it out.

Revising the Essay

Beginners labor to get their thought into words and, having accomplished so much, they rest from their labors. If asked to try another way of saying it, they simply can't. They make a sentence the way they would make a brick, and they can no more revise a sentence than they could a brick. But the professional writer knows that his medium is fluid. When he has a first draft, his job has just nicely begun. Now he will work on his essay as a sculptor would work on a rough clay figure, shaping it nearer and nearer to a perfect realization of his subject.

A good example of the fluidity of prose in the hands of a master is shown in the essay "Thoreau at Work: the Writing of 'Ktaadn,'" page 247. If you have time, first go and read "Ktaadn" (it's the first section of Thoreau's book *The Maine Woods*), and then read the account of how he wrote it.

A briefer example, from the first draft of "Ktaadn," is a passage of the essay which would have appeared in print thus:

> "We at length drove into the scow used as a temporary ferry boat, which had now returned, and had already shoved off some rods when a tin pedlar appeared on the bank and hailed us, earnest to carry his cases still further into the woods. I disdained of ever searching the wilderness with him in company but the boatmen were fain to put back and take him in."   *Unpublished Journal*[1]

The passage appears in the first draft in this form:

~~was~~
"We at length drove into the scow ~~which is~~

which
used as a temporary ferry boat ~~with and~~ had

~~we~~
now returned and ~~the two boatmen~~ had already

shoved off some rods when a tin pedlar appeared

~~the boatmen~~
on the bank and hailed us ∧ earnest to carry

I disdained of ever searching the wilderness with him in
his cases still further into the woods —∧   company but

the boatmen
~~we~~ were fain to put back and take him in."

1. By courtesy of the Henry W. and Albert A. Berg Collection of the New York Public Library.

Notice the evidence that Thoreau did more than just correct this passage. First he wrote "scow which is used," then "scow which was used," then "scow used"—that group of words went through three forms in Thoreau's mind. "The two boatmen had" becomes "we had," which becomes simply "had." Notice also that as the passage was first written, a key idea was missing—the idea of Thoreau's reaction to this unexpected company—so a long addition is made, beginning "I disdained," to set that idea in the passage. Finally, after all these changes, the whole passage was crossed out. None of it appears in the final essay, for Thoreau had decided that the tin pedlar did not, after all, add to the basic point or theme of his essay.

Though it is true that good expository prose has the flow and swing of good conversation, it also has the advantages of second thoughts. It can be condensed, or "folded thick"; it can be made more smooth, precise, and clear than our thoughts are likely to be on first utterance. It can have the advantage of spontaneity and at the same time the advantage of careful reworking. Every writer will develop his own habits of revision, but there are some principles which ought to govern you while you are developing your habits:

1. Always work from larger units to smaller units. Start with the whole essay. Forget your original outline now. Read the essay through and ask whether the major blocks of statement are in the right order and the right proportion of size and emphasis. Ask yourself if all the major statements are needed or if you have any which, like Thoreau's tin pedlar, should be dropped as not helpful.

2. Be true to your subject, and forget your ego. Your essay will not bleed if you lop off part of it. Be heroic in defense of truth, not in defense of yourself as a clever writer. If your essay needs major surgery, take a pair of scissors and cut it up into sections so that you can rearrange them or discard some of them or insert something between two of them. Paste the parts onto separate clean sheets, so you'll be working with pages of regular size. If a new page comes between page 5 and page 6, call it 5A rather than renumbering all the subsequent pages. Above all, keep the process fluid until what you have to say is said right.

3. Once the large blocks of material are decided on, type up the whole essay in a working draft, triple-spaced, and revise it again. A professional writer will often work through several drafts this way, penciling in revisions which his secretary incorporates in a new typescript, and then revising that. Not all of us can afford the luxury of a secretary, and not every writing job is worth that much revision; but the more important the job is, the closer you should approximate this professional method.

Revise now for paragraph sense, sentence logic, exact diction, smoothness of style, clear transitions. Make your essay the clearest and most forceful communication of your subject that you can. The proper time to polish, notice, is after the blocks of material are decided on; you must go from large to small units or else risk polishing a paragraph you're not even going to retain. *How* do you revise? That's a skill you must learn — a skill which teachers of composition do not usually teach, although it is essential to good writing. A good deal of this book is devoted to developing that skill, as you'll see in the chapters on the paragraph, the sentence, etc.

Now is the time, too, for checking spelling, punctuation, grammar, and so on, and for looking up dates and other exact details. Pick up now the marginal notes you made to yourself during the first writing, and work them out.

4. Finally, when the working draft is as good as you can make it, put it away. Let it cool off as long as is practical before typing the final draft. While your head is full of your subject, it's easy to deceive yourself into thinking that you've captured it and expressed it on paper. When you come back to it cold, you can read it much more critically and catch errors or lapses you wouldn't have noticed before. After a final delayed check, you can type your essay and send it forth to your readers with some confidence.

The three-step process of writing which has been described in this chapter is an efficient process for any job of expository writing. If you have all the time you need to write a book, an article, or a term paper, do it this way. If you have just one week to write an essay, and a lot of other things to get done that week, approximate this method the best you can. Write the essay at the beginning of the week, but check it over and type it at the end. If you are writing a business letter or a six-minute essay answer in an examination, you still have time for the three necessary steps: plan, write, revise. You can still, even under this kind of pressure, go on to something else and then come back to what you have written for a final check. Whatever your writing job, you'll do it better if you acknowledge that it *is* a job, and if you see the job as necessitating an orderly three-step process of getting something said clearly and precisely for the benefit of a reader.

Exercises

"Assign problems, not subjects." Here are examples of problems which leave each student free to select his own subject.

1. In an essay of not more than 500 words, describe a person with whom you are familiar, in such a way as to answer the question "What kind of person is he?" Give illustrative details. Include biographical details such as place of birth, schooling, etc., only if they help answer the central question.

2. In an essay of not more than 500 words, comment on any event currently in the news. Draw your material from at least two different newspaper accounts of the same event. Clip out the newspaper stories and attach them to your essay so the teacher can judge how well you have selected and presented the evidence.

3. Describe in detail something you think is wrong with the school you attend. Suggest means of improvement. Be careful to choose a problem for which you can suggest a practical solution.

CHAPTER TWO

Seeing the Skeleton

An essay must have deliberate structure, for the benefit of both the reader and the writer. For if it is true that the reader needs to be guided through the subject in order to read well, it is equally true that the writer must have a previous overview of his essay in order to write well.

I once noticed, in the office of a publisher, a poster advertising a new textbook in elementary mathematics. The poster showed two ways of looking at a tree: first in full leaf and then completely leafless. The tree in full leaf is the final tree, as it were, the finished tree, the tree whole and living; but the leafless tree is also interesting, for when the leaves are removed, we can see the basic structure, the principle, as it were, of that tree. Similarly, the poster suggested, one can see the essence of a mathematical problem if the words, like the leaves, are removed and the problem is stated abstractly in mathematical symbols. It is equally helpful to a writer to comprehend his essay, that more or less complex statement he is about to make, by the use of some abstracting device which strips off words and sentences and shows only the skeleton.

The old-fashioned formal outline is one abstracting device for showing the skeleton, and anyone who habitually makes formal outlines before writing does not need to learn another device. But I have found reason to distrust the formal outline. First, it does not abstract enough — it includes too much detail. For a short piece of writing, it's too cumbersome; for a long one, it includes so much that the essay cannot be seen at a glance. I have found that teaching outlining is in one way like teaching formal grammar: there's little carry-over into writing habits. (In fact, when I was a young teacher I was distressed to find that almost all of my students were first writing their essays and then making outlines from them to hand in to me!)

Let me suggest another method of visualizing an essay (a simpler way of outlining, you may call it), which can be used for the shortest writing job or for long, complicated chapters, and which does actually become a useful part of the writing process.

We start by visualizing the whole essay as a set of boxes. In its simplest form, the system calls for one box for each paragraph of the body of a short essay and one offset box each for the opening and the close (regardless of whether or not these will be separate paragraphs).

Consider this purely abstract skeleton of an essay:

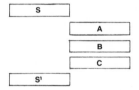

Here S is the opening, boxes A, B, and C are paragraphs of a brief essay, and S[1] is the close. (S, incidentally, stands for *subject,* and one value of the system is that it reminds the writer of the need for openings and closings and of their relationship to the rest of the essay.)

In this hypothetical essay, the writer will make three points about one subject. Perhaps he is giving three reasons for voting for his candidate. Perhaps he has a set of three necessary conditions leading to a conclusion ("If a man knows certain laws of probability, and if he plays only among friends, and if he can afford to lose, then it's all right for him to play stud poker"). Perhaps he is about to tell us the three vital steps in buying a car, or judging a play, or choosing a wife. Whatever his subject, the writer has first determined for himself that he wants to make three points about it, and he has then drawn for himself (either on paper or in his mind) the graphic representation of the essay he's about to write.

He has not, of course, set up the boxes first and then gone looking for three points. He started by brooding over his subject, talking about it, making scratch lists of things he might say, and finally he concluded that he had three basic points to make.

Let's assume that his subject was how to read poetry out loud to a group. (If that was his subject, he chose it because he was already pretty good at reading poems, and had given the matter of how to read them a good deal of thought, and had readers in mind who would want some tips on the process.) Perhaps he began with an almost absent-minded listing of incomplete and unrelated notes:

–Poems must be read out loud to "get" them
–"A Noiseless Patient Spider" vs. "To a Waterfowl"
–Take poetry seriously or don't bother—have to work at it
–Don't read for the lines—just read and let lines take care of themselves
–Poetry is the voice of beauty
–Poetry is not statement but feeling
–Literal meaning tied down first, then look for other levels
–Allusions—what to do about them
–"A person should not sound like a book."
–The time Sue recited "How Do I Love Thee?" & why class broke up
–First work out *meanings*
–Pitch voice to back of room
–Look up—eye contact impt.
–Sound should echo sense
–Project the poem, not yourself

After making such a list, the writer feels an understandable frustration, which is in one sense greater the better he knows the subject. Everything is part of everything else, and all are parts of an amorphous whole. He has not learned his subject as a neat, well-organized body of knowledge; he has accumulated it as a complex and largely unverbalized tangle of experience, example, habit, attitude, precept, perception, supposition, personal preference, and fact. About this largely nonverbal and unorganized "subject," he must now make a clear and coherent statement.

First, he broods over his scratch sheet, to see if he can begin pulling things together in groups. The second stage of his notes might look like this:

reading to the group	don't read for the lines person should not sound like book: Sue pitch voice to back of room eye contact
analysis of poem	literal meaning first allusions work out levels of meaning
from meaning *to proper reading*	poetry is feeling — examples here: sound should echo sense → "Spider" project poem, not self — "Waterfowl"
throw these out?	take poetry seriously poetry the voice of beauty

It is a help to a writer, at this point, to remember that he has a reader who wants to know something about the subject. With such a reader's needs in mind, the writer can begin to arrange his grouped notes, to see what they are good for and how they must be selected and ordered.

Another help for the writer at this point is to realize that he must so order his materials that he can see his own essay in advance. How many major points does he need? How many boxes will there be in his graphic representation? This he will decide by balancing out two factors.

First, what are the steps the reader will have to go through if he is really going to put the essay to work and read some poetry by the suggested method? Second, how close can the writer come, without distorting the subject and the process, to a set of no less than three nor more than five major headings?

Three, four, or *five.* Unless the subject really demands fewer headings, or more, it's an excellent rule to present your statement in three, four, or five steps. Most subjects are too complex to be handled all at once, with no divisions. A division into two headings is natural for some subjects, but too simple for most, and tends to monotony. A divison into three, four, or five headings gives room for dealing with complex subjects but does not present the reader with more points than he can keep in mind all at once.

It's no accident that so many folk tales, in all cultures, have been told in units of three parts: three brothers each in turn fighting the dragon, or three raids by Jack upon the giant's castle, or three wishes and their consequences. *Three* is a mystic and magic number, a number that balances the simple and the complex, a humanly satisfying number. *Four* is a familiar number, the number of the four winds and the four seasons — a good, solid, square number. (Why do we speak of the *four* points of the compass and the *four* seasons, out of the infinite number of points in the circle and in the natural year?) *Five* is the number of segments you see when you cut an apple in half and the number of fingers on a hand. "Nature loves the number five," as Emerson reminds us. *Three, four, five:* large enough to give a sense of fullness and development, small enough to be comprehended and remembered. Don't be pedantic about it; don't distort the subject to fit an arbitrary number. It takes more than five to encompass some subjects, such as the deadly sins. But stick to three, four, or five where you reasonably can, for your reader's sake.

This is not to suggest that the subject be simplified. On the contrary, the suggestion is that the *presentation* of the subject be simplified, which is all the more important the more complex or deep the subject. (We shall not accuse Beethoven of oversimplifying his music because his symphonies are presented in three or four movements.)

Our writer, having brooded over his subject with his reader's needs in mind, decides that the advice he has to give his reader logically falls, or can be seen as falling, into three parts: How to analyze a poem, to get the meaning; how to work out from the meaning the proper tone, pace, and emotional pitch; how to deliver the poem orally. Not an easy subject at all, you see, but it absolutely must be worked out in advance and focused around a few major points. Now the writer is ready to draw his set of boxes:

```
┌──────────────────┐
│        S         │   reading poems to group
└──────────────────┘
      ┌──────────────────┐
      │        A         │   analysis of poem
      └──────────────────┘
      ┌──────────────────┐
      │        B         │   sound from sense
      └──────────────────┘
         ┌──────────────────┐
         │        C         │   mechanics of delivery
         └──────────────────┘
┌──────────────────┐
│        S¹        │
└──────────────────┘
```

The order in which the major points will appear is determined, in this case, by the logic of chronology: the order of
steps in the process under examination. Many subjects do
not in themselves suggest an order; they must be *given* an
order, just as they must be *given* the division into a small
number of major points. Here, too, the reader's needs must
govern. It helps to remember that reading an essay should
be an experience, a discovery, even in some sense an adventure. Order should be dramatic. First *this,* then *this,* then
this happens (narrative, or chronological). Not *this,* not even
this, but THIS! (climactic). Concede *this,* then *this,* then
this, then see where you come out (inductive). *This* seems
true; *this* other challenges it; combining them with modifications brings us closer to truth (dialectic). Keep in mind
that your essay should be an adventure in discovery for the
reader, and order will not be a problem. The boxes will fall
into a meaningful A, B, C.

Of what advantage is it to the writer to abstract his essay
thus into a set of boxes? First, it's a guarantee to himself
that he's thought the subject out and knows what he wants
to say, *without having killed off spontaneity by working out all
the details in advance.*

Second, it forces him to consider order and proportion in
advance. Since the proposed essay on poetry will have only
three points, the proper order of which is easily decided,
there's no great problem here, but even in so simple an
essay it pays to consider such things in advance.

Third, it encourages him to remember the proper function of the parts and their relationship to each other. A, B,
and C are parallel but separate steps. A plus B plus C adds
up to S (a method of reading poetry). S and S¹ must establish and re-establish that subject.

The function of S, the opening, is to establish a subject, set a mood, catch the reader's interest, and possibly indicate how the subject will be developed in the essay. The function of S¹, the closing, is to leave the reader with the major idea or theme clearly in mind. The essay on poetry must not end with the idea that poetry is beautiful, or that Whitman is a great poet, or that too regular anapestic tetrameter is hard to read. It must leave the reader with the idea that he has just run though a system for reading poetry.

Will the conclusion have to be a separate paragraph? That's hard to say in advance. If the essay ends with the last step of a simple process, there's little danger of the reader forgetting the main idea. If the subject is complex and the essay long and the last section of the essay interesting in itself, then the reader does need a separate concluding paragraph to summarize and bring him back to the theme. We must decide entirely by estimate of the reader's needs as he comes to the end of the essay.

Seeing his essay as a set of boxes also reminds the writer of the points within the body of the essay where the reader will need particular kinds of help. When the writer goes from A to B, the reader must be taken along, must know what B will be and how it is related to A and to S. In the essay on reading poetry, the writer must find a way of saying, "Now that we've completed one step in the process of reading poems aloud, we turn to the second step, which is the working out of the way sound and sense are related in the poem in question." He won't say it just like that, for readers do not like to be reminded flat-footedly that they are being guided through a subject. But one way or another, that is the signal he must give the reader at this point, as his boxes serve to remind him.

To see an essay thus in advance is to provide a channel for the first draft. In writing a first draft, the writer must above all be free from having to stop to think about steps which could be considered before or after the first draft. Matters of style, the checking of factual details, mechanics of spelling, and other particular points are properly taken out of consideration in the writing of a first draft and held until later. Matters of structure and order are also properly eliminated, decided first, in order to make a framework or channel through which the writer's spontaneous thoughts can flow freely, uninhibited, striking all kinds of sparks along the way, but always guided by the framework which was constructed beforehand.

The device of seeing an essay as a set of boxes can be moved up and down the scale of magnitude. A, B, and C, which in the example above represent paragraphs, might in a briefer piece of writing represent points to be made within one paragraph. If the writer is a student taking an examination, to see his one-paragraph answer thus structurally will save him from rambling. Going up the scale of magnitude, if the essay is a long one, A, B, and C might each represent a *group* of paragraphs, or numbered sections of a long essay, or even chapters in a book. The way to use the system, in this case, is to form a new set of boxes, expanding each box of the original set into a set of its own, as you come to each section in the writing. (Some writers will prefer to work out the whole essay in detail in advance and write the whole first draft without interruption; but for most writers, and especially those who are blocked or frustrated, the step-at-a-time system works better.)

The author of the essay on reading poems, when he comes to box A of his set, representing "How to analyze a poem before reading it out loud," will break down this subject before he writes about it, as if it were in itself a small essay. He started, we recall, with only these few notes on the subject represented by A:

analysis of poem { literal meaning first
                       allusions
                       work out levels of meaning

Now he thinks this subject out. How *does* one analyze a poem? Casting his mind over the process as he is familiar with it, he asks himself what the reader of a poem should look for. First, the literal meaning, which he can get at best through the dramatic situation: Who is speaking? Who is doing what where? Second, the meanings of key words, ambiguous or puzzling words, and formal allusions. Third, the effect of symbolic details. Fourth, the overtones, or higher levels of meaning.

At this point, the writer is ready to restate A something like this, using the same system of boxes as before:

S	analysis of poem
A	literal meaning: dramatic situation
B	words and allusions
C	mood, tone
D	deeper levels
S¹	

At this point, if not sooner, it becomes clear to the writer that this section of his essay could be expressed in any length, from a paragraph to a whole book. He must keep his eye on the whole job, the whole essay, the original set of boxes, and not get lost in this one section. If his main object is to tell people how to read poetry out loud, he must keep this section strictly under control. It is only one part of his essay, and the other parts, B and C, are more important to him.

Now the writer is ready to write section A, letting this part of his subject out in a first draft within the framework he has devised for it. After that, he will move on and develop section B in the same way, and write that. And so on.

Remember, though, that the point of the system is to make it possible for the writer to see what he's about to do and still keep the first draft spontaneous. If the system is used pedantically, it will be cumbersome rather than helpful. Here, as in so many situations, it is the approach that is important, not a precise formula. "The letter killeth, but the spirit giveth life."

There is no magic in these boxes. No rabbits come out of them. They will not make an ignorant writer wise, a lazy writer industrious, nor a turgid writer lucid. Used as one flexible method of seeing where you are going without killing off spontaneity, the boxes will serve their purpose.

It must be said that these boxes are not intended as a method for analyzing the essays of others. They *may* prove useful to you in your reading, but their great advantage is in helping you visualize your own job of writing. It is interesting to examine the box-skeletons of other people's writing, as we are about to do, but the point is not to judge the writers of those essays by how well their essays do or do not fit the system. The point is to demonstrate that any writer of good exposition has, in one way or another, developed his ideas in a coherent structure which can be seen in the final writing, and to suggest that the efficient way to develop structure is to do it before you write.

Let's start with an example of relaxed, informal, and apparently spontaneous writing, "A Funny Thing Happened on the Way to Antigua," by Russell Baker, which we mentioned in Chapter 1.

[1]Let me say at the outset that I am one of life's most consistent losers. Although I have been moderately successful at my work and earn a comfortable living, I am basically the sort of person to whom nothing good has ever happened.

[2]Without belaboring the point I will simply note that the first car I ever owned was the last Hudson ever made, and that my second was an Edsel. It should be obvious that I am a man of considerable pessimism and negligible expectations.

[3]Accordingly, when my wife and I decided last autumn to splurge on a winter in Antigua, I hadn't the least hope that the thing would come off, but I was mildly curious to see what disaster would intervene. Well, sir, it started with finger smudges on the stairway wall. But let me backtrack a bit.

[4]Two years ago we were living in a small box in the suburbs. The children had begun to grow leggy and I had developed this terrible sensation of living a totally boxed life. Inside our box we were all cramped into small interior boxes filled with even smaller boxes.

[5]One could stare at the box that talked, or go into the kitchen and ponder the box that cooked, or escape on the box with wheels. My analyst diagnosed a dangerous obsession and advised a move. And so we sold the place and bought an enormous old box of the kind they don't build any more.

6The sense of enboxment subsided at once, and I even began to develop a fondness for the old place. Well, as I was saying, we had booked for Antigua when my wife remarked on the finger smudges on the stairway wall paint.

7We must have this wall papered with something washable, she said, and called a wallpaper man. When he arrived he shook his head mournfully and warned that it would be a bad mistake to paper until certain cracks in the plaster had been repaired.

8My wife called a plasterer, who agreed to examine the cracks within a fortnight. "Hm," he said, "you've really got cracks. Bad cracks." My wife, who was naturally alarmed, asked him to examine the really prepossessing cracks which we had always taken for granted in the north bedrooms and shower stall.

9"Yes, sir," he said, "these are really some cracks." "What do you think caused them?" asked my wife. "Could be," he mused, "you got termites under the north end of the house and they've eaten away all the underpinnings."

10He thought it would be a mistake to undertake major crack repairs until the foundation had been thoroughly examined. Seven weeks later a carpenter agreed to give us an appointment. At the north end of the cellar he tore away some beaverboard ceiling and exposed perhaps twelve feet of suspended sawdust.

11"You had termites, all right," he allowed. "Look at this beam." He handed me a palm full of sawdust. "Will the dining room fall through?" asked my wife. "Not so long as you stay out of there," he said.

12He thought that the damage was reparable, although it would require electricians to relocate the overhead wiring during the operation. The cost? "It'll be a right good bit," he said. "About the cost of a month in Antigua?" I asked. "Just about," he thought.

Here are twelve paragraphs, short and informal. But you can easily see the brief essay, if not the paragraphs, falling into three sections, each offering an explanation of why the writer never got to Antigua. First, he is by nature a misfortunate man, for whom all such plans go awry. Second, he bought an old house. Third, a chain of discoveries about the house led to the admission that the vacation money had to go for repairs.

```
┌─────────────────┐
│       S         │ Antigua?
└─────────────────┘
        ┌─────────────────┐
        │        A        │   misfortunate man
        └─────────────────┘
        ┌─────────────────┐
        │        B        │   old house
        └─────────────────┘
        ┌─────────────────┐
        │        C        │   series of discoveries
        └─────────────────┘
┌─────────────────┐
│       S¹        │ no trip to Antigua!
└─────────────────┘
```

Section C is in itself developed clearly in three points (notice how like a fairy tale it is in structure, in three acts each leading into the next and all to the climax): smudges to cracks to termites; or, if you prefer, wallpaper man to plasterer to carpenter.

```
┌─────────────────┐
│       S         │ repairing the house
└─────────────────┘
        ┌─────────────────┐
        │        A        │   smudges → wallpaper man
        └─────────────────┘
        ┌─────────────────┐
        │        B        │   cracks → plasterer
        └─────────────────┘
        ┌─────────────────┐
        │        C        │   termites → carpenter
        └─────────────────┘
┌─────────────────┐
│       S¹        │ there goes the money
└─────────────────┘
```

The point of this analysis is not to suggest that the writer arrived at this structure by the use of the box system (he seems to have as low an opinion of boxes, in fact, as Malvina Reynolds, who wrote a song called "Little Boxes Made of Ticky-Tacky") nor that he must necessarily have used *any* kind of formal outline. Russell Baker is a professional writer who draws on not only a talent for writing but a developed skill. For such a writer, the process of seeing structure in advance is so automatic a part of the writing process that we must expect that he developed the structure of this brief essay in his head rather than on paper, and by so habitual a process that the structure seemed to come to him of its own accord. This is only to say that for any skilled craftsman the basic techniques of his craft become natural. Alexander Pope, looking back on a career of writing poetry, could not remember the learning process and declared that as a child he "lisped in numbers, for the numbers came." Any expert makes his job look easy — that's one way you can tell he's an expert. Beginners, however, soon discover that the use of techniques before they become habitual must be a conscious and even a painful process.

"Those move easiest who have learned to dance," as Alexander Pope also tells us, and though the skillful dancer does not have to think about where his feet are going, there was a time when he did have to think about them, and learn the steps. The entire system of this book, including the box system of graphic representation of the essay, is most useful for those who have not yet learned to move easily in writing, those for whom the numbers come not, but must be coaxed into existence.

To take another example, more formal in purpose (if not in tone), here is the opening section of the Foreword to *Mastering the Art of French Cooking*. Here the authors, Simone Beck, Louisette Bertholle, and Julia Child, had the advantage of readers who already knew the purpose of this piece of writing and were already interested — otherwise they would not be reading the foreword to the book. That simplified the problem of the opening, certainly, but the writers' job was not simple. They wanted to explain the book: what it is, how the writers approached the subject of French cooking, how readers should use the book, what attitudes users of the book should bring to it, how it is different from other books about French cooking. A large and complex subject, you see. An unskillful writer would have great difficulty developing it into a clear, concise, coherent structure. See how well the authors succeeded:

[1]This is a book for the servantless American cook who can be unconcerned on occasion with budgets, waistlines, time schedules, children's meals, the parent–chauffeur–den-mother syndrome, or anything else which might interfere with the enjoyment of producing something wonderful to eat. Written for those who love to cook, the recipes are as detailed as we have felt they should be so the reader will know exactly what is involved and how to go about it. This makes them a bit longer than usual, and some of the recipes are quite long indeed. No out-of-the-ordinary ingredients are called for. In fact the book could well be titled "French Cooking from the American Supermarket," for the excellence of French cooking, and of good cooking

in general, is due more to cooking techniques than to anything else. And these techniques can be applied wherever good basic materials are available. We have purposely omitted cobwebbed bottles, the *patron* in his white cap bustling among his sauces, anecdotes about charming little restaurants with gleaming napery, and so forth. Such romantic interludes, it seems to us, put French cooking into a never-never land instead of the Here, where happily it is available to everybody. Anyone can cook in the French manner anywhere, with the right instruction. Our hope is that this book will be helpful in giving that instruction.

²Cooking techniques include such fundamentals as how to sauté a piece of meat so that it browns without losing its juices, how to fold beaten egg whites into a cake batter to retain their maximum volume, how to add egg yolks to a hot sauce so they will not curdle, where to put the tart in the oven so it will puff and brown, and how to chop an onion quickly. Although you will perform with different ingredients for different dishes, the same general processes are repeated over and over again. As you enlarge your repertoire, you will find that the seemingly endless babble of recipes begins to fall rather neatly into groups of theme and variations; that *homard à l'américaine* has many technical aspects in common with *coq au vin,* that *coq au vin* in turn is almost identical in technique to *boeuf bourguignon;* all of them are types of fricassees, so follow the fricassee pattern. In the sauce realm, the cream and egg-yolk sauce for a *blanquette* of veal is the same type as that for a sole in white-wine sauce or for a *gratin* of scallops. Eventually you will rarely need recipes at all, except as reminders of ingredients you may have forgotten.

³All of the techniques employed in French cooking are aimed at one goal: how does it taste? The French are seldom interested in unusual combinations or surprise presentations. With an enormous backbround of traditional dishes to choose from (*1000 Ways to Prepare and Serve Eggs* is the title of one French book on the subject) the Frenchman takes his greatest pleasure from a well-known dish impeccably cooked and served. A perfect *navarin* of lamb, for instance, requires a number of operations including brownings, simmerings, strainings, skimmings, and flavorings. Each of the steps in the process, though simple to accomplish, plays a critical role, and if any is eliminated or combined with another, the texture and taste of the *navarin* suffer. One of the main reasons that pseudo-French cooking, with which we are all too familiar, falls far below good

French cooking is just this matter of elimination of steps, combination of processes, or skimping on ingredients such as butter, cream—and time. "Too much trouble," "Too expensive," or "Who will know the difference" are death knells for good food.
⁴Cooking is not a particularly difficult art, and the more you cook and learn about cooking, the more sense it makes. But like any art it requires practice and experience. The most important ingredient you can bring to it is love of cooking for its own sake.

The *tone* of this foreword is relaxed and friendly, as if the authors were simply talking to us. In fact, the tone is very carefully colloquial: the writers use the expression *out-of-the-ordinary* where they could have used the more concise word *exotic,* presumably because *exotic* is not colloquial enough. But though they seem to be talking spontaneously, the ladies have put this foreword together as carefully as any of their recipes.

¶1	S	written for enjoyment for those who love to cook
	A	technique, not exotic ingredients, the main thing
¶2	B	techniques fall into groups and patterns
¶3	C	goal of technique: perfect taste
¶4	S¹	technique + love of cooking = good food

Because their readers already know, in general, what the subject of the foreword must be, and are already interested, S does not require a separate paragraph. S and the opening of A are united, which may throw you off if you are trying to analyze the selection. But once that is seen, notice how carefully the authors guide the reader, how gently, in the midst of conversation, they nudge him to the central idea.

They start with the idea of the American housewife who has time to *enjoy* cooking. Paragraph 1 builds to the idea that "the excellence of . . . cooking . . . is due . . . to cooking techniques." Paragraph 2 (Section B) begins "Cooking techniques include. . . ." Paragraph 3 (Section C) begins "All of the techniques employed in French cooking are. . . ." Paragraph 4 (Section S¹) restates the theme of technique, as "practice and experience," and ties that theme to the opening idea, S, the love of cooking. Under the relaxed, colloquial rambling, in short, is a careful, deliberate plan. Under the leaves is the skeleton of the tree, giving it form and focus.

If we move the box technique along the scale of magnitude, we find that the same care has gone into the construction of Section **A**, for example, as if it were an essay in itself:

S	for those who love to cook: instructions
A	recipes longer, more detailed than usual
B	common ingredients, not exotic
C	technique the important thing
D	no romantic nonsense
S¹	this book gives instructions

This foreword is an interesting example of that kind of writing which hides its own technique under a casual style. Note that because the purpose is more formal than that of "A Funny Thing Happened on the Way to Antigua," the structure is a bit more obvious: the material is organized into paragraph units more clearly; paragraphs 2 and 3 have openings which clearly relate them to the central idea; paragraph 4 is a tying-up of the central idea.

The more formal the purpose of a piece of writing, the more we expect it to be organized into careful paragraphs, each a clear step in the development of the thought, and the more apparent the *structure* of the essay will be. We have seen an informal letter, written for a newspaper column, and the foreword to a cookbook. Now let's take another step in the direction of formality and look at a quite formal brief essay, Thomas Huxley's "Hypotheses" (from his *Science Primer,* 1885):

[1]When our means of observation of any natural fact fail to carry us beyond a certain point, it is perfectly legitimate, and often extremely useful, to make a supposition as to what we should see, if we could carry direct observation a step further. A supposition of this kind is what is called a *hypothesis,* and the value of any hypothesis depends

MAN IS TRAPPED

upon the extent to which reasoning upon the assumption that it is true, enables us to explain or account for the phenomena with which it is concerned.

[2]Thus, if a person is standing close behind you, and you suddenly feel a blow on your back, you have no direct evidence of the cause of the blow; and if you two were alone, you could not possibly obtain any; but you immediately suppose that this person has struck you. Now that is a hypothesis, and it is a legitimate hypothesis, first, because it explains the fact; and secondly, because no other explanation is probable; probable meaning in accordance with the ordinary course of nature. If your companion declared that you fancied you felt a blow, or that some invisible spirit struck you, you would probably decline to accept his explanation of the fact. You would say that both the hypotheses by which he professed to explain the phenomenon were extremely improbable; or in other words, that in the ordinary course of nature fancies of this kind do not occur, nor spirits strike blows. In fact, his hypotheses would be illegitimate, and yours would be legitimate; and, in all probability, you would act upon your own. In daily life, nine-tenths of our actions are based upon suppositions or hypotheses, and our success or failure in practical affairs depends upon the legitimacy of these hypotheses. You believe a man on the hypothesis that he is always truthful; you give him pecuniary credit on the hypothesis that he is solvent.

[3]Thus, everybody invents, and, indeed, is compelled to invent, hypotheses in order to account for phenomena of the cause of which he has no direct evidence; and they are just as legitimate and necessary in science as in common life. Only the scientific reasoner must be careful to remember that which is sometimes forgotten in daily life, that a hypothesis must be regarded as a means and not as an end; that we may cherish it so long as it helps us to explain the order of nature; but that we are bound to throw it away without hesitation as soon as it is shown to be inconsistent with any part of that order.

¶1	S	hypothesis a supposition that explains phenomena
¶2	A	used in daily life (example)
¶3	B	used in science, but scientist remembers
	S¹	to discard it if it fails to explain phenomena

In this brief, formal essay, we see a simple and efficient structure. Section S defines *hypothesis* as a supposition which explains phenomena without direct evidence. A and B are two areas of human activity in which hypotheses are common; since the two sections are parallel and similar, both A and B open with *Thus* . . . , showing that they both have the same relationship to S. B is more important to Huxley than A; in fact, A is important only because it is more familiar to the reader. Therefore, Huxley puts B last, following A (climactic order). The essay is brief, and the ending comes round to the main theme neatly, so S^1 does not need to be a separate paragraph.

"A Funny Thing Happened on the Way to Antigua," "Foreword," and "Hypotheses" are very different pieces of writing. The level of formality varies; the tone and style vary; the visibility of the skeleton varies, from one to another. And this is proper, for these selections were written by different people, in different moods, for different readers. But never forget what the three have in common, beneath their differences. Each of them has structure. Each has been carefully worked out as a problem in organization. Each has a skeleton, an architecture. Each of them *had* to have a structure, for the writer's sake as well as the reader's.

Exercises

1. How much of Agnes de Mille's essay "Rhythm in My Blood" (page 146) is the opening? How much is the close? What does the opening do to set the subject, establish the tone, and catch the reader's interest? How does the close ensure that the reader will have the central idea clearly in mind?

2. Answer the same questions about an essay of your own (preferably one you are about to hand in) as are asked about Agnes de Mille's in exercise 1.

3. What are the major divisions of thought in the essays "The Long Snowfall" (page 217) and "Introduction" (page 133)? How are the divisions made obvious to the reader?

4. Develop an idea for an essay through the following preliminary steps: scratch list, primary set of boxes, one box expanded into a set of boxes.

CHAPTER THREE

Thinking in Paragraphs

There is probably no advice modern writers need more than the precept "Think in paragraphs!" If you once concede that it is useful to "clump" your thoughts, so that they become a coherent series of statements rather than a meandering stream or an amorphous mass, then the value of thinking in paragraphs is clear, but I find nothing more foreign to the habits of beginning writers than this.

One reason we tend not to think in paragraphs is that historically, in some kinds of writing, the paragraph has been shrinking and shrinking until it has practically disappeared or is preserved only as a vestigial organ. In newspaper writing, especially, the habit of thinking in paragraphs has been almost abandoned. To see this, compare a newspaper article of the year 1711, Joseph Addison's piece on superstition (page 126), with a newspaper article of the year 1965, Russell Baker's essay (page 124). Both are brief, witty essays on current customs. Addison's is developed in six steps, embodied in six paragraphs (one of them 535 words long). Baker's, written two and a half centuries later, is developed in a much looser form, with a conscious air of just talking out thoughts as they come to him; the longest paragraph has only 56 words, and the paragraph divisions do not correspond to the three major units of thought. (See page 26.) As a matter of fact, it would be fair to say that in this kind of writing the paragraph has really ceased to exist; the indentations mark pauses for breathing, or a visual breaking-up of the column. A newspaper copy editor feels free to break up a writer's paragraphs merely because he judges that things look better in smaller units.

Some critics have related the shrinking of paragraphs to the increasingly fast tempo of modern life, as if readers had time only for smaller and smaller units, and it is certainly true that in our times readers are generally in a hurry. But it is *not* true that a reader can take in the same idea more quickly when it is arbitrarily broken into smaller units than when it is presented to him in conventional paragraphs.

Let's try an experiment. First, read the opening passage of Oliver P. Pearson's "The Metabolism of Hummingbirds" with new and random paragraphing—not a word changed but the paragraph divisions multiplied. The experiment is a fair one because Pearson's style is so lucid and his subject so concrete that we can make sense of the passage without his paragraphs. The only question is, can we read the passage as easily, or as well, without those paragraphs?

First, then, the opening of Pearson's essay, arbitrarily broken up into small units:

Version A

¹The living rate of an animal depends on its size: the smaller the animal, the faster it lives.

²This does not necessarily mean that its life span is shorter (a man is smaller than a horse), but pound for pound the more diminutive animal eats more food, consumes more oxygen, produces more energy—in short, has a higher rate of metabolism.

³Each gram of mouse tissue, for example, metabolizes much faster and uses much more oxygen per minute than each gram of an elephant's tissues. If the elephant's cells were to live at the pace set by mouse cells, the ponderous animal would be unable to dissipate the resulting heat rapidly enough.

⁴It would perish within a few minutes from overheating.

⁵Life has been compared to the flame of a candle. The candle's wax combines with oxygen from the air and produces heat and carbon dioxide.

⁶The rate at which the flame burns can be measured by any of these four factors: its consumption of wax or oxygen or its production of heat or carbon dioxide.

⁷Similarly, one can measure how "alive" an animal is, how intense are its life processes, by determining how fast it consumes food or oxygen or how fast it produces heat or carbon dioxide.

[8]For practical reasons the easiest and most satisfactory yardstick is oxygen consumption. Such measurements have been made on a host of animals from protozoa to mice to elephants.

[9]We are interested here in the small end of the scale.

[10]Among the warm-blooded animals about the smallest is the hummingbird—some species of hummingbirds weigh no more than a dime.

[11]As we should expect, the hummingbird has the highest rate of metabolism of any bird or mammal.

[12]In a resting hummingbird each gram of tissue metabolizes 15 times as fast as a gram of pigeon and more than 100 times as fast as a gram of elephant.

[13]When the metabolism rates of various animals are plotted on a chart, the curve goes up steeply at the small-animal end, and it indicates that at 2.5 grams the rate of metabolism would be infinitely rapid.

[14]No bird or animal so small could exist without resorting to some metabolic legerdemain unknown to its larger relatives, for it simply could not eat fast enough to avoid starvation.

A reader gets the general meaning of this passage. He may even be trained, as readers of most newspapers are, to read such passages without ever noticing the lack of logic of the paragraphing. But whether he notices it or not, the reader suffers. First, *he* must do the work of putting ideas together, of making larger clumps of them and seeing the relationships between them. Unit 4 is obviously part of the idea expressed in unit 3; unit 6 is a continuation of the thought of unit 5. The reader can make such connections for himself. But he does not make the connections as quickly, as consciously, or as efficiently as the writer could have made them, since the reader is in a hurry, does not know the subject as well, has not thought about the logical structure of the essay, and is in all probability not so seriously concerned with the subject as the writer is. The reader, therefore, does not put the ideas together as well as the writer could and does not see the relationship or the progression of ideas as clearly as he should. In short, the reader suffers from fuzziness of communication.

Now examine the same passage *with* paragraphs, as Pearson wrote it:

[1]The living rate of an animal depends on its size: the smaller the animal, the faster it lives. This does not necessarily mean that its life span is shorter (a man is smaller than a horse), but pound for pound the more diminutive animal eats more food, consumes more oxygen, produces more energy—in short, has a higher rate of metabolism. Each gram of mouse tissue, for example, metabolizes much faster and uses much more oxygen per minute than each gram of an elephant's tissues. If the elephant's cells were to live at the pace set by mouse cells, the ponderous animal would be unable to dissipate the resulting heat rapidly enough. It would perish within a few minutes from overheating.

[2]Life has been compared to the flame of a candle. The candle's wax combines with oxygen from the air and produces heat and carbon dioxide. The rate at which the flame burns can be measured by any of these four factors: its consumption of wax or oxygen or its production of heat or carbon dioxide. Similarly, one can measure how "alive" an animal is, how intense are its life processes, by determining how fast it consumes food or oxygen or how fast it produces heat or carbon dioxide. For practical reasons the easiest and most satisfactory yardstick is oxygen consumption. Such measurements have been made on a host of animals from protozoa to mice to elephants.

[3]We are interested here in the small end of the scale. Among the warm-blooded animals about the smallest is the hummingbird—some species of hummingbirds weigh no more than a dime. As we should expect, the hummingbird has the highest rate of metabolism of any bird or animal. In a resting hummingbird each gram of tissue metabolizes 15 times as fast as a gram of pigeon and more than 100 times as fast as a gram of elephant. When the metabolism rates of various animals are plotted on a chart, the curve goes up steeply at the small-animal end, and it indicates that at 2.5 grams the rate of metabolism would be infinitely rapid. No bird or mammal so small could exist without resorting to some metabolic legerdemain unknown to its larger relatives, for it simply could not eat fast enough to avoid starvation.

Now we can see that Pearson has developed his thoughts in three steps, representing three points he wants to make:

(1) The smaller the animal, the higher the rate of metabolism. (2) Rate of metabolism can be measured by oxygen consumption. (3) The hummingbird is probably as small as it is possible for a warm-blooded animal to be and has the highest rate of metabolism.

An exceptionally good reader could have seen these three steps in Version A, but most readers simply would not. Pearson has presented each step in a paragraph, each isolated and developed as if it were a miniature essay. At the end of each paragraph, one can pause and think over so much of Pearson's ideas, because each paragraph is a real unit of ideas. If the reader has trouble figuring out any point, he goes back over one clearly defined paragraph and works it out there.

The very fact that two sentences are in the same paragraph is a signal to the reader of their relationship. In Version A, the relationship of unit 9 to either 8 or 10 is not clear. In Version B, it is clear that "We are interested . . ." begins a new thought and that "Among the warm-blooded . . ." begins the development of that thought.

If even so concrete a subject as Pearson's needs paragraphing for efficient communication, think how important paragraphing is to less concrete subjects. Think what a hodgepodge the "Foreword" on page 130 would be if it were not set in paragraphs! There is simply no question that the reader of expository prose needs paragraphs if communication is to be efficient; so it is incumbent on the writer of exposition to develop the habit of thinking and writing in paragraphs.

Expository Paragraphs

Writing in paragraphs does not mean grouping sentences arbitrarily. The word *paragraph* originally meant a mark in a passage of dialog to indicate that one person's speech is ended and the following words are spoken by another. The word means primarily the visual sign, in modern exposition the indentation, but the function of that sign has always been to indicate a shift in voice or a shift in ideas. The expository paragraph is a real entity, with a logical unity. It has, in fact, what we can call an organic unity, and if your mind runs that way, you can see a striking resemblance between a paragraph and an organic cell.

Looking at living cells under a microscope, as students of biology are sometimes shown the cells in the tail of a live goldfish, you see structural units. Each cell is, of course, made up of smaller constituents which can be seen moving within it: nucleus, ectoplasm, endoplasm, etc. Each cell is also one incorporated bit of a large living whole. Nevertheless, the cell is visibly a unit, and cells are spoken of as the building blocks of organic life. Paragraphs, like cells, can be seen as made up of internally functioning constituents, but they can also be seen as distinct units which are the building blocks of exposition.

Visualize a paragraph as if it were an organic cell — just for fun, to get the idea of a paragraph set in our heads. A normal expository cell, or building block, or paragraph, can be imagined thus:

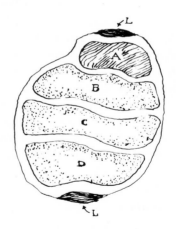

The two L's, at top and bottom, are the links by which the paragraph is bound to adjacent paragraphs and thus to the whole organism, the essay. A is the nucleus, the governing idea or topic which both justifies and determines the paragraph, gives it identity. B, C, and D are units of development, the particular ideas which expound or explain the topic. (The number of these will vary from paragraph to paragraph.)

If we were to visualize Pearson's first paragraph (Version B, page 38) in this way, we'd notice that the top L is missing, since there is no preceding paragraph to link it with. A, or the nucleus of this paragraph, is the idea that the smaller an animal is, the higher its rate of metabolism will be. There are two units of development, B and C, the application of the basic idea first to mice and then to elephants. The bottom L is the idea of heat, which links the paragraph to the idea of a hot flame in the next paragraph.

If we look at Pearson's second paragraph in the same way, the top L is the idea of flame, linking with the idea of heat in the preceding paragraph. The nucleus is the central idea that the burning of a candle is analogous to organic metabolism. The two units of development are the idea that a candle's rate of burning is measurable and the idea that metabolic rate is measurable. The bottom link is the idea of a scale on which such measurements have been made. In the third paragraph, the top link is the idea of the scale again, the nucleus is the idea of animals at the small end of the scale — and so on, each paragraph an organic unit, one of the living blocks which constitute exposition.

One of the working definitions of a paragraph is that it consists of a group of sentences about one sentence. This suggests that in a typical paragraph the theme, or topic, or nucleus, is stated in one sentence (though in practice it often occurs in more than one or is only implied) and that the other sentences say something about that theme. The commonest methods of "saying something" about the theme are often classified: We say that paragraphs are developed by particularization, by example, by definition of terms, by contrast and comparison, by analysis, by classification, by narration. Pearson's first paragraph is developed by example (the examples of the mouse and the elephant). His second is developed by comparison (the analogy of flame and organic metabolism). His third is developed by particularization (the particular details of metabolism). It is useful to consider the internal constituents of paragraphs in this way, as the analogy to the organic cell suggests, but I find these classifications not very useful in the actual process of writing — they are not often consciously used by writers. On the other hand, the whole relationship of the nucleus to the development is of the utmost importance. In broad terms, that is the relationship of the general and the particular in exposition, such a basic subject that it must have its own chapter (see Chapter 4).

We must candidly admit that not all paragraphs fit the foregoing description neatly; not even all the paragraphs in Pearson's essay will perform for us as obligingly as the first three. In practice, not every idea that a good writer decides is worth setting off as a paragraph is worth developing (Pearson's seventh is a good example — see page 213). Sometimes a paragraph break comes where it does, apparently, because the writer felt a paragraph was getting too long and therefore separated out an idea which might have been included (Pearson's sixth paragraph, for instance). The paragraphs of an essay must not be monotonously alike, either in length or in structure. But thé basic type, the model, the pattern, is the expository paragraph as we have described it, and this pattern a writer must study until it becomes habitual with him, the type from which he departs only for variation.

Only for variation? Well, not quite. There are paragraphs whose function is not expository at all, in the sense of stating or developing ideas, and these paragraphs are not constructed like the expository model. Their function is to give the reader information not about the subject but about the essay, to provide transition and emphasis, keeping the reader aware of what the essay is doing.

Paragraphs of Transition and Emphasis

In Oliver Pearson's essay on hummingbirds, the entire seventeenth paragraph (see page 215) is this:

In the face of two such unthinkable alternatives, any laboratory answer may seem foolish. But we can at least attempt a calculation, if only for the amusement of playing with the figures.

The purpose of this paragraph is not to develop an idea but to steer the reader's attention from one subject of discussion to another. Such a paragraph serves exactly the same purpose as the turn signals on cars. "We have been talking about theories of how hummingbirds cross the Gulf of Mexico; now hold onto your hat, because we're making a fast, sharp turn into the subject of how laboratory observations of metabolic rate can be used to test theories of action in the field."

In Erich Fromm's essay "Is Love an Art?" (page 172), the ninth paragraph consists of only nine words:

What are the necessary steps in learning any art?

Here, too, the purpose is to guide the reader through the essay rather than to develop an idea. At the same time, expressing this guidance in the form of a question startles the reader a bit, and expressing it as a very brief sentence set off as a paragraph among fairly long expository paragraphs gives the question tremendous emphasis, lights it up with the strongest of spotlights.

Note that it would not be possible for the paragraph of transition or the paragraph of emphasis to have their proper effect on the reader if they did not occur as exceptions to the established pattern of typical expository paragraphs.

We must think of the writer's job of communicating with a reader as a twofold process: Developing ideas, imparting information, expounding opinion, and such expository processes are only half the job; at the same time, the writer is constantly thinking of himself as a guide through a subject. The writer and the reader find themselves together in a subject very much as if they were in the midst of a thick forest. To the reader, who is a newcomer to this forest, all is confusion as he looks around—nothing but trees in all directions, and no directions known. To the writer, these are familiar woods—he has lived in them and knows his way about in them. He tells the reader, "Look—that big rock over there marks the way out of the woods. From its top we can see a lone pine tree, and we head for that, and from there we can see glimmers of light at the edge of the forest."

Part of the process of guidance is the use of transitional and emphatic paragraphs, but such paragraphs must not be considered as separate devices. They are part of the whole method of guidance, which also includes a certain trick of grouping paragraphs and a certain way of linking up the threads of discourse which run through the paragraphs of an essay.

Paragraphs in Groups

If a coherent group of sentences is a paragraph, what is a coherent group of paragraphs? We must call it simply a paragraph-group, but there really ought to be a specific name for it, for this is one of the important tools of the expository writer. In an essay of more than a few paragraphs, the writer develops his thoughts by a series of clearly defined, coherent groups of paragraphs, each forming one step in his discourse.

To see paragraph-groups at work in an essay, let's examine the paragraph pattern of "The Metabolism of Hummingbirds." Start with the basic pattern of the whole essay, expressed as boxes:

```
  S          metabolism of hummingbirds
        A          measuring metabolism: the scale (¶1-3)
        B          eat all day — hibernate all night (¶4-10)
        C          energy consumption: at rest,
                   hovering, flying (¶11-15)
        D          can they cross the Gulf? (¶16-18)
  S¹       (¶19)
```

The order of the parts, we note in passing, is from general to particular: from metabolism as a process, to metabolism by day and by night, to a particular problem involved with metabolism during one activity. Each of the parts, A to D, is expressed as a paragraph-group in the finished essay.

The first group consists of three solid, typical expository paragraphs, getting across presumably new ideas by careful and full development of each paragraph.

When he began the second group, at paragraph 4, Pearson faced a particular problem. How should he let the reader know that the discourse was now switching not just to a new paragraph but to a whole new paragraph-group? The editor of the magazine in which Pearson's article first appeared helped the reader by leaving a space between the third and fourth paragraphs and starting the fourth with a large, emphatic capital letter. Sometimes either writer or editor may assign numbers to paragraph-groups within essays, and the number 2 might well have appeared here. Usually, though, the reader must be guided only by the words in the paragraphs themselves.

Pearson helped his readers by using at this point a transitional paragraph:

> The hummingbird wins the honor of living at a rate faster than any other animal at the cost of an enormous food consumption. The bird must devote much of its day to gathering food, mainly nectar and insects. But what happens at night? Hummingbirds are not adapted for night feeding. If their intense metabolism continued undiminished through the night, as it does in other birds, they would be in danger of starving to death before morning.

Notice that "wins the honor of living at a rate faster than any other animal" has nothing to do with the immediate subject of the new paragraph-group. The writer could have introduced the new subject with the statement: "The hummingbird has an enormous food consumption." Nor did we need to be told that the hummingbird lives faster than other animals—we had already learned that in the previous paragraph-group. The idea is included here (quite possibly inserted during the process of revision, by the way) in order to carry us smoothly from the subject of high metabolic rate to the idea of food consumption and how the bird gets through the night without eating. In the rest of the paragraph, Pearson brushes aside the subject of daytime feeding, as if to say, "I must mention this, of course, since food consumption is the subject, and since I can't talk about *night* without suggesting *day;* but the bird's daytime habits present no problem, so I'll say as little about them as possible and get on to the real problem—how the hummingbird gets through the night—and to that problem I now invite your attention."

Paragraph 4 and the six which follow are tightly bound together in a paragraph-group. The reader slides easily from one paragraph to the next, the transitions all being smooth and suggesting that each paragraph is closely connected in subject to the one before and the one after it.

¶ 4 { "... in danger of (starving to death) before morning."

¶ 5 {
"The trick by which hummingbirds avoid (overnight starvation) ..."

"... a metabolism (level) only one fifteenth as rapid as the daytime rate."

¶ 6 {
"Now this is the (level) at which. ...."

"... from dusk to (dawn.)"

¶ 7 {
"Before (daybreak.) ...."

"... (dart off in search of food.)"

¶ 8 {
"That hummingbirds (behave in the same way) in nature. ...."

"... (retreat at night) into caves."

¶ 9 { "We know of no other bird that (hibernates overnight.) ...."

¶10 { "The metabolic profit which a hummingbird gains by (nocturnal hibernation) ..."

Notice how each transitional phrase links the paragraph to the preceding paragraph, not to a preceding paragraph-group. For example, the first sentence in paragraph 8 contains the phrase "the same way." Even if all we had was the opening sentence of this paragraph, we would know that the paragraph had to be part of a group, not starting a new group, for "the same way" seems so clearly to refer to some "way" just mentioned. If the paragraph had started "That hummingbirds hibernate in nature in the same way as they do in laboratories under our observation . . . ," then the reference would be to the whole subject of hibernation in laboratories, and we would have the impression of glancing back over a whole group of paragraphs (as we did at the beginning of paragraph 4), but within this paragraph-group Pearson has quite properly given us no such break: The subject of one paragraph slides easily into that of the next.

At the same time, the writer is constantly, within this paragraph-group, repeating key words and synonyms of those key words, not only for the transitions we've just noted but to keep the reader on the main line of thought, to keep the thread of discourse clear. Far from being afraid of repeating himself, he goes out of his way to repeat key words for this purpose. The word *hummingbird* appears 14 times in this paragraph-group, the word *bird* 9 times, and pronouns referring to hummingbirds no less than 24 times, making 47 iterations of the idea of hummingbird in seven paragraphs. The idea of metabolism, expressed in forms of the words *metabolism, metabolism level, oxygen consumption,* etc., occurs 14 times. These two concepts, of course, are central to the essay and run through all the paragraph-groups. Central only to this paragraph-group are the idea of night and the idea of hibernation, since the main point of the group is that hummingbirds pass the night in a torpid state similar to hibernation. Notice how often these key ideas are repeated, how they run through all the paragraphs of the group:

¶ 4 { ". . . at night? . . . night feeding . . . through the night . . . before morning."

¶ 5 { "The trick [i.e., hibernation] . . . overnight . . . before nightfall . . . for the night . . . metabolism had dropped . . . middle of the night. . . ."

¶ 6 { ". . . hibernate . . . at night . . . of hibernation . . . torpid . . . insensible . . . congealed . . . hibernation . . . from dusk to dawn. . . ."

¶ 7 { "Before daybreak. . . ."

¶ 8 { ". . . at dusk . . . torpid . . . at night . . . at night. . . ."

¶ 9 { ". . . hibernates overnight . . . torpor. . . ."

¶10 { ". . . nocturnal hibernation . . . hibernate . . . most of the night . . . hibernating at night."

Within the next paragraph-group, there is a similar ease of transition from one paragraph to another. There is a similar repetition of key words and phrases, though of course the words repeated are different from those in this paragraph-group.

If the whole essay on hummingbirds were given to a sensitive reader with one paragraph left out, and if the omitted paragraph were also given to the reader, he could tell where it would have to go—between which paragraphs it had been left out. The key words would help him decide to which paragraph-group it belonged; the transitional links would help him find its proper place in the group—and this quite apart from any help that his understanding of the subject might give him.

After paragraph 10, Pearson moves into a new paragraph-group, this one concerned with relative rates of energy expended by birds at rest, hovering, and flying. Again, the group is introduced by a transitional paragraph:

When the hummingbird is not sleeping, it is eating, and it does this entirely on the wing. How strenuous is it for a bird to fly? Hummingbirds can hover in a small space, and this attribute makes them ideal subjects for investigation in laboratory confinement.

"When the hummingbird is not sleeping. . . ." An interesting clause. It refers, obviously, to more than "hibernating at night," in the preceding paragraph; it casts a glance backward over the whole paragraph-group in which the idea of night and sleep has been central and thus prepares us to leave that group and go on to another. (If the writer had wanted to link this paragraph only to the one preceding, he might have said, "When the hummingbird is not thus hibernating at night. . . .") The writer in these transitional paragraphs is like a hiker who, having attained the summit of a hill, now looks back over the way he has come, then forward into the new scene opening before him.

We must notice that Pearson here takes us from one subject to another not by any logical connection but by a gimmick. He wrenches us, in fact, from one to another, though the casual reader will not feel the wrench. Look at the progression: (1) We've been talking about sleep; (2) When these birds don't sleep, they eat; (3) They eat on the wing; (4) Our new subject, by a happy coincidence, is the amount of energy needed to keep a bird on the wing. Once we are in on the secret, as expository craftsmen watching a fellow craftsman, we see what he's up to. The idea of *eating* has no function in this paragraph at all, except to serve as a stepping stone to take us from the idea of *hibernation* to the idea of *on-the-wing*. That is not to say that Pearson has done wrong; quite the contrary — we must commend him for the pains he has taken to carry the reader from the idea of one paragraph-group to the idea of the next group.

We should expect, on investigation, to see the same mechanics at work in any good piece of exposition: the paragraphs parts of paragraph-groups, the groups clearly introduced and clearly defined, and the reader guided skillfully through groups and through paragraphs, with the goal itself, the central idea of the whole essay, always before his eyes.

Another excellent example of the way the thread of discourse is carried through paragraphs and paragraph-groups can be seen in Erich Fromm's "Is Love an Art?" (It begins on page 172, but if you haven't yet read it, don't do so now; it will be all the more striking to see first how intelligible the discourse can be without reading the essay.) Let's quote only the key statements of each paragraph of Fromm's essay, indicating at the same time the number of words in each paragraph to show how much has been left out:

¶ 1 (52 words)   "Is love an art? . . . or a pleasant sensation?"

¶ 2 (50 words)   "Hardly anyone thinks that there is anything that needs to be learned about love."

¶ 3 (178 words)   "This peculiar attitude is based on several premises. [The first premise is. . . .]"

¶ 4 (238 words)	"A second premise behind the attitude that there is nothing to be learned about love is the assumption that. . . ."
¶ 5 (333 words)	"Closely related to this factor is another. . . ."
¶ 6 (211 words)	"The third error leading to the assumption that there is nothing to be learned about love lies in. . . ."
¶ 7 (126 words)	"This attitude—that nothing is easier than to love—has continued . . . in spite of. . . ."
¶ 8 (58 words)	"The first step to take is to become aware that love is an art. . . ."
¶ 9 (9 words)	"What are the necessary steps in learning any art?"
¶10 (243 words)	"The process of learning an art can be divided conveniently into two parts . . . , theory . . . and practice. . . ."
¶11 (109 words)	"First I shall discuss the theory of love . . . and secondly . . . the practice. . . ."

We can see the structure of the essay so clearly, just from these brief quotations from fairly long paragraphs, that we can be pretty sure the essay must fall into three sections:

¶ 1–2	Introduction of main question: Does one have to learn how to love?
¶ 3–6	Why some people think love does not have to be learned.
¶ 7	(Transition)
¶ 8–10	The method of learning love as an art.

There are, apparently, two important paragraph-groups here (¶ 3–6 and ¶ 8–10), each developing one of the two sides of the question or, rather, telling us first why one argument is faulty and then why the counterargument is sound. We note, especially, how at the beginning of paragraph 7 Fromm glances back over the subject of the whole preceding paragraph-group — "This attitude — that nothing is easier than to love . . ." — which is followed, presumably, in the rest of paragraph 7, by a forward look at the next subject.

It's time now to come back to our examination of the paragraph as a unit, to look closely, after all this, at what's going on inside one specific paragraph. Here is the third paragraph of Fromm's essay:

This peculiar attitude [that loving does not need to be learned] is based on several premises which either singly or combined tend to uphold it. Most people see the problem of love primarily as that of *being loved*, rather than that of *loving*, of one's capacity to love. Hence the problem to them is how to be loved, how to be lovable. In pursuit of this aim they follow several paths. One, which is especially used by men, is to be successful, to be as powerful and rich as the social margin of one's position permits. Another, used especially by women, is to make oneself attractive, by cultivating one's body, dress, etc. Other ways of making oneself attractive, used both by men and women, are to develop pleasant manners, interesting conversation, to be helpful, modest, inoffensive. Many of the ways to make oneself lovable are the same as those used to make oneself successful, "to win friends and influence people." As a matter of fact, what most people in our culture mean by being lovable is essentially a mixture between being popular and having sex appeal.

This paragraph illustrates many of the things we've said about paragraphing. The opening phrase, "This peculiar attitude," is the link which binds the paragraph to the one preceding, for it refers to a statement in paragraph 2 ("Hardly anyone thinks that there is anything that needs to be learned about love."). The statement "This peculiar attitude is based on several premises . . ." is the introduction to a paragraph-group (¶ 3 – 6) in which the premises will be presented. Fromm could have said "three premises" rather than "several," but he apparently felt that this would be too cut-and-dried. For the same reason, he has not made the transitional passage a separate paragraph but the opening of the paragraph in which the first premise is examined. (Note that immediately after the first sentence he could have said, "The first premise is . . . ," and continued with the second sentence.)

The topic, or nucleus, of this individual paragraph is expressed in the passage "Most people see the problem . . . how to be lovable" (sentences 2 and 3). Then follows a sentence telling the reader how this paragraph will be developed: ". . . they follow several paths." The rest of the paragraph tells us what these paths are, thus developing in detail the idea expressed in the nucleus.

Obviously this paragraph cannot be judged as an independent unit, taken out of context. It works as part of a paragraph-group and as part of an essay, as a good paragraph should.

At what point in the process of writing an essay should a writer have all these ideas about paragraphs in mind?

If you were to study this chapter carefully, and apply its principles to the study of several of the essays in Part II, and keep all this fresh in mind as you sat down to write — you would very likely be unable to write at all. While you are actually engaged in writing, you must not be overwhelmed by the theory of writing. If you take a familiar word and stare at it intensely, it may go all funny on you, become strange and unfamiliar and unusable, and the same is true of paragraphs or any other unit of language. But that must not worry you. If you stare at your feet, you can't dance, either, but people do learn how to dance.

There are two ways to make use of the theory of paragraphs. The first is to think about paragraphs, to be interested in them and how they work, to notice them as you read, and thus to etch into your mind the idea of the paragraph. If you do this, you'll find your own thoughts flowing into paragraphs as you write, for our preconceptions largely determine how we think. In this way, even though you keep the process of writing as spontaneous as you possibly can, thinking not of the mechanics of writing but only of the subject, the theory of paragraphs will be working for you. The second way of using the theory of paragraphs is to check your paragraphing consciously and deliberately during revision. The third step in writing, the conscious revision, is the time to think about mechanics. An essay worth writing well is worth checking several times, the checker looking for different things each time. Use one careful check-reading to examine your paragraphs and paragraph-groups, to see that they really are paragraphs, that they really state ideas and develop them, that the transitions are expressed and the key words emphasized — in short, that each paragraph is at one and the same time a clear unit of thought and a part of a closely woven web of intelligent discourse.

Exercises

1. Retype one of your own essays omitting all paragraph divisions. Later, see if you can distinguish the paragraphs clearly enough to divide it properly.

2. Consider paragraphs 10 through 12 of "On Being the Right Size" (page 204) as a paragraph-group. What passage in paragraph 10 tells us that we are starting a new group? What passage in paragraph 11 links with paragraph 10? What passage in paragraph 12 links with paragraph 11? What passage in paragraph 13 tells us that one paragraph-group has been concluded and a new group is starting? What key words or phrases run through paragraphs 10 through 12?

3. In an essay of your own which is long enough to use paragraph-groups, ask the same kind of questions about one group as are asked about "On Being the Right Size" in exercise 2.

CHAPTER FOUR

General and Particular

Some of the elements of exposition which we have discussed are separable; that is, they are appropriate to separate
steps in the process of writing—for instance, *organization,
first draft,* and *revision.* The subject of this chapter is not
separable in any such sense; it must be part of the writer's
technique in all aspects of his job, from thinking out the
whole essay to planning and writing paragraphs and making
decisions about style and diction. On whatever level we
consider exposition, we find that it balances, as it were,
between two poles, as a man balances on his two legs when
he walks. These poles, opposite but complementary, are the
general and the *particular.*

To show at once how the balance is achieved and why it is
important, I offer two brief examples:

1. (Brooks Atkinson is describing the art of Charlie Chaplin; see
page 170.) "To be fully articulate he has always needed hostility—
ferocious foremen, brutish police, villainous thugs. . . ."

2. (Rachel Carson is describing the deposits of sediment on the
ocean floor; see page 220.) "One thing seems probable—the sediments have been unevenly distributed both in place and time. In
contrast to the 12,000-foot thickness found in parts of the Atlantic,
the Swedish oceanographers never found sediments thicker than
1000 feet in the Pacific or in the Indian Ocean."

Chaplin "has always needed hostility." That's an interesting remark, as all good generalizations tend to be, but it's
not clear—we don't know in any detailed or specific sense

what it means. The mind of the reader starts up with interest, with expectancy, at such a statement. We are interested, but we are also waiting, saying silently to the writer, "How are you going to prove that?" or "How does that work out?" What, exactly, is meant by *hostility?* The rest of the passage clarifies the thought by showing how it can be particularized; it shows us some precise meanings for the word *hostility* as used in this context. Without these particulars, the general remark might well be interesting to the reader, but he could never in any satisfactory way understand it.

On the other hand, if Atkinson had said only, "Chaplin has always needed ferocious foremen, brutish police, and villainous thugs," we would not be able to add up the three constituents and come to the proper conclusion—the essence—the thing these three have in common in the mind of Brooks Atkinson. You can test this quickly enough: Read the sentence to a friend and ask him what, in this context, the three have in common, then watch him wrestle with the problem of generalizing from these three particulars.

The same principle holds in the passage by Rachel Carson: The general and the particular must both be there, in complementary polarity, for the communication to be efficient. To say only "In contrast to the 12,000-foot thickness found in parts of the Atlantic, the Swedish oceanographers never found sediments thicker than 1000 feet in the Pacific or in the Indian Ocean" would leave the reader wondering what purpose the statement had—what it proved, how it was supposed to be taken. (He might take it as a comment derogatory to Swedish oceanographers!)

To say only "the sediments have been unevenly distributed . . ." would leave us tantalized by an interesting generalization but completely unable to understand it because we would have only the vaguest notion of what the writer meant by *unevenly.* Very few readers indeed would gather from the general statement that some of the sediment found in the Atlantic is twelve times as thick as any found in the Pacific. Again, both general and particular are needed for communication.

Generalizations are interesting because they abstract out of the particulars conclusions that are not stated by the particulars. A generalization is the distillation of facts, the sum of specific numbers. Sometimes, as in the passage by Rachel Carson, the generalization is simply a convenience, pointing to what the writer is interested in. Sometimes it is a real discovery, the result of the human mind brooding over facts until something new is hatched, some new idea which was not there before. When Brooks Atkinson considers all those familiar cops and foremen and thugs in the Charlie Chaplin movies and comes up with the conclusion that Chaplin *needs* hostility, he delights us with the insight, the discovery, the new understanding he has given us of familiar facts. To make such generalizations, the writer must be familiar with his subject and must have thought about his subject. His generalizations are the something he has to say about that subject.

Therefore, the generalizations of good writers are almost always interesting, even though we do not yet understand them.

"Hardly anyone thinks that there is anything that needs to be learned about love." *Erich Fromm — see page 172*

"The reading of the story contained in the sediments has only begun." *Rachel Carson — see page 223*

"In those days there was no such thing as a bad movie show." *Brooks Atkinson — see page 169*

"Every worker recognizes his own devices." *Agnes de Mille — see page 148*

"The first truly American literature grew out of the tidewater culture of the early republic." *Bernard DeVoto — see page 133*

"When TV appeared, the motion-picture people put up a struggle." *Elia Kazan — see page 164*

In all such statements, the reader sees interesting beginnings; he is eager to go on and get the details. He needs to go on, to go further into the subject, because generalizations, while they can give us flashes of insight, cannot give us clear understanding without the particulars.

I have often used in writing classes a little ploy I learned from S. I. Hayakawa's *Language in Action.* I tell the class to imagine that I am a foreigner with only a rudimentary reading knowledge of English, and that I have come across a word I do not know, so I ask them. What is *red?* Invariably the answer is, "It's a color." Then I say, "Ah, very interesting. But, please, what is a color?" Then we get wound up in all kinds of intricacies involving wave lengths and reflection and other recondite matters, all of which, of course, throw the poor foreigner into spasms. The solution, as sooner or later a student always points out, is to explain the meaning of *red* not by getting more general but by getting specific: "*Red* is the way this dress looks, and this apple, and this fire-engine — what they all have in common."

One of the things that semanticists, Hayakawa and others, have done for us is to point out that words form, as it were, ladders, mounting from the specific to the general through various levels of abstraction. If we start with *Fido,* we might mount, rung by rung, to *Airedale,* to *dog,* to *pet,* to *domestic animal,* getting more and more abstract at each step.

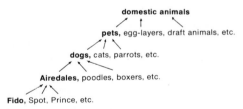

The usefulness of abstractions is that they enable us to think and talk about groups and classes of phenomena, leaving out individual cases. The weakness of abstractions is that, though they leave out individual cases, they derive meaning only from the specific steps of the ladder beneath them, and two people using the same abstraction may be thinking of quite different specifics. If you and I both say *pet,* you may be thinking of dogs and cats, but I may be thinking of otters and lemurs, and a third person might think of lion cubs. So if one of us says, "Pets are easy to take care of," there may be a genuine misunderstanding.

This kind of misunderstanding of abstractions plagues people in important ways. Any lawyer can testify that the general terms of a contract do not always mean the same thing to the two contracting parties. During the 1950's Russia and the United States formally agreed that a democratic form of government is proper and should be guaranteed to various peoples, but they came to serious misunderstandings over the implementation of the agreements because the word *democratic* suggested different specifics to each nation.

Abstractions and generalizations are absolutely necessary, in exposition and elsewhere. But in order for people to understand each other, whether they are parties to an international treaty or businessmen making a contract or the writer and reader of an essay, the abstract and general must be tied down to the specific, the particulars.

The application of this principle to the making of paragraphs is obvious. Almost any generalization which the writer judges interesting enough to tell a reader can stand as the first sentence of a paragraph, and the rest of the paragraph can consist of the particulars which bring the generalization to vividness, clarity, and understanding. Take the sentence by Elia Kazan, quoted above. Kazan, in his essay "Writers and Motion Pictures," built it into a paragraph in just this way.

> When TV appeared, the motion-picture people put up a struggle. They didn't give up easily. First they pretended that it wasn't there. Then they tried to combat it with every conceivable technical novelty. They tried big screens in all sorts of ratios of width to height. They tried the third dimension, with and without goggles. They tried multiple sound sources and bigger budgets. As I write, the novelty is long long long pictures. They tried just about everything except the real novelty: three-dimensional material, new and better stories.

Now the generality comes to life, and in ways that could not have been anticipated. It turns out that Kazan had his tongue in his cheek, that the tone of the generalization was ironic. By detailing the inadequate and diversionary tactics of "the motion-picture people," Kazan has earned, as it were, his generalization. It's the generalization that gives us the interesting subject, but it's all those details about screen shape, goggles, and so on that tell us how to take the generalization, and it's the details that give the passage its punch. In the same way, the exact particulars give body, point, and punch to the essay "The Metabolism of Hummingbirds," which we considered at length in Chapter 3. All those precise details—those scientific measurements, those observations of particular birds—not only get the point across but strengthen that point immeasurably by convincing the reader that the writer knows what he's talking about.

Looking back at some of the paragraphs we considered in Chapter 3, we can see that expository paragraphs (as distinguished from the transitional and emphatic) are all built up of general and particular.

Look at the first paragraph of "The Metabolism of Hummingbirds," for example:

The living rate of an animal depends on its size: the smaller the animal, the faster it lives.

This does not necessarily mean that . . . (A), but . . . (B). . . . For example, . . .

First the general statement, then the clarification of its meaning and an example.

Consider the third paragraph of Erich Fromm's essay, leaving out the transitional matter at the beginning:

Most people see the problem of love primarily as that of being loved, rather than that of loving, of one's capacity to love. Hence the problem to them is how to be loved, how to be lovable.

In pursuit of this aim they follow several paths. One is . . . (A). Another is . . . (B). Other ways are . . . (C, D, etc.). Many of the ways are. . . .

First the general statement, then the examples which bring it to life.

Handbooks specify methods of developing paragraphs, as I've commented before: development by classification, exemplification, analysis, comparison and contrast, definition, etc. These are all useful as exercises in the balancing of general and particular, so long as you remember that this is what such devices are for: They flesh out the skeleton; they add up the numbers; they carry us down the abstraction ladder to solid ground; they bring generalizations to life. Consider the relationship of general and particular in this paragraph by Fromm:

The third error leading to the assumption that there is nothing to be learned about love lies in the confusion between the initial experience of "*falling*" in love, and the permanent state of *being* in love, or as we might better say, of "standing" in love. If two people who have been strangers, as all of us are, suddenly let the wall between them break down, and feel close, feel one, this moment of oneness is one of the most exhilarating, most exciting experiences in life. It is all the more wonderful and miraculous for persons who have been shut off, isolated, without love. This miracle of sudden intimacy is often facilitated if it is combined with, or initiated by, sexual attraction and consummation. However, this type of love is by its very nature not lasting. The two persons become well acquainted, their intimacy loses more and more its miraculous character, until their antagonism, their disappointments, their mutual boredom kill whatever is left of the initial excitement. Yet, in the beginning they do not know all this: in fact, they take the intensity of the infatuation, this being "crazy" about each other, for proof of the intensity of their love, while it may only prove the degree of their preceding loneliness.

Fromm has not taken us to the completely specific. He does not say, "I once observed two young people in my neighborhood, Jack Smith and Adele Jones, who fell madly in love. . . ." There are a great many possible levels of abstraction on the abstraction ladder; it is not always necessary to bring your thoughts all the way down to one individual case but only down far enough, to a level of specificity which will make your generalizations clear.

Presumably Fromm, in writing this paragraph, started with the general statement that *falling* in love is often confused with *being* in love, and then worked his idea out into enough details to enable the reader to follow him, to know in detail what he was talking about. Unless—and this is more likely—unless it happened the other way around, long before the writing of the paragraph, when Fromm was observing the behavior of people and said to himself, "Yes, their love is intense, all right, but it doesn't last," and after observing the particulars came to the general conclusion. For this is, after all, what a writer does first. In the process of making himself in some degree an expert on his subject, he examines the evidence, and, brooding over it with creative imagination, he arrives at generalizations. These he is eager to present to his reader, but he knows that he cannot build an essay or a paragraph from his conclusions alone: he must make judicious use of the evidence. As an observer, he went from particular to general in order to *know* (think how many particulars it took to enable Oliver Pearson to say with such confidence, "The smaller the animal, the faster it lives"); as a writer, he builds from general to particular in order to *explain.*

If a writer is blocked, as so many student writers are, the dynamite that will break the log jam is labeled *particulars.* If you know a subject well enough to write about it, you can make a statement. If you are a blocked writer, the trouble is that you make a generalization and then stop. But if you can imagine a reader saying, "Say, that's an interesting thought. What's the evidence? How did you arrive at that conclusion?" you can start building a paragraph, or an essay.

Imagine any of the writers whose essays are included in Part II sitting down to write and feeling blocked and frustrated. (It happens!) Imagine the muttering which takes place:

"Come on now, blast it! Stop cracking your knuckles and sharpening pencils, Pearson (or Fromm or DeVoto)! You know something about metabolism, after all (or love or American literature)! What's the most important thing you've learned? That the metabolism of hummingbirds is intricately related to their size (or that love is an art or that Mark Twain brought the American heartland into literature)? All right, then. All you have to do is answer the questions, 'How do you know?' 'What's the evidence?' Give the answer, in enough detail, and you've got an essay. So—start thinking about particulars and let's see how the essay grows out of them."

Whether you start with the particulars, like T. S. Eliot's Prufrock walking

> through certain half-deserted streets,
> The muttering retreats
> Of restless nights in one-night cheap hotels
> And sawdust restaurants with oyster-shells[1]

and let the particulars lead you (as Prufrock did not have the courage to do) to "an overwhelming question" or whether, like Elizabeth Browning, you start with a general question, "How do I love thee?" and then, realizing the need for particulars, immediately add, "Let me count the ways" — in either case, as a writer, you must remember that in framing a paragraph or framing an essay the complementary polarity of general and particular gives your reader both the insight and the understanding that he needs.

Exercises

1. In paragraphs 6, 7, and 8 of "Give Slum Children a Chance" (page 189), underline the general statements which must be supported by specific examples. How well is each of them supported?

2. Make three general statements about people which you believe to be true. ("College students are. . . ." "The older generation seems to ignore. . . ." "Americans are different from Germans in that. . . .") Under each statement, list at least three examples which could be used as evidence to convince a reader that the general statement is tenable.

---

1. From "The Love Song of J. Alfred Prufrock" in *Collected Poems 1909 – 1962* by T. S. Eliot. By permission of Harcourt, Brace & World, Inc., and Faber and Faber Ltd.

CHAPTER FIVE

The Sentence

I have postponed until a late chapter consideration of the sentence, the subject with which many handbooks start. From a writer's point of view, the sentence is not something which can be discussed in isolation but something which works within paragraphs and essays.

It is true that the study of sentences as independent structures can be in itself both useful and fascinating. This branch of inquiry, which we call *grammar,* is a noble part of human learning, and it is not without cause that many brilliant minds are devoted to the study of grammar and to the development of new grammars (that is, new systems for analyzing sentences). But grammar is not a subject to consider while writing. You should be able to tell a grammatically correct sentence from an incorrect one, of course (a good handbook, such as those listed in Chapter 8, will help you develop this ability if you don't yet have it), and we could all profit from intensive study of grammar — to which the books of grammar listed in Chapter 8 are excellent introductions. But as writers, and while writing, we consider sentences from a point of view different from that of the grammarian. Our concern is not with the analysis of sentences, but with how sentences work within essays to make communication efficient.

From the writer's point of view, then, how do sentences work? Perhaps in school you were taught the old rule-of-thumb definition: "A sentence is a group of words that expresses a complete thought." Starting with this definition in mind, let's examine a few specimens of what we are talking about — the sentence as it is actually used in standard writing. Let's look at seven specimens from the essays in

Part II, each of which is at least punctuated as if the writer thought of it as a sentence:

1. "So with composing."   *De Mille, page 154*

The first specimen is what is known as a sentence fragment, this one having neither subject nor verb. Good writers use such fragments occasionally. In English classes they are usually banned on the grounds that students should cultivate the habit of writing in sentences, which is quite proper since most of the fragments that students construct are accidental and infelicitous. Notice that the quoted words, though they make excellent sense within Miss de Mille's essay, make no sense at all when they are isolated.

2. "He cannot and he may not."   *De Mille, page 157*

3. "And his output was, to put it charitably, not any better."
                                            Kazan, page 164

4. "His very lineaments show it."   *DeVoto, page 135*

5. "But what is of perhaps even more fundamental theoretical importance is how much there is for man to learn."   *Geertz, page 187*

Specimens 2, 3, 4, and 5 are grammatically correct sentences (though two of them start with coordinating conjunctions, a practice which many English teachers frown upon). But none of these sentences expresses a complete thought. In most of them we find pronouns (*he, he, his, his, it*) whose meaning cannot reach us, for we have no way of knowing to whom or to what they refer. In 3 and 5 we have words expressing comparison, but we can't understand them because one side of each comparison is missing. What "his output" is no better *than,* we cannot tell, nor what that is which "how much there is for man to learn" exceeds in importance. In short, it is clear that none of these sentences was intended to stand alone, or to make sense alone.

Furthermore, we cannot even tell what the common verbs and nouns mean in these sentences. "He cannot," indeed!

Cannot *what?* And what is "output"? Electric current? Money? Friendliness? All of these sentences are designed to be parts of larger structures. They make sense only if we put them back into their essays. Not one, by itself, expresses a complete thought nor, indeed, *any* comprehensible thought.

6. "The Mississippi, the Ganges, and the Nile, those journeying atoms from the Rocky Mountains, the Himmaleh, and Mountains of the Moon, have a kind of personal importance in the annals of the world."

Thoreau, page 246

The sixth specimen is more promising. It does make a comprehensible statement. It has no grammatical links to other sentences. If you were trained in the old method, you will feel that it expresses a complete thought. But your feeling will be only a feeling, not a rational conclusion. If you look at the sentence more closely, you'll notice that it is puzzling. In what sense can these rivers be said to have a *personal* importance in history? Why are just these three rivers mentioned—because they are typical? Because they are the best examples? Because the statement is true only of them? And why mention their sources? Do the sources affect the meaning of the statement? We can answer all these questions if we put the sentence back in its essay; we can answer none of them so long as the sentence is considered in isolation.

7. "Life has been compared to the flame of a candle."

Pearson, page 211

Here's a sentence which sounds so self-contained and independent that it might be an epigram. Surely here we have found a sentence expressing a complete thought? But exactly what does it mean? In what way is life like the flame of a candle? The sentence cannot tell us. To know that, we must read the sentences which follow this one in Pearson's essay.

We must conclude that for a writer, at any rate, a sentence is far from an independent or complete unit of exposition or of thought. It is true that epigrams can stand alone: "Early to bed and early to rise makes a man healthy, wealthy, and wise," for example, or "Rome wasn't built in a day." It is also true that in daily life we can communicate in single sentences: "The next stop is Forty-Eighth Street"; "Pass the butter"; "Someone is at the door." But expository writing is not epigrams, nor daily life, nor theoretical patterns. In expository writing, the sentences are the units of which paragraphs are built. We must study the expository sentence in its native habitat, at work within the paragraph.

The Sentence in the Paragraph

One function of sentences in the paragraph is, as we have seen in the chapter on General and Particular, to develop the central thought of the paragraph by giving details, or particulars, or examples. We must now note another, concomitant function: to keep the flow of discourse smooth and clear. How we link the ideas in one sentence to those in another, how we lead the reader around the curves of thought from sentence to sentence, how we cluster our ideas into sentences so that each represents a clear step in the development of the central idea—these determine how clearly and forcefully we lead the reader through the subject, which is another way of saying that they determine how efficient our sentences are.

To see the truth of this, let's look first at a paragraph in which the reader is *not* skillfully guided and then at the same paragraph written skillfully. I have taken the liberty of rewriting three paragraphs, one each by James Baldwin, Bernard DeVoto, and Henry Thoreau, so as to break up the flow of discourse and reduce the element of guidance. By comparing these inept paragraphs with the originals, we can see how the writers have put their sentences to work in the service of paragraphs.

First, a paragraph from Baldwin's essay, as an unskillful writer might have written it:

[1]It is useful, furthermore, to remember in the case of Hemingway that his reputation began to be unassailable at the very instant that

his work began to decline. ²From that decline it never recovered. ³This period in Hemingway's work begins with the publication of "For Whom the Bell Tolls." ⁴What a boyish and romantic and inflated book that is! ⁵Hindsight allows us to say that it marks Hemingway's abdication from the effort to understand evil. ⁶The evil that is in the world is many-sided, and requires effort to understand. ⁷To say that he stopped trying to understand it is exactly the same thing as saying that he somehow gave up the effort to become a great novelist.

Here are seven sentences. Each one contains ideas which the writer wants to express, but the sentences seem somehow to be at war with each other rather than working together. The trouble is that they contain several ideas but don't show us which of these ideas are central and which are subsidiary, or how the subsidiary ideas are related to the developing central idea. In other words, the flow of discourse is blocked.

Sentence 2 sounds like the introduction of an important idea, which will be developed. But then sentence 3 states a different idea as if *that* were the theme to be developed. If we examine the paragraph closely, we'll probably conclude that the central idea is Hemingway's decline and that Baldwin wants to make two statements about it: when it began, and in what it consists. If that is so, then sentences 2, 4, and 6 cannot be permitted to stand as separate sentences, for they are not *directly* related to the central idea.

In a proper paragraph, in other words, we must make each separate sentence part of the development of the central thought and put all subordinate or modifying or explanatory ideas *within* sentences that help express the central thought. In that way, the flow of discourse will run through all the sentences and not be obstructed or turned aside by any one sentence. That's easy to say, of course, but not always easy to accomplish: it is what a skillful writer works for in revising his sentences, making sure through whatever exasperating effort that in the final draft the thought flows effortlessly. Look at the way Baldwin wrote the paragraph in question (page 139):

¹It is useful, furthermore, to remember in the case of Hemingway that his reputation began to be unassailable at the very instant that

his work began that decline from which it never recovered—at about the time of "For Whom the Bell Tolls." [2]Hindsight allows us to say that this boyish and romantic and inflated book marks Hemingway's abdication from the effort to understand the many-sided evil that is in the world. [3]This is exactly the same thing as saying that he somehow gave up the effort to become a great novelist.

Notice how the idea of *For Whom the Bell Tolls* is tucked into the statements about decline, since it is an illustrative idea rather than a central one. The reader is now led through three steps: (1) reputation began to be unassailable at instant of decline; (2) decline began with abdication of effort to understand evil; (3) i.e., with abdication of effort to be a great novelist.

(Incidentally, I hope it's not necessary to point out that I am not here concerned with whether or not you agree with Baldwin's assessment of Hemingway but only with how he makes sentences.)

How does a writer achieve sentences which keep the discourse flowing? By thinking in paragraphs—that is, by keeping clear in his own mind the central idea of the paragraph and making each sentence say something about that. The time to be sure you are achieving such smoothness of discourse is during revision, of course, not during the writing of the first draft, but it is also true that the more conscious you are of the need for such sentences, the more your thoughts will tend to flow into them even during the uninhibited writing of a first draft.

Look now at a paragraph of Bernard DeVoto's, first at a part of that paragraph as he did *not* write it:

[1]Lincoln's feeling for the continentalism of the American nation was so intense that it almost transcended the transcendent facts. [2]It was a deposit in the very cells of his bones. [3]It came from the soil of the Great Valley itself. [4]Lincoln was, as Herndon rightly says, one of the limestone men. [5]Such men were tall, gaunt, powerful, sallow, and saturnine. [6]When the wilderness on both sides of the Ohio comes under the plow, such men appear in quantity. [7]In fact, there are enough of them to constitute a recognizable type. [8]Lincoln's radical democracy, too, was wrought from the experience of the Great Valley. . . .

Notice the way sentences 5, 6, and 7 lead us *away* from the central idea, which concerns Abraham Lincoln, and into the idea of "the limestone man" as a type. Notice the wrench with which sentence 8 has to pull us back to the idea of Lincoln and into what seems such a different idea about Lincoln that it might belong to a different paragraph. Now look at the way Bernard DeVoto wrote the whole paragraph, of which the preceding passage represents only about the first half:

[1]Lincoln's feeling for the continentalism of the American nation was so intense that it almost transcended the transcendent facts. [2]It was a deposit in the very cells of his bones from the soil of the Great Valley. [3]He was, Herndon rightly says, one of the limestone men, the tall, gaunt, powerful, sallow, saturnine men who appear in quantity enough to constitute a type when the wilderness on both sides of the Ohio comes under the plow. [4]His radical democracy was wrought from the experience of the Great Valley. [5]In his ideas and beliefs as in the shadowed depths of his personality there is apparent a new articulation of American life. [6]His very lineaments show it. [7]When you turn from the Jefferson nickel to the Lincoln penny as when you turn from Jefferson's first inaugural address to any of Lincoln's state papers, in the flash of a total and immediate response you understand that you have turned from one era to a later one. [8]You have turned from the tidewater republic to the continental empire.

DeVoto, page 135

Notice how DeVoto's third sentence has subordinated the limestone type to the idea of Lincoln. Notice also how the whole paragraph leads to an idea of which Lincoln himself is only an example, but how right up to that last sentence your mind is kept clearly on Lincoln:

1. "Lincoln's feeling. . . ."
2. " . . . his bones. . . ."
3. "He was. . . ."
4. "His radical democracy. . . ."
5. "In his ideas. . . ."
6. "His very lineaments. . . ."
7. " . . . the Lincoln penny . . . Lincoln's state papers. . . ."

Every one of these seven sentences, in other words, is a statement about Lincoln. The last sentence, number 8, which is a generalization from the facts about Lincoln, is thrown into sharp relief, given a great emphasis, by the fact that after so many statements about Lincoln, this statement broadens out to encompass an idea of which Lincoln is only a part. (Contrast this effect with the confusion which results from a *pointless* generalization, such as sentence 6 of the first version on page 68.)

We can admire this paragraph for other elements besides the sentences — beginning with the interesting idea here expressed, the insight into American types. One element, which reminds us of the importance of general and particular, is the imaginative rightness of the details — what makes this paragraph stick in a reader's memory is likely to be the idea of the tall, gaunt, powerful, sallow, saturnine limestone man, together with the wonderfully familiar evidence of the Lincoln penny. These details support and vitalize the generalities beautifully. But notice how the communication of these generalizations and details is made smooth and forceful by the sentence patterns. And notice how the *rightness* of sentences 3 and 6, for instance, can be judged only within the context of the paragraph in which they appear.

Turn now to a paragraph by Henry Thoreau, again starting with a version which he did *not* write:

[1]The Mississippi, the Ganges, and the Nile, those journeying atoms from the Rocky Mountains, the Himmaleh, and Mountains of the Moon, have a kind of personal importance in the annals of the world. [2]The heavens are not yet drained over their sources. [3]The Mountains of the Moon sent their annual tribute to the ancient Pharaohs without fail. [4]They still send their tribute to the modern Pasha. [5]The rest of his tribute he must collect at the point of the sword. [6]The footsteps of the first travelers must have been guided by rivers. [7]They are the constant lure, when they flow by our doors, to distant enterprise and adventure. [8]By a natural impulse, the dwellers on their banks will at length accompany their currents to the lowlands of the globe. [9]They will explore, at the rivers' invitation, the interior of continents. [10]Rivers are the natural highways of all nations. [11]They level the ground and remove obstacles from the path of the traveler. [12]They quench the

traveler's thirst. ¹³They bear him on their bosoms. ¹⁴Along the banks of rivers occurs the most interesting scenery. ¹⁵Rivers flow through the most populous portions of the globe. ¹⁶In the river valleys we find that the animal and vegetable kingdoms have attained their greatest perfection.

There are interesting ideas here, but the flow of these ideas from writer to reader is awkward and disjointed. Notice how the flow of discourse is broken by sentence 3, since we have no way of seeing how it relates to sentence 2, and how sentence 5 leads us away from the central idea, and how sentences 14, 15, and 16 seem to have wandered away from the immediate thought.

What is the central idea of the paragraph? Not rivers only, and not the marvelous attractiveness of rivers only, but the way rivers entice and serve the traveler—a fit theme for the opening of Thoreau's account of his river voyage. In the paragraph as Thoreau wrote it, notice the skillful way in which the sentences keep the reader's mind first on the enticing idea of the sources of rivers and second on the idea of the traveler and what the river does for him, subordinating all other details to these:

¹The Mississippi, the Ganges, and the Nile, those journeying atoms from the Rocky Mountains, the Himmaleh, and Mountains of the Moon, have a kind of personal importance in the annals of the world. ²The heavens are not yet drained over their sources, but the Mountains of the Moon still send their annual tribute to the Pasha without fail, as they did to the Pharaohs, though he must collect the rest of his revenue at the point of the sword. ³Rivers must have been the guides which conducted the footsteps of the first travelers. ⁴They are the constant lure, when they flow by our doors, to distant enterprise and adventure; and, by a natural impulse, the dwellers on their banks will at length accompany their currents to the lowlands of the globe, or explore at their invitation the interior of continents. ⁵They are the natural highways of all nations, not only leveling the ground and removing obstacles from the path of the traveler, quenching his thirst and bearing him on their bosoms, but conducting him through the most interesting scenery, the most populous portions of the globe, and where the animal and vegetable kingdoms attain their greatest perfection. *Thoreau, page 246*

Thoreau's sentences are longer than DeVoto's or Baldwin's, but in this passage, as in the others, the pattern of sentences follows the same logic: Keep one central idea in mind, and lead the reader through that idea, sentence by sentence. Therefore the ideas about what lies along the banks of rivers, which may be very interesting in themselves, are not allowed to reach the reader as ideas in themselves but are strung on the thread of the idea of adventurous travel.

In my discussion of the three paragraphs so far, I have really made only one comment: that it is necessary, for the reader's sake, to bring ideas together in effective sentences. There are many more lessons to be drawn from the use of sentences in these paragraphs. For instance, I have not represented the need for taking apart sentences which inefficiently combine *different* ideas.

An unskillful writer might have run together the ideas in DeVoto's third and fourth sentences: "He was, Herndon rightly says, one of the limestone men . . . even his radical democracy being wrought from the experience of the Great Valley." Or he might have jumbled together Thoreau's second and third sentences: "The heavens are not yet drained over the sources of these rivers, or the sources of any of the world's rivers, those guides which conducted the footsteps of the first travelers, but the Mountains of the Moon still send their annual tribute. . . ." Here, of course, the writer must see that he has jumbled together *two* steps in the discourse and has to separate them.

But in practice this is not a serious problem. Writers don't have much trouble *separating* ideas, once they have seen the need of making the sentences logical steps in discourse, but we all have trouble, even the most skillful of us, in *uniting* ideas into logical steps. I have not been unfair in suggesting that the ineffective writer will use many more sentences than he should; the hypothetical bad writer who used seven sentences where Baldwin used three, eight where DeVoto used four, and sixteen where Thoreau used five does represent the common fault of unskillful writers, who make their readers take in ideas in fragments and sort them out for themselves. In effect, such writers say to their readers, as a certain advertising executive is reputed to have said to his subordinates, "I've given you the apples; now you bake the pie."

Groups of Sentences

If a paragraph is fairly long, it may contain more than one basic idea. It may, for instance, contrast two different ideas. Whenever more than one idea is developed in a paragraph, the sentences must be carefully formed to show this. They must be "clumped," as groups of paragraphs are "clumped" within an essay (see Chapter 3). Consider, for example, the opening paragraph of Clifford Geertz's essay, "The Transition to Humanity." (The whole essay is reprinted on pages 177–188; here we need only abstract out the elements under consideration.)

In this paragraph, Geertz is contrasting two theories about man's relationship to the other animals. After introducing the whole subject in the first three sentences of the paragraph, he develops each theory in a group of sentences and keeps the reader aware that he is doing this by signaling the "clumping" of the sentences.

Group 1
- Sentence 4: Some students, especially those in the biological sciences, . . . have tended to stress. . . .
- Sentence 5: They see evolution as . . . they tend to view. . . .
- Sentence 6: What strikes them is. . . .

Group 2
- Sentence 7: However, students in the social sciences . . . have tended to view [man] as unique. . . .
- Sentence 8: Man is. . . .
- Sentence 9: Only he . . . only he . . . only he . . . only he. . . .
- Sentence 10: He has. . . .
- Sentence 11: Only he. . . .

By parallel structure and by the repetition of key words, Geertz keeps the reader aware that in sentences 4 through 6 he is considering one topic, in 7 through 11 another.

Style and the Sentence

It is convenient to take up under the heading of sentences the subject of style, since it is in the revision of our sentences that we most consciously work for style. Many good books have been written on this single subject — some of the best are described in Chapter 8. A serious writer will keep such books beside his bed or in his traveling bag, for style is an enchanting subject for the writer. Style is the music of language, the sound of the writer's voice, the life breath of exposition. But more important for our purposes here, style is also the practical matter of saying what you mean concisely and precisely — a plain bread-and-butter necessity for the writer.

Achieving Conciseness. The first rule of style in this sense is conciseness. Achieve conciseness, and all other expository virtues shall be added unto you. The fewer the words with which you can express a given thought clearly and gracefully, the more highly charged with meaning your words will be and the more you will seem to know what you are talking about. Therefore, if you can express a thought well in nine words, you must never let yourself use ten.

Verbosity is a fault unfortunately encouraged by the practice of padding out essays to assigned minimum lengths. I remember once many years ago taking an essay into class and scolding the student author for padding it with unnecessary words, only to have him say angrily, "You told me I had to write five hundred words!" For myself, I have solved this problem by always assigning *maximum* word limits. Write *no more than* five hundred words on such and such a problem. Then I scold students for not getting more said within that limit. But any student can solve the same problem for himself, even if he is assigned essays of minimum lengths, simply by refusing to play meaningless games with himself and by disciplining himself to make each sentence say as much as possible.

The best friend of the writer who has a completed first draft is his blue pencil. Go through your essay rigorously, and simply cross out every word that isn't needed to get your thoughts expressed clearly. (I'm talking about the excision of *words,* now, not *ideas.*)

Suppose Thoreau had come across the following in his manuscript:

The natural phenomena which we call rivers must have been the faithful guides which conducted the footsteps of the first fearful but expectant travelers.

Considering the passage in the light of the whole essay and the whole paragraph — considering, that is, exactly what it was he was trying to get said — he would use his blue pencil thus:

~~The natural phenomena which we call~~ rivers must have been the ~~faithful~~ guides which conducted the footsteps of the first ~~fearful but expectant~~ travelers.

In another essay, the idea of *faithful* guides or the idea of *fearful* travelers might have been needed; here, since the author is talking about guides and travelers in general (faithful or unfaithful, fearful or fearless), the words can only confuse the reader. On the other hand, although Thoreau could have cut out "the footsteps of" and said "which conducted the first travelers," he would not have wanted to, because the idea of footsteps suggests the idea of adventure, as well as the idea of the simplest kind of travel, so this phrase would stay in the sentence. As for "the natural phenomena which we call," that *must* come out, for it conveys no meaning at all. Such meaningless expressions clutter up most writers' first drafts, but they must not clutter up the final communication.

Suppose Bernard DeVoto had found this in his first draft:

His outstanding and radical type of democracy was painfully wrought from the life-long experience of what we call the Great Valley.

He would have to wield his pencil to this effect:

His ~~outstanding and~~ radical ~~type of~~ democracy was ~~painfully~~ wrought from the ~~life-long~~ experience of ~~what we call~~ the Great Valley.

It looks easy here, but any writer can testify how hard it is to spot all the phrases like *type of* and weed them out.

Many a student essay contains passages like this one:

About the end of the first half of the nineteenth century, between the Mexican War and the frightful upheaval we call the Civil War, something happened in American literature. For some reason or other, within this short period, there appeared many of the best works of some of our country's very best writers. For this reason, this period has been designated the period of the American Renaissance.

Here are 67 words, which can be reduced immediately by a blue pencil to 32:

Between the Mexican War and the Civil War there appeared many of the best works of some of our best writers. For this reason, this period has been designated the American Renaissance.

That's far from a finished passage yet, but it is already on the way to force and polish, and the writer, having cleared away the dead words, can see more clearly what he has said and can think about saying it better. He will probably think over the word *designated,* for instance, and search for a better word, though in the first version *designated* did not sound so bad, being lost in all the bombast.

Students always object at this point that I am asking them to prune out all the *beauty* from their writing, all the grace and force. We should remember Hemingway's statement that style is a matter of architecture, not interior decoration; it must grow from the subject itself, not be added with a flourish. Conciseness is to style what streamlining is to airplanes: at once a utility and a means of beauty.

Besides blue-penciling, there's another way of working towards conciseness. The principle is this: A sentence can always be reduced to a clause; a clause can always be reduced to a phrase; a phrase can always be reduced to a word; a word can always be left out. For instance:

(*sentence*)   We entered the valley on our third day out from Ramapo. SPREAD OUT BEFORE US, THE VALLEY WAS A BEAUTIFUL SIGHT.

(*clause*)   On our third day out from Ramapo, we entered the valley, WHICH LAY SPREAD OUT BEFORE US, A BEAUTIFUL SIGHT.

(*phrase*)   On our third day out from Ramapo we entered a valley OF GREAT BEAUTY.

(*word*)   On our third day out from Ramapo, we entered a BEAUTIFUL valley.

(   )   On our third day out from Ramapo, we entered the valley.

Which of these levels of reduction is the proper one? That can be answered only within a particular paragraph, by checking the passage against the central idea. The point is to come as far down the scale as you can with lesser ideas, leaving the major ideas expanded and emphatic.

There are other rules for achieving conciseness, which I think of as the trouble-shooter's rules, to be used when you find yourself tangled and bogged in your sentences. When in such trouble, try these:

1. Change indirect statements to direct. (For "There appeared many books," try "Many books appeared.")

2. Change impersonal constructions to personal. (For "Teaching is a profession encumbered by . . . ," write "Teachers are encumbered by . . ."; for "Objections have been received," write "Customers have objected"; for "Compilation of data on the subject of achievement scores is delayed pending release of pertinent information by the office of the president," try "Until the president releases. . . .")

3. Make the logical subject of your statement the grammatical subject of the sentence. (For "There are reasons

which have been cited for teacher dissatisfaction," write "The main reasons for . . . are . . ." or "Mr. Jones cites the following reasons . . ." or "Teachers are dissatisfied because. . . .")

These rules are not for constant use—that would make your prose stilted and mannered—but for getting you out of briar patches and mudholes.

One of the most important ways of achieving conciseness is always to use the exact and forceful *word*, but the whole subject of word choice we must leave for Chapter 6.

Achieving Grace. If the first virtue of style is conciseness, the second is grace. It's impossible to distinguish entirely between these two elements, but it is valuable to see the writer's job as including grace, which means saying things not only clearly but well.

One means of grace in exposition is deliberate repetition, either of words or of sentence patterns. In Chapter 3, we saw how writers repeat key words and themes to keep the reader on the track (see especially pages 45 to 48). On page 69 we noted how the pronouns referring to Lincoln keep DeVoto's sentences related to the theme.

Where repetition is accidental, it is awkward and annoying. An old rule says you shouldn't use the same noun, verb, adjective, or adverb twice within three lines. So far as it applies to accidental and meaningless repetition, this is sound. No one would leave this passage in his essay:

When the sonnet is considered historically we see that throughout most of English history there have been two basic kinds of sonnet: the Petrarchan sonnet and the Elizabethan sonnet, each popular in its own historical period.

On the other hand, no one would object to the repetition in this passage:

Charity suffereth long and is kind; *charity* envieth not; *charity* vaunteth not itself, is not puffed up.

Or in this one, in which we find not only the repetition of *words* but also that repetition of *structure* called parallelism:

Four score and seven years ago our fathers brought forth on this continent a new *nation,*

> *conceived* in liberty
>> and
>
> *dedicated* to the proposition that all men
>> are created equal.

Now we are engaged in a great civil war, testing whether that *nation,* or any *nation*

> so *conceived*
>> and
>
> so *dedicated*

can long endure.

The use of such repetition, of word and structure, cannot be reduced to rules. We can only be conscious of it as a skill every writer must develop to a degree, and we can note that it is a natural human habit to fall into repetitive patterns of language under the influence of strong feeling. ("I've begged and pleaded and argued with you," I heard a mother say recently to her recalcitrant child, "and the more I beg and plead and argue with you, the more you don't listen to me!")

We can study the patterns of repetition in what we read and thus sharpen our awareness of them. Consider the opening of Melville's *Moby-Dick:*

Call me Ishmael. Some years ago—never mind how long precisely—having little or no money in my purse, and nothing particular to interest me on shore, I thought I would sail about a little and see the watery part of the world. It is a way I have of driving off the spleen, and regulating the circulation. Whenever I find myself growing grim about the mouth; whenever it is a damp, drizzly November in my soul; whenever I find myself involuntarily pausing before coffin warehouses, and bringing up the rear of every funeral I meet; and especially whenever my hypos get such an upper hand of me, that it requires a strong moral principle to prevent me from deliberately stepping into the street, and methodically knocking people's hats off—then, I account it high time to get to sea as soon as I can. This is my substitute for pistol and ball.

Here the repetition of word and structure gives the passage the effect of high dignity; if you read the passage aloud, you find yourself chanting it. But even in less highly ambitious and rhetorical prose, you will find the same kind of pattern, though working more quietly. Consider the repetitive pattern of Bernard De Voto's paragraph, quoted on page 69 above:

```
Lincoln's feeling   || was so intense . . .
                    || was a deposit . . .

                    || the limestone men
He was one of       || the  ||  tall
                              gaunt
                              powerful      men . . .
                              sallow
                           || saturnine

                                    || ideas . . .
                          || in his || beliefs . . .
There is apparent   ||
                          || in the shadowed depths . . .

|| When you turn from . . .
|| when you turn from . . .
|| you have turned from . . .
|| You have turned from . . .
```

Sentence Length. It's interesting to note, in the opening of *Moby-Dick,* how Melville has varied the length of his sentences. Against the stark, abrupt "Call me Ishmael" rises the long, swelling reiteration of *whenevers.* If we count words in the first five sentences of the novel, the variation is striking:

sentence	number of words
#1	3
#2	40
#3	15
#4	87
#5	8

To a certain extent, this variation expresses the highly emotional state of the narrator, but that's not a complete explanation. You can see the same kind of variation in DeVoto's paragraph:

sentence	number of words
#1	19
#2	18
#3	39
#4	12
#5	22
#6	5
#7	48
#8	11

What an emphasis is thrown on sentence 6 ("His very lineaments show it") by the length of the sentences coming before and after! The ebb and flow of discourse is suggested by the variety of these sentences, as you can hear if you read the paragraph out loud.

Achieving the proper length and variety in sentences can no more be reduced to rules than can achieving the proper pattern of repetition. The important thing is to be aware of the need for both and to be familiar with the practice of other writers (especially those you admire). Judge yourself by the music — that is to say, the *tone* of the passage and its fitness for the expressed idea. Expository prose must follow the rule which Alexander Pope enunciated for poetry:

'Tis not enough no harshness gives offence;
The sound must seem an echo to the sense.

In good exposition, we hear the voice of the writer, for style is, finally, the voice of the man himself.

The Style Is the Man Himself

If you stop to think about it, you can easily distinguish the different personalities behind the writings we have cited as examples so far and, indeed, behind all the essays in Part II. Notice the tense, earnest, preaching, dogmatic style of James Baldwin; the pugnacious style of Bernard DeVoto; the nervous, finger-snapping, off-the-top-of-the-head style of Elia Kazan; the slow, thoughtful style of Agnes de Mille; the precise statements of Oliver Pearson, based squarely on evidence; the solid, generalizing style of Clifford Geertz; the style of Thoreau, which seems barely restrained from rushing in all directions as his thoughts lead him out into poetic relationships and connections.

What personality will your readers apprehend through your writing? Don't try to be a personality, or what they will apprehend will be the effort and the phoniness. Relax. Talk to your reader. Let out your first draft uninhibitedly. Revise your sentences so that they not only carry the central thought but also sound right to you. You will come through, never fear. You are not a machine, nor a god, nor a talking statue in a tableau: You are one particular person, and if you learn to speak frankly and honestly in your expository prose, the style of your sentences will inevitably be you and nobody else.

Your sentences are an extremely important element of your writing. Take time to go over every piece of writing once just to check for sentence structure, for the logic of sentence order, and for the music of the sentences, the way your sentences carry the tone of your own voice.

Exercises

1. In the following paragraph, the sentences are inefficiently constructed. Rewrite the paragraph, keeping the ideas in the same order in which they are stated but grouping them efficiently into sentences. Compare your finished version with the original paragraph, on page 157.

The folks who think only of money are cynical. They pretend, cynically, that they don't care. However, they get stomach ulcers and they become alcoholics. These facts prove that they care, and show how much they care. It isn't a matter of what work is done. What's important is *how* the work is done. It is vital to everyone to know that his work is necessary. We must know that our work is done to the best of our ability. That's true of any work—whether we make soap operas or wash floors. It is only when the dust is swept under the rug that the process of disintegration sets in.

2. Revise one of your own essays by striking out all unnecessary words. Select at least two words or phrases which could be left out but which you prefer to retain. Explain why you want to keep them.

CHAPTER SIX

The Word

In most people's minds, the word is *the* unit of discourse: Speaking and writing are thought of as ways of using *words.* We say "He has a way with words," or "What's the good word?" or "Let thy words be few." When Polonius asks Hamlet "What do you read, my lord?" the answer is "Words, words, words." To say "He has a way with paragraphs," or to substitute *sentence* in any of these sayings, would spoil the effect. And though the preceding chapters emphasize the importance of the whole essay, and the paragraph, and the sentence, the universal feeling that the *word* is basic is certainly sound. If you want to write well, you must choose the right words.

Words are the writer's tools. They must be kept clean and sharp and used skillfully. The good writer values his words, takes care of them, uses them with precision, as any good craftsman uses the tools of his trade. A clumsy or careless writer, like a clumsy carpenter, lets his tools get dull or uses them in the wrong places, and generally neglects them.

Many people who write are simply insensitive to words. They use expressions like "In our modern world of today," without noticing that "In our world" or "In the modern world" or "In the world of today" or simply "Today" would express the idea more sparsely, cleanly, and forcefully. They will say "That's slightly ridiculous" or "His idea is most unique," without noticing that they have thereby blunted the edges of *ridiculous* and *unique.* They will say "As you infer" when they mean *imply,* or use *affect* when they mean *effect,* or *convince* when they mean *persuade,* or *credible* when they mean *credulous.* They will let their sentences get cluttered up with meaningless words, as in "Let's have lunch together *in terms of* next week" or "*In the case of* John Milton, *he* was *a man who was* determined to be a great poet."

Let's understand each other on this point. There is a snobbish kind of insistence on correctness for social reasons which has nothing to do with what I'm talking about here. Many people think they have to "watch their language" around English teachers, in order not to make social blunders. That's pure nonsense, and most English teachers, though too polite to say so, are embarrassed by it. What I'm concerned with here is not "correctness," but preciseness in the use of the tools of communication.

No one has perfect command of English. Writers must always, forever, be learning more and more about words. Beginning writers misuse words — that's only natural. Some few students, such as the one who wrote "Occupation-wise there is coming about somewhat of an equality of women," are so insensitive to words that they'll never be really skillful writers, but we are all only relatively skillful, and we must all keep learning.

There's a false feeling about writing which keeps many people from expressing themselves as well as they can. I think of it as a kind of stage fright. When people unaccustomed to public speaking address a group, they often go all stiff and resort to big words, sweeping generalities, trite ideas pompously spoken, windy bombast — under the impression that the occasion calls for high dignity and rhetorical elegance. Similarly, people of common sense and interesting ideas often go bombastic when they write, producing trite, inflated, fuzzy, unnatural English — thinking they have to make an impression — when they should be simply communicating with people.

Much more of the foggy and imprecise language that gets into print, however, is deliberate. James Baldwin says (page 140), "We live in a country in which words are mostly used to cover the sleeper, not to wake him up." *Mostly* is perhaps too harsh, and the custom is certainly not confined to one country, but the observation is an important one. In advertising and in politics, especially, writers often use words not so much to communicate ideas as to impress the reader or to make the reader feel differently about something than he would if we expressed ourselves plainly. "The reply is negative," we sometimes say, meaning simply "No." Or "Illumination is required to be extinguished in these premises on termination of business," meaning "Put out the lights when you leave." Or "Our financial requirements are being projected in the minimum need area of two millions of dollars," meaning "We need two million dollars."

The *New York Times* of March 24, 1965, carried the report of a real-estate agent who deplored the term *loft* and suggested that the profession should change "Loft for Rent" to "Commercial or Industrial Space for Rent." Perhaps he's right. When *Thunnus saliens* was called *horse mackerel*, it did not sell very well, but when the same fish is called *tuna*, it sells quite satisfactorily, and we may presume that when it is called *Chicken of the Sea*, it's irresistible, for a rose by another name does *not* always smell as sweet.

In politics, as George Orwell tells us in detail in "Politics and the English Language," words are used as often to disguise meaning as to clarify it. Consider such odd terms as *clean bomb*, for example. And notice how the human implications are concealed by *policy of deterrence, low megaton yield,* or *equalization of population.* In time of war, soldiers sometimes come to distrust all big words. Remember Hemingway's statement in *A Farewell to Arms?*

I was always embarrassed by the words sacred, glorious, and sacrifice and the expression in vain. We had heard them, sometimes standing in the rain almost out of earshot, so that only the shouted words came through, and had read them, on proclamations that were slapped up by billposters over other proclamations, now for a long time, and I had seen nothing sacred, and the things that were glorious had no glory and the sacrifices were like the stockyards at Chicago if nothing was done with the meat except to bury it. There were many words that you could not stand to hear and finally only the names of places had dignity. Certain numbers were the same way and certain dates and these with the names of the places were all you could say and have them mean anything. Abstract words such as glory, honor, courage, or hallow were obscene beside the concrete names of villages, the numbers of roads, the names of rivers, the numbers of regiments and the dates.[1]

The lesson is clear. Propaganda is not communication. If your purpose is communication, you must use words so that they really communicate. You can use abstract words, honorable words, dignified words if you really have something abstract, honorable, or dignified to communicate, but not otherwise.

Precision and Liveliness

First of all, you must keep your language clear and precise. Don't use more words than you need.

Words are like leaves, and where they most abound,
Much fruit of sense beneath is rarely found,

as Alexander Pope says.

Avoid the use of those ready-made phrases which come to mind easily because they are so trite and common but which usually don't mean anything, such as "under the circumstances" or "consideration must be given to" or "in view of the fact that" or "It is not unreasonable to expect that." Avoid as much as possible the use of counters, or verbal slugs, which have no readily definable meaning, such as "in the *case* of," "the *thing* that," "a *definite* advantage." Look out for the currently fashionable slug especially; though it is everyone's language today, it will be forgotten tomorrow. Not long ago, we often heard "in terms of population" or "in terms of entertainment" or "in terms of finances." Recently, these were popularly changed to "population-wise" or "entertainment-wise" or "finance-wise." What will take their place tomorrow, who knows?

Can you imagine Thoreau saying, "In terms of desperation, the great majority of people manage to appear deceptively quiet, surface-wise"? Or how about that fine old

1. Reprinted with the permission of Charles Scribner's Sons from *A Farewell to Arms* by Ernest Hemingway (page 190, 1957 ed.). Copyright 1929 Charles Scribner's Sons; renewal copyright © 1957 Ernest Hemingway.

proverb, "Typically, people who are experiencing misery derive a sort of comfort from fellow human beings, company-wise"? They go much better, somehow, as "The mass of men lead lives of quiet desperation" and "Misery loves company."

Keep your words lively, active, and natural. Keep them tied to specifics. Notice the liveliness and vitality of this passage, in which Thoreau describes a section of the Concord River:

> . . . Many waves are there agitated by the wind, keeping nature fresh, the spray blowing in your face, reeds and rushes waving; ducks by the hundred, all uneasy in the surf, in the raw wind, just ready to rise, and now going off with a clatter and a whistling like riggers straight for Labrador, flying against the stiff gale with reefed wings, or else circling round first, with all their paddles briskly moving, just over the surf, to reconnoitre you before they leave these parts; gulls wheeling overhead, muskrats swimming for dear life, wet and cold, with no fire to warm them by that you know of, their labored homes rising here and there like haystacks; and countless mice and moles and winged titmice along the sunny, windy shore; cranberries tossed on the waves and heaving up on the beach, their little red skiffs beating about among the alders; — such healthy natural tumult as proves the last day is not yet at hand.   *Page 242*

Notice how the *tumult* is carried by the active verbs and verbals: *agitated, keeping, blowing, waving, rise, going off, clatter, whistling, flying, circling, briskly moving, reconnoitre, leave, wheeling, swimming, warm, rising, tossed, heaving, beating.* Notice the perfect rightness of *wheeling* in "gulls wheeling overhead," catching in one word the action of the seagulls circling there, looking down, with outstretched wings supported by the wind. And the rightness of the words about the ducks, first uneasy, ready to rise, and then going off all together, making a clatter with their wings. The sharp and active impression we get of those ducks is partly the result of Thoreau's knowing his subject well, his familiarity with the way ducks behave, and partly the way he has built the sentence in a headlong rush, and partly this rightness of word choice — all these working together.

Thoreau's subject is a tumultuous one, and to that extent the subject is easy to present in sharp and active terms. But good writers get the same clear, sharp effect in dealing with other kinds of subjects, too. See how Elia Kazan gives us sparse, active language in a description of a static scene:

I remember my first day at lunch in the Twentieth Century Fox commissary. I was told that Mr. Zanuck ate in state, flanked by his producers, behind the closed doors of the executive dining room. I didn't care about them. To me, the figures of glamour were the famous directors — gods! There they were, ranged along the best wall, looking out over the enormous dining room, each at his reserved table with his favorite waitress, also reserved. The center tables were taken by the stars. They were surrounded by their favorites and sycophants: make-up men, hairdressers, stand-ins, agents, girl or boy friends. At other prominent tables sat the big men of the back lot, the cameramen. Each had his heads of departments, his gaffers and key grips and so on: a Homeric catalogue.

Only after several weeks did I notice and explore a sorry group at a remote table. Their isolation was so evident that it seemed planned. There was no mixing with this group, no table-hopping to their table. They seemed out of place. Their dress was tamer. Few had the fashionable sun tan that a Beverly Hills success carries right to his grave. They laughed in a hysterical way, giddy or bitter. The writers. . . .

Page 160

As in the Thoreau passage, the words do not create an effect by themselves. Here, the nervous sentences, the dramatic way everything is presented as the successive discoveries of an enchanted observer, the choice of eloquent details and the suppression of all others, all are necessary to the effect. But so are the words. All simple words, you observe, except for *sycophant* and *Homeric catalogue* and the technical words *gaffer* and *grip* — the rest are all words one might use in informal speech. A few very apt words: the directors are *ranged* along a wall, as if on exhibition; the writers are a *sorry* group; Zanuck is *flanked* by his producers. The specific lists of those who surround the stars and cameramen give us an effect of great specificness of understanding. The action words keep the passage lively: *ate, flanked, closed, ranged, looking, taken, surrounded, sat, notice, explore, planned, mixing, table-hopping, carries, laughed.* (To get a lively appreciation of the skillfulness of this passage, do the exercise on page 107.)

Notice how few adjectives these writers use. (Mark Twain said, "As for the adjective: when in doubt, leave it out." Voltaire said, "The adjective is the enemy of the noun," since adjectives always qualify or modify nouns and thus prevent them from standing strong and free.) If we distinguish between intensifiers (modifiers intended to make the noun or verb more emphatic) and qualifiers (modifiers which change the meaning or add a meaning), these writers use qualifiers sparingly and intensifiers practically never, and so should you. Not *very strong spray,* but *spray;* not *very healthy* or *definitely healthy,* but *healthy;* not *majestically flanked,* but *flanked;* not *eager table-hopping,* but *table-hopping.* Choose the right word, and leave it alone to do its job. Modify only when you need to add a meaning: *labored homes, countless mice, healthy natural tumult, first day, executive dining room, best wall, enormous dining room.*

Taking out dead words is a matter of conscious revision, and we must assume that both Thoreau and Kazan had some deadwood in their first drafts which they later eliminated. Choosing the exact word is a process not so easily learned or consciously controlled. Words "come to us" as we write. We can select the best that come — the most precise and forceful. We can send back an unsatisfactory word and hope that a better one will be sent up to replace it. But we must prepare ourselves, in advance, to be able to think of precise words. We must pay attention to words in our reading and use the writer's reference tools to improve our knowledge of words.

When Joseph Addison, in his essay on superstition, says "I . . . began to consider my self, with some Confusion, as a Person that had brought a Disaster upon the Family" (page 127), he is using the word *disaster* in a particular way, conscious at once of its common meaning and its origin. A disaster is a calamity. But the word *disaster* comes from *aster,* or *star,* and the stars, according to the superstitions Addison is talking about, govern the fates of men. A *disaster* is a calamity that results when the stars are in an unfortunate position according to astrology, a calamity caused by the stars. If you know the basic meaning of the word, you get more meaning from the passage and are amused by Addison's playful choice of the word. Furthermore, if you know the meaning of the Greek word *aster,* "star," you will have a finer appreciation of *aster,* the flower shaped like a star, and *astronomy,* the study of stars, and *astronaut,* the man who sails out among the stars (by combination with *nautes,* the Greek word for "sailor," with allusion to the heroic *Argonauts,* who sailed the ship Argo on adventures into the unknown world), and even *asterisk,* the punctuation mark that looks like a star.

One of the most fruitful games a writer can play is the study of words—their precise meanings, their origins, the stories behind them. Not that he will collect strange and esoteric words, if he is interested in communication, but he will be interested in the words people really use and will indulge his curiosity, thus amusing himself and sharpening his tools at the same time.

A writer playing this game will notice that the word *breakfast* is composed of two words and means breaking one's fast, or eating after fasting all night—once he has noticed this, he won't ever again say "Is breakfast ready?" without thinking of the breaking of a fast. He will learn to use the etymologies, or word histories, in dictionaries. He will browse through the dictionary, looking for the histories of common words. Take the word *bus,* for instance. It comes from *omnibus.* Looking up that word, he finds it is a Latin word meaning "for all." A *bus* is for everybody, as distinguished from a taxi or a private car. That's no great discovery, of course, but the word has more meaning now; it's not just an arbitrary sound.

Take the word *nonchalant. Webster's Seventh New Collegiate* says:

non·cha·lant \-'länt\ *adj* [F, fr. OF, fr. prp. of *nonchaloir* to disregard, fr. *non-* + *chaloir* to concern, fr. L *calēre* to be warm — more at LEE] **:** apparently unconcerned or indifferent **syn** see COOL — non·cha·lant·ly *adv*

The dictionary's key to abbreviations helps us read this cryptic report, to trace the word back through French to Latin, and to understand a *nonchalant* person as one who is not heated, or concerned—one who is cool. Similarly, we find that *superfluous* means "running over," *supercilious* means "raising an eyebrow," and so on.

By persisting in this game, one discovers all kinds of interesting stories behind words, stories that enrich our understanding of words and make them more precise for us. A *daisy* is the "day's eye." A *dandelion* is *dent de lion,* or "lion's tooth" (named for the jagged leaf). *Sweet alyssum* is a cure for *lyssa,* or rabies (according to an old belief).

The *derrick* you see working on construction jobs is by a grim joke named after an English hangman, Mr. Derrick, of more than three hundred years ago. *Panic* is the fear felt in the presence of the great god Pan. The *starboard* side of an airplane or boat is the right side as you face forward, because the *steer board,* or steering oar of a boat, was put into the water on that side in the days before rudders. To *inculcate* a belief means to grind it in with your heel. To *ostracize* someone means to vote against him by putting your oyster shell on the pile. The *corollary* of a logical proposition is a gift, something added free, because flowers (or *corollas*) are given as gifts. A *fanatic* is one who has taken a vow at the altar (or *fane*), like Hannibal swearing to destroy the Romans.

Carne is meat, as in *chili con carne.* So *incarnate* means "embodied or made flesh," and *carnival* is *carne vale,* or "farewell to meat," the last fling of indulgence in meat-eating (and other delights) before the fasting season of Lent. *Cardinal* means "hinge"; so the *cardinal* numbers are the basic ones, on which the others swing; a *cardinal* in the church holds a key office (or "hinge office"); since cardinals wear robes of a certain shade of red, that shade is called *cardinal red.* Since an American bird has feathers of that color, he's called a *cardinal.* Since this bird is common around St. Louis, the St. Louis ball team is the *Cardinals.*

Such games the writer plays in his spare time, simply because he likes words. Another game he can play with the dictionary is *synonyms,* or distinguishing the different shades of meaning of closely related words. Leafing through the dictionary, he sees here and there word groups introduced by the abbreviation *Syn.* and followed by explanations of the differences between synonyms. What's the difference between *sinister* and *baleful*? Or *baleful* and *malign*? How about *origin, source, inception,* and *root*? Or *covetous, greedy, acquisitive, grasping,* and *avaricious*? Or *lovable* and *amiable*? Or *irony, sarcasm,* and *satire*? Your dictionary knows!

Appropriateness

Of the various possible words to express a thought, how do we decide which to choose? Should we say "a most attractive girl," "a gorgeous creature," or "a knockout"? All are correct, in their proper places.

Many people assume that the dictionaries are collections of correct words only, acceptable words, elegant words, with all improper words carefully omitted. *"Ain't* ain't in the dictionary," our elders used to admonish us. But the lexicographers who compile the dictionaries consider themselves record-keepers, historians, not arbiters. They record what people do, not what they ought to do.

We can get some help in appropriateness from the dictionaries, it's true. Many dictionary entries include usage markings. For instance, I have just opened the dictionary quite at random and found eleven definitions of the word *iron,* of which four have usage markings:

Chem[ical]. a ductile . . . metallic element.
Slang. a pistol.
Archaic. a sword.
Med[ical]. a preparation of iron . . . used as a tonic.

Also, I find the word *ain't* in *Webster's Seventh New Collegiate,* with this note: "now used in dialect or illiterate speech." The word *to bust,* meaning *to burst,* is listed as "inelegant," and a *buster,* meaning something huge, is called "slang." *Dove* as a past tense of *dive* is "colloquial."

Such helpful markings appear in the dictionaries, but they are not plentiful enough to give us all the help we need with appropriateness of diction. We must add to the regular dictionaries those special dictionaries of usage listed in Chapter 8. And we must constantly develop our own sensitivity to the way good writers use words.

It goes almost without saying that in a formal situation you will use formal English. No one would use the same style or the same words in a job application, a memorial speech, a college essay, an article in a college newspaper, and a letter to an intimate friend. You can trust your feelings in these matters, to a large extent, but take two precautions:

First, it's always a good idea to have a friend read over your essay, especially if you're lucky enough to have a friend whose writing you admire, to get his comments on your choice of words.

Second, remember that it is better to use a specific and forceful word than a polite but empty word. Empty words sound insincere. What you write should have the sound of a real human voice.

Notice the unusual but expressive way the word *sandpapering* was used in an editorial in the *New York Times* (June 7, 1965) that commented on the retirement of Michael J. Murphy as Police Commissioner of New York City.

. . . The P.C.'s job is always rough, and Commissioner Murphy took more than the usual share of sandpapering as civil rights and other demonstrations swept the city, [with] complaints of police brutality.

The editors of the *Times* believe, apparently, that the best diction is a diction at once lively, colloquial, and precise.

Jargon

All special interest groups develop their own vocabularies, which the linguist calls *jargons*. (*Jargon* also means "gibberish," but that's a different use of the word.) When a grammarian talks shop to grammarians, a photographer to photographers, one short-order cook to another, one nuclear physicist, or medical student, or cab driver, or chess player, or fan dancer, or cyberneticist to his or her fellows, they quite naturally and properly use words which outsiders wouldn't understand. As long as they are talking to each other, that's fine. But when they try to communicate with outsiders, the trouble starts. Some people live and breathe their specialties, and the jargon of their in-group becomes their whole language, so that they can hardly communicate at all with outsiders. (I once knew a jazz musician of whom this was true, and also a professor of sociology; you find such people in all kinds of specialties.) When the first American astronauts held news conferences, the newspapers were kept busy explaining for their readers such terms as *booster, thrust, G's* and such expressions as "All systems were go."

A good writer is conscious of the fact that his jargon is not a universal language, and he either avoids using special words or uses them in such a way as to make their meanings clear. Notice, for instance, how Oliver P. Pearson, in "The Metabolism of Hummingbirds," has explained his terms: "Pound for pound the more diminutive animal eats more food, consumes more oxygen, produces more energy—in short, has a higher rate of metabolism" (page 211). That is a beautifully unobtrusive way of being sure the reader knows what *metabolism* means without insulting his intelligence or talking down to him or getting all heavy and saying, "The term *metabolism,* which I shall have occasion to use frequently in this article, must be defined." Pearson might have taken for his motto that shrewd saying of Pope's, "Men must be taught as if you taught them not." When Pearson uses a phrase like "the metabolic profit which a hummingbird gains by nocturnal hibernation," every word is intelligible because he has suavely made sure that we know what they mean.

Oliver Pearson is a master craftsman at translating the jargon of his field into the general language—a talent far too rare. Clifford Geertz, if not quite so brilliant in this respect as Pearson, is still efficient—if he were not, "The Transition to Humanity" would be so much Greek to most readers. In the first few pages of this essay appear the words *anthropology, culture, Homo sapiens, critical point theory, hominidization, primate line, primatologist,* and *Pithecanthropus erectus.* Some of these are vaguely familiar, of course, but

Geertz unostentatiously pins them all down to the precise meanings we must understand in order to follow his line of discourse.

Metaphor

One of the ways in which a writer makes his meaning clear is by the use of metaphor. Clifford Geertz, explaining the critical point theory, says, "Man's humanity, *like the flare of a struck match,* leaped into existence" (page 179). Later, explaining a different concept, he says, "*Like the cabbage it so much resembles,* the *Homo sapiens* brain, having arisen within the framework of human culture, would not be viable outside of it."

The metaphor (or simile, or brief analogy—to the writer they are all one tool), comparing the unknown picturesquely to something known, enables us to perceive and possess the unknown, to make it known. All writers use metaphors; when they are well used, they are extremely effective devices for communication.

". . . the weeds at the bottom gently bending down the stream, shaken by the *watery wind.* . . ."   *Thoreau, page 246*

". . . [the hummingbird] was completely torpid and allowed itself to be picked off *like a ripe fruit.*"   *Pearson, page 213*

". . . two people . . . suddenly let *the wall between them break down.* . . ."   *Fromm, page 174*

"[We] bought an enormous old *box.* . . ."   *Baker, page 125*

"The Long *Snowfall*"   *Title of Rachel Carson's essay*

". . . [a bird] about as smoothly plump and compact *as a pebble that has been whirled in a pot-hole.* . . ."   *Muir, page 225*

". . . words are mostly used *to cover the sleeper, not to wake him up.*"   *Baldwin, page 140*

Our language is rich in poetic metaphor, as a casual browsing in H. L. Mencken's *American Language* makes delightfully clear. Think of the poetic exactness of idea behind the expressions *hot rod, sugar-daddy, apple polisher, big shot, love nest, egghead, dog-eared, pussyfooting, flannel-mouth, puddle-jumper, whirlybird.* Note the force of the metaphor used as an epigram in the following passage from a newspaper feature story:

[Lyndon Johnson] is able enough, experienced enough, knowledgeable enough to be President—perhaps a great president. But he has not yet met the test set forth crisply by Harry Truman. *"If you can't stand the heat,"* Mr. Truman said, *"get out of the kitchen."* . . . President Johnson . . . will have to prove that he can stand the heat. *New York Times, July 7, 1965*

When the metaphor is expanded into an analogy, it sometimes catches an author's meaning beautifully, as in Pearson's analogy of organic metabolism and the flame of a candle. Alexander Pope once explained the relationship of reason and passion by saying that passion is the wind in the sails, without which a boat cannot move, and reason is the compass, without which it cannot stay on course.

A number of cautions must be made here. First, since analogy is a *poetic* device, not a *rational* one, it is of no logical value as argument; an analogy cannot *prove* anything but can only strengthen feelings or clarify apperception. J. B. S. Haldane, in "On Being the Right Size" (page 204), draws an analogy between the physical size of organic beings and the size of political or economic institutions, an analogy which can strengthen feelings if you already have them but cannot prove or demonstrate or argue that institutions follow the same natural laws as physical organisms.

We must remember that a metaphor is a picture. If we look at a picture too often, we no longer see it, and so it is with a metaphor. But if the reader does not see the picture, the metaphor does not work. There are three degrees of freshness. There are dead metaphors, which no longer operate as pictures or comparisons at all. The word *companion* used to suggest an image of people eating together. The word *lady* implied an image of the woman of the house baking loaves of bread for her men. But most people don't see these pictures when the words are used, for we no longer use them metaphorically.

There are dying metaphors, which can be called trite and boring pictures, pictures we are so tired of that they are more likely to irritate than to enlighten. "Strong as an ox"; "a square meal"; "as cool as a cucumber"; "the shackles of the past"; "the ship of state"; "on the downward path"; "the game of life"; "the hand of Fate"; "put your shoulder to the wheel"; "toe the line." These, obviously, we should weed out ("weed out" is pretty trite too, come to think of it!) during revision, since they *are* trite and therefore do not communicate as metaphors.

The third class is the new, fresh metaphor, which really makes us see things freshly, such as those listed on page 96.

One more caution. Just as a photographer must avoid unintentional double exposures, so the writer must avoid mixed metaphors, and for the same reason. I remember a politician who said, "The New Deal is a snake in the grass gnawing at the roots of the ship of state!" Recently a student wrote that he had "taken a giant step towards his goal on the ladder of life." Sometimes writers carelessly jam together two trite metaphors: "We've got to get down to grass tacks" (*grass roots* or *brass tacks*); "You hit it right on the nutshell"; "Here's looking down the hatch." When you are conscious of metaphors, such monsters will not survive your revision. Neither will such inept and unconsciously grotesque metaphors as one of my students made when he said, "While fishing off the town dock, I caught the eye of a beautiful blonde."

Enough said!

Exercises

1. For any group you belong to (professional group, hobby group, school group, family, etc.) make a list of words or phrases outsiders would not understand. Define or explain each one.

2. Keep a list of all the metaphors you hear spoken in a single day. Classify them under the headings "Trite" and "Fresh."

3. Write a brief essay giving the history of one of the following words, drawing your information from historical dictionaries:

bunk (meaning "nonsense")
boycott
macadam
clown

CHAPTER SEVEN

Exercises

It is customary to equip handbooks of English — usually after each chapter or section — with "exercises" to be used by teachers as tests to see if the students have understood each section or as remedial assignments for students having trouble with, say, comma splices or sentence fragments or the punctuation of quotations. As such, exercises are proper and useful, but it has always seemed to me that they should be vastly more useful than they commonly are.

Let's consider exercises in the broadest sense. Think of ballet dancers loosening up their muscles at the barre, or pitchers warming up in the bull pen, or any practitioner of physical arts and skills — opera singers, tightrope walkers, cross-country runners, guitar players, magicians, jugglers, card dealers, gunslingers, ropers, archers, actors, billiards players, weight lifters — all developing their special skills. Exercises are not for any of these a punitive or meaningless or elementary practice but part of a way of life, and so should they be for writers.

Considered in this context, exercises are not just teachers' gimmicks. Here, as in so many scholastic activities, the ambiguous role of teachers in our schools has sometimes distorted the function of the activities. Our teachers have to be not guides and coaches only (as they should be) but also judges and disciplinarians. (The very word *discipline,* a fine old word which used to suggest the relationship between a *disciple* and a *master* in any field, has been corrupted by the official relationship of teacher and student and now means imposing order on unruly classrooms or meting out punishment.) You must forget the idea of exercises as semipunitive teaching devices if you want to get anything of value out of them. Think of exercises as something *you* can use, not as something *teachers* use. The best thing a teacher can help you do, in the use of exercises as in anything else, is to outgrow the need of a teacher, but you will not outgrow the need of exercises.

A good exercise is designed to strengthen a specific skill which the writer himself knows he needs—you must feel the need of an exercise before it can be worth doing. The best exercises are administered, performed, and judged by the writer himself. Think of a tennis player consciously developing his backhand stroke by banging a tennis ball against a wall—all by himself and of his own volition, because he wants to perfect that skill. That's an ideal example of exercising, and it suggests three characteristics of any good exercise: (1) It must be clearly and specifically useful; (2) it must be positive, to develop a skill; and (3) the person doing it must be able to see for himself how well he is doing. (If you do a set of "exercises," then hand them in and wait for the teacher to mark them and pass them back so you can see how many you have right, you have been taking a test, not doing an exercise.)

Benjamin Franklin tells us in his *Autobiography* that when he was about sixteen years old he decided to teach himself how to write. Not having a master in this field, he had to develop a system for himself, and being of a shrewd, inventive turn of mind, even as a youngster, he devised a scheme so useful that we may take it as a model.

About this time I met with an odd volume of the *Spectator*. It was the third. I had never before seen any of them. I bought it, read it over and over, and was much delighted with it. I thought the writing excellent and wished, if possible, to imitate it. With this view I took some of the papers, and making short hints of the sentiment in each sentence, laid them by a few days, and then, without looking at the book, tried to complete the papers again, by expressing each hinted sentiment at length, and as fully as it had been expressed before, in any suitable words that should come to hand. Then I compared my *Spectator* with the original, discovered some of my faults, and corrected them. But I found I wanted a stock of words, or a readiness in recollecting and using them, which I thought I should have acquired before that time if I had gone on making verses; since the continual occasion for words of the same import, but of different length, to suit the measure, or of different sound for the rhyme, would have laid me under a constant necessity of searching for variety, and also have tended to fix that variety in my mind, and make me master of it. Therefore I took some of the tales and turned them into verse, and, after a time, when I had pretty well forgotten the prose, turned them back again. I also sometimes jumbled my collections of hints into confusion, and after some weeks endeavored to reduce them into the best order, before I began to form the full sentences and complete the paper. This was to teach me method in the arrangement of thoughts. By comparing my work afterwards with the original, I discovered many faults and amended them; but I sometimes had the pleasure of fancying that, in certain particulars of small import, I had been lucky enough to improve the method or the language, and this encouraged me to think I might possibly in time come to be a tolerable English writer, of which I was extremely ambitious.

Forget for the moment Franklin's hints about the usefulness to a prose writer of exercises in poetry. (The hint will one day be acted upon and the writing of poetry again made customary in the schools, as it once was, but that's too radical a suggestion for the present.) Think of the importance of his idea that we should construct our exercises in such a way as to be able to compare our results with the way a successful writer has done the same thing, and thus be able to judge for ourselves how well we are doing without the irrelevance of "marks" or the delay of a teacher's grading.

I'm about to suggest some specific exercises, but only as examples of how to do it yourself, how to make your own exercises for your own use. Part of this approach is the importance of considering any piece of writing in context. I have already suggested that sentences should not be judged in isolation but only as functioning parts of essays. So, taking your cue from Franklin, base your exercises on essays you admire and are familiar with, so that you are constantly aware of the context, the total problem, the mood of the passage, the proportionate importance of the various ideas, and so on. Base your exercises on essays you have read, and check the results against the originals. Using this approach, you can develop exercises in all aspects of expository writing, but the method is especially suited to the development of those qualities needed in revising essays, such as the achievement of conciseness, liveliness of style, skillful parallel structure, sentence sense, logical paragraph development, and precision of word choice.

Conciseness. Here's how it works. Suppose you want to work on conciseness of style—and you should want to, for it's the most useful of skills. Take a passage you admire from a well-written published essay. (Not a *great* piece of writing, please. Great art has a crystalline quality which makes it harder to analyze for method.) Take a good, efficient, lively piece of exposition. Select a brief passage, and rewrite that passage in loose, wordy style, with the sentences chopped up into childish ones. A day or so later, take your passage and revise it. Remembering the general point of the essay and the proportionate importance of the passage, turn it into as concise and smooth a passage as you can. Then compare it with the original, sentence by sentence and word by word. The point is *not* to see how close you can come to the exact words of the original but to see how the author has solved problems you have also wrestled with and to compare your efficiency with his. You'll be amazed, the first time you try this, at how illuminating a process it is—how much you will learn both about the author's style and about your own.

For example, take the opening paragraph of Rachel Carson's "The Long Snowfall" (page 217). If I were to make an exercise of this paragraph, for myself, I'd first rewrite it thus, keeping all the ideas and the order of presentation but breaking down the style and the sentences:

Every part of the earth is different from the others. Every part has its own atmosphere, one that is peculiarly its own. You might call it a quality, or perhaps a characteristic, which is peculiarly its own. So it is with every part of the air, and also with the sea. Take the floor of the deep sea, for instance. Whenever I think of that floor, one single and overwhelming fact possesses my imagination. That fact is what we call the accumulation of sediments. In my imagination I see always the downward drift of materials—a drift which is steady and unremitting, coming from above. Down it comes, flake upon flake. It settles upon the floor of the sea layer upon layer. This process has been going on a long time—in fact, for a span of years which must be measured in the hundreds of millions. This process will continue to go on far into the future—for as long as there are any seas and any continents.

This version has 169 words in 12 sentences. To use it as an exercise, try revising it, stating the same ideas as concisely as possible and in the smoothest of sentences. Note how many words and how many sentences you use. Then compare your version with Rachel Carson's and see how beautifully she has packed a lot of ideas into a few smooth sentences. Notice also how fitting the *music* of her sentences is when read aloud.

The trouble with this exercise, for your purposes, is that the text to be revised was made by *me*, and so it represents the kind of sloppy writing *I* need to wrestle with. It would be much better to turn a passage of Rachel Carson's essay into your own variety of sloppiness and start from that.

The more skillful the writer is in the element you are working on, the more striking the lesson of such an exercise will be. Probably the best essay in Part II on which to base exercises in conciseness and sentence structure is Oliver Pearson's "The Metabolism of Hummingbirds." Here's Pearson's second paragraph, exploded into loose language and sloppy sentences in a version containing 207 words in 8 sentences. See how well you can revise it, and compare your revision to his original on page 211. (I'll tell you in advance, though perhaps I shouldn't, that the original passage contains 116 words in 6 sentences.)

The process of biological life has been considered to be comparable to the process by which a candle burns. The candle burns by the following process: the wax of the candle combines with oxygen, which it obtains from the air. The combination of wax with oxygen results in two products: heat and carbon dioxide. If you want to measure the candle's rate of burning, you can use any of four factors as a basis:

1. consumption of wax
2. consumption of oxygen
3. production of heat
4. production of carbon dioxide.

Now, in the same way, if you want to measure how "alive" any animal may be—by which we mean how intense its biological life processes are, measure any one of the following:

1. How fast does it consume food?
2. How fast does it consume oxygen?
3. How fast does it produce heat?
4. How fast does it give off carbon dioxide?

Of these four possible measurements, the easiest and most satisfactory one, for practical reasons, is how fast it consumes oxygen. And we find that measurements of the rate of oxygen consumption have been made on a host of animals. The subjects range all the way from the tiny protozoa to mice, and all the way from mice to the ponderous elephant.

Grace. Suppose what you want to develop is not conciseness but the use of parallel structure and repetition. Then find a passage in which these are used well, rewrite it in a way that eliminates parallels and repetition, and later revise the passage to achieve them. People quite naturally use these rhythmic devices in moments of high emotional pitch. That's why Lincoln's Gettysburg Address is more rhythmic than his inaugural addresses. For the same reason, writers of expository prose tend to rhythmic repetition and parallels (and often to short sentences) in the closing passages of their essays, when the discourse surges upward to a finale. So take as a base for an exercise the last paragraph of Agnes de Mille's "Rhythm in My Blood" or the last paragraph of the selection from Bernard DeVoto's "Introduction." You might rewrite Miss de Mille's closing paragraph into something like this:

The individual cannot, and indeed may not, demand a certificate of quality before starting, but must work on faith. Only his conscience must be listened to (that will be stern enough, in truth); no other voices must be heard, for listening to critics, or to friends, or even consulting one's business interests may mean to be lost. The individual can only pray that his own tastes and passions will be common to many other people, though even so one must suit oneself first, before every other person, which means to marry the girl of one's heart despite the family, since the alternative is to bed down for life with a wench not of his choosing.

As you revise this passage, remember that Agnes de Mille based her paragraph on short sentences, on the repetition of the pronoun *he,* and on action words. Try it yourself, and compare the result with her version on page 158.

Liveliness. How about an exercise in vividness and liveliness of style? To make such an exercise, follow Franklin's method exactly. Reduce the original to a series of notes, or "hints," in the same order as in the original, and later expand these notes into a full expository passage. For instance, here are the "hints" of the contents of Rachel Carson's third paragraph:

Oceanic sediments come from:
1. deposits from rivers, throughout geologic eons
2. volcanic dust settling from upper atmosphere
3. sand from coastal deserts, carried by winds
4. gravel, pebbles, small boulders, shells, carried by glaciers and drift ice
5. bits of meteors (including iron and nickel)
6. limy and silicious shells and skeletons of minute animals of upper waters of oceans
   a. numbered in billions
   b. most widely distributed of sources of sediment

Try your hand at expanding that to a one-paragraph statement, and compare the result with the original passage on page 218 (which, by the way, contains 173 words in 7 sentences; try to state the ideas in something like this degree of expansion). Note that Rachel Carson has included, besides the raw information, a sense of drama, of liveliness, which is part of her charm as a writer. Notice how *active* her passage is.

Organization. For a workout in the skills of selection and order, take any good passage of description of a subject which is presented spatially, reduce it to a map or spatial diagram, and use that for an exercise. Elia Kazan's "Writers and Motion Pictures" is a good subject. Try this, for an exercise:

Using the first-person point of view, describe the commissary of Twentieth Century Fox from the following diagram and notes, in about 200 words (Kazan used 206, in 17 sentences and 2 paragraphs), putting the various items into the best possible order but emphasizing the isolation of the writers:

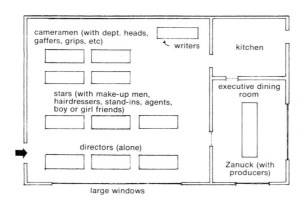

Notes:
1. Table-hopping is customary at all tables but that of the writers.
2. Writers laugh differently—hysterical, giddy, bitter.
3. Writers wear less colorful clothes.
4. Writers have less sun tan. Tan is fashionable; the others cultivate deep tans.
5. Directors can see out over the whole room.
6. Directors reserve tables and waitresses.
7. The others shun the writers.
8. The observer didn't notice the writers for several weeks.

To get a more thorough workout in organization, break down an essay into notes, putting each note on a 3 x 5 card; then shuffle the cards and play a kind of solitaire on a large table or the floor, rearranging the cards until their order is the best, which means the most logical arrangement of the subject and the most dramatic presentation of that subject to a reader; and finally compare your organization with the author's. (Incidentally, it's a useful device when you're having trouble organizing your own essay to play the same kind of solitaire with your own notes.) Here's a breakdown of the contents of Bernard DeVoto's "Introduction." To play the game, first transfer each of these starred items to a separate 3 x 5 card, then shuffle the cards and go ahead.

(NOTE: The cards in this group should be lettered E in the upper left-hand corner, meaning that each of these items concerns the East, the tidewater culture. You need not, of course, keep them all together in the final organization of the essay.)

*Eastern period more homogeneous than any other period of American culture.

*Jefferson the classic type: see his first inaugural address and the Jefferson nickel.

*Jefferson looks like Roman consul, on stamps, coins.

*Architectural style: classical.

*U.S. Constitution embodies Roman virtues, ideas.

*Statue of George Washington (by Horatio Greenough) in toga, like Roman consul.

*Classic American writers: Emerson, Poe, Thoreau, Melville, Hawthorne, Whitman—grew up in classical period of tidewater culture.

*East fails to realize center of gravity shifts westward.

*Civil War results from East's failure to think continentally.

(NOTE: The cards in this group should be lettered MW, meaning that each of these items concerns the Midwest, or heartland, or Great Valley.)

*Life centers around great river (Mississippi), turns away from Europe. MW called "Egypt of the West."

*New kind of country: landscapes, rivers, sky, wind, water, space and distance, soil, climate, conditions of life.

*Settlers come from East to MW in two streams: from South and from New England.

(NOTE: These two cards should be lettered FW, meaning that both of these items concern the Far West.)

*Oregon, California developing beyond western mountains.

*Logically part of continental nation; "implicit" from signing of Louisiana Purchase.

(NOTE: The cards in this group should be lettered L, meaning that each of these items concerns Abraham Lincoln.)

   *L understood continental unity of the U.S.

   *L one of the "limestone men" (Herndon) — a Midwestern type.

   *L's democracy comes from experience of the Great Valley.

   *L is the typical man of the Great Valley — see his state papers and the Lincoln penny.

This exercise takes a good deal of time and persistence, but when you compare your organization to DeVoto's (pages 133–137), you'll have a lively sense of his skill in ordering materials dramatically, a sense of what any good writer goes through in organizing serious writing. You may arrive at a different order than his—there's no one "right" way to arrange these materials—and you may even prefer your own arrangement. The value of the exercise comes not from finding a right answer but from checking your arrangement of materials against that of a professional.

If you want a workout in the skills of transition—of taking a reader smoothly from one item to another and one subject to another—arrange these same cards in the order DeVoto himself uses, and then write the essay. Compare your transitions to his. (You may have cause to appreciate a statement DeVoto once made, that a good writer is made by "ten years of terrible discipline.")

Diction. Exercises in diction are the easiest to set up for yourself. Whenever you notice a particularly effective word, copy the sentence it appears in, and substitute a less effective word. Underline the word so you can quickly remember which word is at stake. (You could put the sentence, with the substituted word, on a 3 x 5 card, and write the original word on the back of the card for quick reference.) Later, try to find the best possible word for that slot. The point is not to recall the exact word the author used but to think of a good one, one that fits the context of the sentence in the whole essay. Check your choice against the original. (At the very least, this exercise will give you an enlightened sense of that author's talent for word choice.)

Henry Thoreau is a good writer to use for diction exercises. But don't use his technical words, such as *blue-joint, sedge, pipe-grass.* And don't use his puns, such as the word *out* in "men . . . who were out not only in '75 and 1812, but have been out every day of their lives." (*To be out,* you gather, means in one sense to be enlisted under arms in a military campaign.) Look for vivid and lively words which you might want to use yourself.

1. "For a long time, they made the most of the driest season to get their hay, working sometimes till nine o'clock at night, *earnestly swinging* their scythes in the twilight round the hummocks left by the ice." *See "Concord River," paragraph 1, page 240.*

2. "And there stand all around the alders, and birches, and oaks, and maples full of *life* and sap." *Paragraph 2*

3. "Concord River is *noted* for the gentleness of its current." *Paragraph 4*

4. "For the most part, it *flows slowly* through broad meadows." *Paragraph 4*

5. "The *slow stream* of the Concord meadows *passes* thus unobserved through the town, without a *sound* or a pulse-beat." *Paragraph 6*

6. "Rivers . . . are the constant *invitation*, when they flow by our doors, to distant enterprise and adventure." *Paragraph 7*

The exercises described so far are only one kind of workout, one approach to the whole subject of developing skills by practice. Two other kinds I've found useful are analytical exercises and assigned projects.

Analytical exercises are easy to set up for yourself. They consist of marking off, in any essay, the elements you are concerned with. For instance, it's instructive to study the way essays open. Start with the previously stated assumption that an ideal opening would state the subject clearly, suggest how the subject will be developed, attract the reader's interest to the subject, and set the mood or tone of the essay, all within the first paragraph or the first few paragraphs. Take a number of essays, and as you read each one, mark in the margin how much of it is the opening; then mark in the opening section the parts that perform the various functions of an ideal opening. (Some parts may perform more than one function at a time.) Be careful to allow for the context of the essay in your final judgment. The writer of an introduction to a book, or of a set of instructions for the purchaser of a machine, does not have to explain to his reader why he is writing, or why the reader should be interested, or what the general subject is; but the writer of a magazine article or a college essay must justify himself and establish a claim to the reader's attention.

Try underlining those sections or passages which tell the reader something about the *essay* rather than about the *subject* — all the introductory, transitional, and summarizing passages. Or try circling all the repetitions of a key word or phrase and connecting the circles by straight lines.

Best of all, do these analytical exercises on your own essay, before making the final draft.

Workouts. All these exercises are what we might call drills. The tennis player practicing his backhand is drilling himself in one skill; he is not playing tennis. Similarly, to do the exercises described above is to give yourself drills, workouts in writing skills, but that is not the same thing as actually writing. The best exercise for a tennis player is to play tennis. The more he plays (if he is constantly trying to improve), the better he plays. Drills are useful, advice is often useful, studying the theory of tennis and the style of other players is useful; but the game's the thing. So it is for writing. No teacher can teach you how to write (he doesn't have time to give you the necessary individual attention, for one thing). No book can teach you how to write. Teachers and books have one God-like characteristic: they help only those who help themselves. If you want to develop your skill as a writer, you must write. Write something every day. Write letters, write essays, write articles, keep a journal, take every reasonable opportunity to get things stated in written words. The best exercise of all is a lot of writing.

Some of the assignments I give my students fall midway between drills and full-scale writing. I think of them as workouts (though sometimes a student gets interested in the subject for its own sake and it becomes for him a real writing job); I present some of them here as suggestions for a different kind of exercise from the foregoing.

1. When you read a book, either fiction or nonfiction, write a review in which you explain to someone who has not read the book what kind of book it is, what it covers, what the tone or mood is (a quotation will help), and how effective it is. Set yourself a maximum word limit of four hundred words. Don't waste time recounting the plot of a work of fiction. When you've finished, find a professional review of the same book (use the *Book Review Digest* to locate one), and compare your review with the published one.

2. Describe a jargon. To do this, select any group you belong to that uses words whose meanings would not be apparent to outsiders. (Everyone belongs to such groups, if only in the family or the school.) For at least a week, keep a careful list of all words or expressions you use or hear used which are part of the jargon. Using the list of expressions as your basic material, describe the jargon of the group in an essay.

3. Describe any building with which you are familiar, other than a private home (a school building, church, railroad station, YMCA, civic center). Address your description to a newcomer to the area who will be using the building, and make it a practical description, telling him what goes on in this building and how to find his way around in it. Then, just for fun, write another description of the same building, giving not practical advice but an impression: the tone or personality of the building.

4. If you have a correspondent in a foreign country, here's an interesting project—if you don't, get one or imagine one. Describe any social custom of your own country or area with which your correspondent cannot be expected to be familiar: the way a particular holiday is celebrated, the position of teenagers in the family, what your friends do for relaxation. Or describe for your corre-

spondent a particular amusement park, or subway system, or boat harbor. Or describe skateboards, outdoor movies, summer theater, kaffee klatches, camping vacations. Remember that the reader is not going to do any of these things or visit any of these places but simply wants to know what life is like in your part of the world. Let him know how it really is, not what it ought to be.

5. Take any essay you have written, preferably one you are proud of, and imagine that an editor has said (as editors do), "We'll accept it only if you reduce it to exactly half as many words." Rewrite it in half the length, trying to keep as much of the original idea or information as you possibly can.

6. Take an ordinary flashlight apart and reassemble it. Imagine that the flashlight has recently been invented and is now being marketed for the first time. Write a set of instructions for the purchaser on how to use it, including how to put in new batteries and bulbs, how to keep it from being damaged or becoming run down, etc. Remember, you are not trying to make him buy it — he's already done that. He needs information, not persuasion.

7. Write instructions for playing any card game you are familiar with. Compare your instructions with those published in Hoyle.

The best expository writing is done for a purpose, with a reader clearly in mind and something specific to communicate to him, and the best exercises and assignments must be the same. The best subjects are those on which the writer has done a good deal of thinking, those that have ripened within him, areas in which he is experienced. (This is true in spite of the fact that good expository writing is frequently done not just because someone felt the creative urge but because the writer had a job to do, as student, reporter, historian, or professional writer.) The best exercises and assignments take this into account. It's one more reason why the best exercises are not those arbitrarily assigned to a group but those which the learning writer evolves for himself.

CHAPTER EIGHT

Books for Writers

Every writer needs a few quick-reference books on his desk. Student, teacher, reporter, businessman — whoever you are, if you are to write in any but the most casual way, there are things you'll need to look up during the process of checking and revising what you have written. Matters of spelling, syllabification, punctuation, usage, grammar are not just things to be learned in class; nobody ever gets everything down so pat that he doesn't need reference books. In their zeal to help students make correctness habitual, teachers sometimes unwittingly give the impression that dependence on handbooks is a weakness which a good writer overcomes, but we all need handbooks; it would be foolish to try to memorize everything. Think of rules for writing as you think of telephone numbers: those you use frequently you should know without looking them up; for the others, the important thing is to know where to get them quickly when you need them.

Every writer needs a good desk dictionary, and he needs to know how to use it. To check on the possible meanings of a word; to check on spelling, on the parts of verbs or the plural forms of nouns; to check on how to split a word at the end of a line; to check on whether a word is standard English or slang; to get an understanding of a word through its history; to distinguish between synonyms — for all these, you need a good desk dictionary. I recommend four, any one of which will serve the purpose well.

Webster's Seventh New Collegiate Dictionary. Springfield, Mass.: G. & C. Merriam Co., 1965.

Webster's New World Dictionary of the American Language.
Cleveland: The World Publishing Company, 1956.

The American College Dictionary. New York: Random
House, Inc., 1965.

The Standard College Dictionary. New York: Funk & Wag-
nalls Co., Inc., 1963.

Webster's Seventh is published by G. & C. Merriam Co.,
which has been bringing out Webster dictionaries since
1847. When we say "According to Webster . . ." or "Webster says . . . ," we mean, traditionally, this dictionary and
its predecessors. All the dictionaries listed above include
extra features which are useful if you can remember they're
there: names of famous people, with their dates; names,
locations, and sizes of geographical places (these are separate sections in *Webster's Seventh,* included in the main al-
phabetical listing in the others); explanations of common
signs and symbols, lists of the colleges in the United States
and Canada. *Webster's Seventh* has a list of rhyming words, for
poets. *New World* has forms of address, for letter writers.
Standard has a brief description of traditional grammar and
the new grammars. The *ACD* has a manual of letter writing
and a section on British and American usage. *New World* and
Standard have tables of weights and measures and brief
histories of the English language.

The dictionary is primarily a historical tool: it tells us
how a word has been used. It is much less useful for determining how a word *ought* to be used, though it does give
usage labels such as *obsolete, dialect, slang, inelegant.* If you
want to know when *due to* is correct, or whether *real* can be
used to mean "very," or the difference between *like* and *as,*
or *shall* and *will,* or whether to say *different from, different
than,* or *different to,* dictionaries are inadequate. The handbooks listed later in this chapter include information on
usage, notably glossaries of faulty expressions, but for
adequate information you need a good book on usage. Out
of several titles available, I recommend two as by far the
best:

H. W. Fowler. *A Dictionary of Modern English Usage.* Second edition, revised and edited by Sir Ernest Gowers. London: Oxford University Press, 1965.

Theodore M. Bernstein. *The Careful Writer: A Modern Guide to English Usage.* New York: Atheneum Publishers, 1965.

The first edition of Fowler's *Modern English Usage* has been the purist's bible for four decades. It has been brought up to date by Sir Ernest Gowers, one of the liveliest champions of good English, whose book on style is recommended in a later section of this chapter. Theodore Bernstein is a managing editor of the *New York Times,* a newspaper which another ardent group of purists considers the absolute standard of good American prose usage. Bernstein has the edge over Fowler and Sir Ernest for American usage, since they are primarily concerned with British custom, but usage in the two countries is close enough that either of these books is a useful guide. The Fowler is more concise, the Bernstein more chatty.

I must also recommend as an excellent guide to usage a book which is many other things as well, being a complete handbook:

Porter G. Perrin. *Writer's Guide and Index to English.* Fourth edition, revised by Karl W. Dykema and Wilma R. Ebbitt. Glenview, Ill.: Scott, Foresman and Company, 1965.

Students in freshman English classes carry about with them books which are called handbooks, though they are really not simple handbooks any more but hybrids. For use as handbooks, they contain the basic rules of grammar, punctuation, outlining, paragraphing, footnoting, etc., arranged for quick reference. On the other hand, they are organized into discursive chapters and are assigned for study chapter by chapter. As textbooks for composition courses, they are designed to cover the whole field of writing—grammar, style, research methods, etc., though necessarily they cannot cover any one field thoroughly. Many students get rid of them after the course is over, as they do other elementary textbooks, not realizing that as handbooks they are permanently useful. If you have a handbook from such a course, keep it and use it. If not, you should get one. There are a great many adequate ones on the market; some of the best are these:

Kendall B. Taft et al. *The Technique of Composition.* Fifth edition. New York: Holt, Rinehart & Winston, Inc., 1960.

Porter G. Perrin and George H. Smith. *The Perrin-Smith Handbook of Current English.* Second edition. Glenview, Ill.: Scott, Foresman and Company, 1962.

Porter G. Perrin. *Writer's Guide and Index to English.* Fourth edition, revised by Karl W. Dykema and Wilma R. Ebbitt. Glenview, Ill.: Scott, Foresman and Company, 1965.

The *Writer's Guide* is the best of these for a mature writer; it is written on the assumption that its readers are more skillful in the mechanics and more interested in alternative possibilities than college freshmen usually are.

Handbooks are, among other things, style manuals; that is, you can look up in them the use of italics, or how to punctuate titles, or the proper way to address a letter to a U.S. Senator, or how to make a footnote. But handbooks, because they are useful in so many fields, are complete in none. They are useful guides to the mechanics of manuscript and typescript style, but they cannot compete with the full-scale style manuals. As any good secretary will tell you, style manuals are indispensable. The best and most widely used are these:

U.S. Government Printing Office Style Manual. Revised edition. Washington, D.C.: U.S. Government Printing Office, 1959.

Mary Alexander. *A Manual of Style.* Eleventh edition. Chicago: University of Chicago Press, 1949.

For the college student especially, the following are also useful:

Kate L. Turabian. *A Manual for Writers of Term Papers, Theses, and Dissertations.* Phoenix Books edition. Chicago: University of Chicago Press, 1960.

Kate L. Turabian. *Student's Guide for Writing College Papers.* Phoenix Books edition. Chicago: University of Chicago Press, 1963.

Besides the ready-reference books mentioned so far, which should be on every writer's desk, there are study books that the writer should read to learn more about the writing process.

First, and important for all who want to write, are books on the subject of style (as distinguished from the style manuals, which deal with mechanics). I think every writer, from high school students to professionals, should know William Strunk, Jr., and E. B. White, *The Elements of Style* (New York: The Macmillan Company, 1959), a compact little treatise on how to say things neatly, exactly, and forcefully. The current edition is a tribute by E. B. White, the *New Yorker* writer, to one of his college teachers, Professor Strunk, a colorful champion of good English whose booklet was first published in 1918. The booklet of another crusty old-time champion, David Lambuth, has been similarly preserved in *The Golden Book on Writing* (New York: The Viking Press, Inc., 1964).

Also highly recommended are the following, which go into the subject in more detail:

Sir Ernest Gowers. *Plain Words: Their ABC.* New York: Alfred A. Knopf, Inc., 1954.

Herbert Read. *English Prose Style.* Boston: Beacon Press, 1955.

Robert Graves and Alan Hodge. *The Reader Over Your Shoulder*. New York: The Macmillan Company, 1943.

George Orwell. "Politics and the English Language" in his *Shooting an Elephant and Other Essays*. New York: Harcourt, Brace & World, Inc., 1950.

Lane Cooper, editor. *The Art of the Writer*. Ithaca: Cornell University Press, 1952.

Cooper's book is a collection of essays and passages on writing, by such writers as Aristotle, Plato, Swift, Voltaire, Goethe, Thoreau, Schopenhauer, and Brunetière.

Grammar, as distinguished from usage, is the description of how a language works, what forms and changes of form are meaningful. Grammar is a noble study and a deep one. You can get a brief introduction to it in the handbooks and a brief description of the current systems of grammar in the *Standard College Dictionary*, but if you are seriously interested in learning the grammar of English, go directly to one of these authorities:

James H. Sledd. *A Short Introduction to English Grammar*. Glenview, Ill.: Scott, Foresman and Company, 1959.

George O. Curme. *The Principles and Practice of English Grammar*. New York: Barnes & Noble, Inc., 1947.

Charles Carpenter Fries. *American English Grammar*. New York: Appleton-Century-Crofts, 1940.

What is language? These works describe the basic nature of all languages:

Leonard Bloomfield. *Language!* New York: Holt, Rinehart & Winston, 1961.

Mario Pei. *The Story of Language*. Revised edition. Philadelphia: J. B. Lippincott Company, 1965.

Margaret Schlauch. *The Gift of Language.* New York: Dover Publications, Inc., 1956.

How did the English language develop? The history of the language is not only useful for an understanding of modern English but is fascinating cultural history in itself. Recommended:

Otto Jespersen. *Growth and Structure of the English Language.* Ninth edition. New York: The Macmillan Company, 1960.

Albert C. Baugh. *A History of the English Language.* Second edition. New York: Appleton-Century-Crofts, 1957.

James A. H. Murray, editor. *A New English Dictionary on Historical Principles.* 10 volumes. Oxford: Clarendon Press, 1888–1928.

The last item is a huge dictionary which gives the changing meanings of each word it includes, throughout its history, with illustrative quotations. It is referred to as the Oxford English Dictionary, or OED.

What is distinctive about American English? Consult these:

H. L. Mencken. *The American Language.* The fourth edition and the two supplements, abridged, with annotations and new material, by Raven I. McDavid, Jr. New York: Alfred A. Knopf, Inc., 1963.

Albert H. Marckwardt. *American English.* New York: Oxford University Press, 1958.

William Craigie and James R. Hulbert, editors. *A Dictionary of American English on Historical Principles.* 4 volumes. Chicago: University of Chicago Press, 1936–1944.

Mitford M. Mathews, editor. *A Dictionary of Americanisms on Historical Principles.* 2 volumes. Chicago: University of Chicago Press, 1951.

Every American writer should know the Mencken, which is wonderful for browsing. The two dictionaries, commonly referred to as the DAE and the DA, do for American English what the OED does for English.

Words have interesting histories, as I suggested in Chapter 6. Many books have been written about the stories behind words, but some of the most readily available mix fact and pure speculation without warning. In this field, it's best to stick to the authorities. Recommended:

James B. Greenough and George L. Kittredge. *Words and Their Ways in English Speech.* New York: The Macmillan Company, 1920.

George H. McKnight. *English Words and Their Background.* New York: Appleton-Century-Crofts, 1923.

Ernest Weekley. *Concise Etymological Dictionary of Modern English.* New York: E. P. Dutton & Co., Inc., 1924.

Wilfred Funk. *Word Origins and Their Romantic Stories.* New York: Grosset and Dunlap, Inc., 1954.

The Funk is the best of the popular treatments of the subject.

This list of suggested readings is heavily weighted with studies of the language, on the assumption that while each writer needs to know his own particular subject well, all writers need to know a good deal about the medium of communication they use to present their subjects to readers.

Essays for Study

The essays here collected (with the possible exception of the last one) are specimens of good professional prose. They are presented as examples to be emulated, as subjects to be analyzed, and as raw material to be used for exercises. In reading them, please remember that not one was written to be published in such a collection as this, nor was any of them written to be an example of good prose. Behind each, you must see a particular human being who had something to say to a particular kind of reader.

These essays are as varied in style and tone as the people who wrote them — and what a varied company they would be, if you can imagine all of them together in one room! There are eighteen different voices here, expressing eighteen different personalities. But I hope you will be struck by some underlying similarities, too. Each writer here represented has had an interesting experience or observation which he wants to communicate to a reader. Each wants to get it said vividly, concisely, and exactly. Each is speaking in his own natural voice: people speaking to people. And each wrestles with the problems of selection, organization, order, exemplification, and style.

RUSSELL BAKER

A funny thing happened on the way to Antigua

Russell Baker is a *New York Times* writer. You may call
him a columnist, a feature writer, or an essayist.
When readers of the *Times* see his name at the head
of a column, they expect a witty, shrewd, personal
comment on the passing scene.

LET ME say at the outset that I am one of life's most consistent losers. Although I have been moderately successful
at my work and earn a comfortable living, I am basically the
sort of person to whom nothing good has ever happened.

Without belaboring the point I will simply note that the
first car I ever owned was the last Hudson ever made, and
that my second was an Edsel. It should be obvious that I am
a man of considerable pessimism and negligible expectations.

Accordingly, when my wife and I decided last autumn to
splurge on a winter in Antigua, I hadn't the least hope that
the thing would come off, but I was mildly curious to see
what disaster would intervene. Well, sir, it started with
finger smudges on the stairway wall. But let me backtrack a
bit.

Two years ago we were living in a small box in the suburbs. The children had begun to grow leggy and I had developed this terrible sensation of living a totally boxed life.
Inside our box we were all cramped into small interior
boxes filled with even smaller boxes.

One could stare at the box that talked, or go into the kitchen and ponder the box that cooked, or escape on the box with wheels. My analyst diagnosed a dangerous obsession and advised a move. And so we sold the place and bought an enormous old box of the kind they don't build any more.

The sense of enboxment subsided at once, and I even began to develop a fondness for the old place. Well, as I was saying, we had booked for Antigua when my wife remarked on the finger smudges on the stairway wall paint.

We must have this wall papered with something washable, she said, and called a wallpaper man. When he arrived he shook his head mournfully and warned that it would be a bad mistake to paper until certain cracks in the plaster had been repaired.

My wife called a plasterer, who agreed to examine the cracks within a fortnight. "Hm," he said, "you've really got cracks. Bad cracks." My wife, who was naturally alarmed, asked him to examine the really prepossessing cracks which we had always taken for granted in the north bedrooms and shower stall.

"Yes, sir," he said, "these are really some cracks." "What do you think caused them?" asked my wife. "Could be," he mused, "you got termites under the north end of the house and they've eaten away all the underpinnings."

He thought it would be a mistake to undertake major crack repairs until the foundation had been thoroughly examined. Seven weeks later a carpenter agreed to give us an appointment. At the north end of the cellar he tore away some beaverboard ceiling and exposed perhaps twelve feet of suspended sawdust.

"You had termites, all right," he allowed. "Look at this beam." He handed me a palm full of sawdust. "Will the dining room fall through?" asked my wife. "Not so long as you stay out of there," he said.

He thought that the damage was reparable, although it would require electricians to relocate the overhead wiring during the operation. The cost? "It'll be a right good bit," he said. "About the cost of a month in Antigua?" I asked. "Just about," he thought.

JOSEPH ADDISON

Superstition

Joseph Addison is the great-granddaddy of all
journalistic essayists. Writing in the early eighteenth
century, Addison produced for *The Spectator*
polished comments on the foibles of Londoners, for
their own amusement and edification. His readers knew
him as Mr. Spectator, a ubiquitous, witty observer; he had
a continuing relationship with his readers which did not
have to be established at the beginning of each essay.
As Benjamin Franklin reminds us (see Chapter 7),
Addison was for generations the most admired and
emulated writer of graceful, witty exposition.

GOING Yesterday to Dine with an old Acquaintance, I had
the Misfortune to find his whole Family very much de-
jected. Upon asking him the Occasion of it, he told me that
his Wife had dreamt a very strange Dream the Night before,
which they were afraid portended some Misfortune to themselves or to their Children. At her coming into the Room I
observed a settled Melancholy in her Countenance, which I
should have been troubled for, had I not heard from whence
it proceeded. We were no sooner sate down, but, after having looked upon me a little while, *My Dear*, says she, turning to her Husband, *you may now see the Stranger that was
in the Candle last Night*. Soon after this, as they began to
talk of Family Affairs, a little Boy at the lower end of the
Table told her, that he was to go into Join-hand on *Thurs-*

From *The Spectator,* March 8, 1711. Reprinted in *The Spectator,* Everyman's
Library edition. New York: E. P. Dutton & Co., Inc., 1907.

day. Thursday? says she, *No, Child, if it please God, you shall not begin upon* Childermas-day; *tell your Writing-Master that* Friday *will be soon enough.* I was Reflecting with my self on the Oddness of her Fancy, and wondering that any Body would establish it as a Rule to lose a Day in every Week. In the midst of these my Musings she desired me to reach her a little Salt upon the Point of my Knife, which I did in such a Trepidation and Hurry of Obedience, that I let it drop by the Way; at which she immediately startled, and said it fell towards her. Upon this I looked very blank; and, observing the Concern of the whole Table, began to consider my self, with some Confusion, as a Person that had brought a Disaster upon the Family. The Lady however recovering her self after a little space, said to her Husband with a Sigh, *My Dear, Misfortunes never come Single.* My Friend, I found, acted but an under-Part at his Table, and being a Man of more Good-nature than Understanding, thinks himself obliged to fall in with all the Passions and Humours of his Yoke-Fellow: *Do not you remember, Child,* says she, *that the Pidgeon-house fell the very Afternoon that our careless Wench spilt the Salt upon the Table? Yes,* says he, *My Dear, and the next Post brought us an Account of the Battel of* Almanza. The Reader may guess at the figure I made, after having done all this Mischief. I dispatched my Dinner as soon as I could, with my usual Taciturnity; when, to my utter Confusion, the Lady seeing me quitting my Knife and Fork, and laying them across one another upon my Plate, desired me that I would humour her so far as to take them out of that Figure, and place them side by side. What the Absurdity was which I had committed I did not know, but I suppose there was some traditionary Superstition in it; and therefore, in obedience to the Lady of the House, I disposed of my Knife and Fork in two parallel Lines, which is the figure I shall always lay them in for the future, tho' I do not know any Reason for it.

It is not difficult for a Man to see that a Person has conceived an Aversion to him. For my own part, I quickly found, by the Lady's Looks, that she regarded me as a very odd kind of Fellow, with an unfortunate Aspect: For which Reason I took my leave immediately after Dinner, and withdrew to my own Lodgings. Upon my Return Home, I fell into a profound Contemplation on the Evils that attend these superstitious Follies of Mankind; how they subject us to imaginary Afflictions, and additional Sorrows, that do not properly come within our Lot. As if the natural Calamities of Life were not sufficient for it, we turn the most indifferent Circumstances into Misfortunes, and suffer as much from trifling Accidents, as from real Evils. I have known the shooting of a Star spoil a Night's Rest; and have seen a Man in Love grow pale and lose his Appetite, upon the plucking of a Merry-thought. A Screech-Owl at Midnight has alarm'd a Family, more than a Band of Robbers; nay, the Voice of a Cricket hath struck more Terror than the Roaring of a Lion. There is nothing so inconsiderable, which may not appear dreadful to an Imagination that is filled with Omens and Prognosticks. A rusty Nail, or a crooked Pin, shoot up into Prodigies.

I remember I was once in a mixt Assembly, that was full of Noise and Mirth, when on a sudden an old Woman unluckily observed there were thirteen of us in Company. This Remark struck a pannick Terror into several who were present, insomuch that one or two of the Ladies were going to leave the Room; but a Friend of mine taking notice that one of our Female Companions was big with Child, affirm'd there were fourteen in the Room, and that instead of portending one of the Company should die, it plainly foretold one of them should be born. Had not my Friend found out this Expedient to break the Omen, I question not but half the Women in the Company would have fallen sick that very Night.

An old Maid, that is troubled with the Vapours, produces infinite Disturbances of this kind among her Friends and Neighbours. I know a Maiden Aunt, of a great Family, who is one of these Antiquated *Sybils,* that forbodes and prophesies from one end of the Year to the other. She is always seeing Apparitions, and hearing Death-Watches; and was the other Day almost frighted out of her Wits by the great House-Dog, that howled in the Stable at a time when she lay ill of the Tooth-ach. Such an extravagant Cast of Mind engages Multitudes of People, not only in impertinent Terrors, but in supernumerary Duties of Life; and arises from that Fear and Ignorance which are natural to the Soul of Man. The Horror with which we entertain the Thoughts of Death (or indeed of any future Evil) and the Uncertainty of its Approach, fill a melancholy Mind with innumerable Apprehensions and Suspicions, and consequently dispose it to the Observation of such groundless Prodigies and Predictions. For as it is the chief Concern of Wise-Men, to retrench the Evils of Life by the Reasonings of Philosophy; it is the Employment of Fools, to multiply them by the Sentiments of Superstition.

For my own part, I should be very much troubled were I endowed with this Divining Quality, though it should inform me truly of every thing that can befal me. I would not anticipate the Relish of any Happiness, nor feel the Weight of any Misery, before it actually arrives.

I know but one way of fortifying my Soul against these gloomy Presages and Terrors of Mind, and that is, by securing to my self the Friendship and Protection of that Being, who disposes of Events, and governs Futurity. He sees, at one View, the whole Thread of my Existence, not only that Part of it which I have already passed through, but that which runs forward into all the Depths of Eternity. When I lay me down to Sleep, I recommend my self to his Care; when I awake, I give my self up to his Direction. Amidst all the Evils that threaten me, I will look up to him for Help, and question not but he will either avert them, or turn them to my Advantage. Though I know neither the Time nor the Manner of the Death I am to die, I am not at all sollicitous about it; because I am sure that he knows them both, and that he will not fail to comfort and support me under them.

SIMONE BECK, LOUISETTE BERTHOLLE,
and JULIA CHILD

Foreword

Of the three writers credited with the following
excerpt, the most widely known is Julia Child, whose
lessons in French cooking on the educational television
circuit have won many amused and devoted followers.
Direct, sensible, unassuming, entirely without the glib
suavity we expect on television or the hauteur we
expect of French chefs, she speaks as one intelligent
housewife to another, and the three ladies write in
the same tone. Since the following is part of the
introduction to a book, the writers did not need to
explain why they were writing nor to whom they
addressed themselves.

THIS is a book for the servantless American cook who can
be unconcerned on occasion with budgets, waistlines, time
schedules, children's meals, the parent–chauffeur–den-
mother syndrome, or anything else which might interfere
with the enjoyment of producing something wonderful to
eat. Written for those who love to cook, the recipes are as
detailed as we have felt they should be so the reader will
know exactly what is involved and how to go about it. This
makes them a bit longer than usual, and some of the recipes
are quite long indeed. No out-of-the-ordinary ingredients are
called for. In fact the book could well be titled "French
Cooking from the American Supermarket," for the excel-

lence of French cooking, and of good cooking in general, is due more to cooking techniques than to anything else. And these techniques can be applied wherever good basic materials are available. We have purposely omitted cobwebbed bottles, the *patron* in his white cap bustling among his sauces, anecdotes about charming little restaurants with gleaming napery, and so forth. Such romantic interludes, it seems to us, put French cooking into a never-never land instead of the Here, where happily it is available to everybody. Anyone can cook in the French manner anywhere, with the right instruction. Our hope is that this book will be helpful in giving that instruction.

Cooking techniques include such fundamentals as how to sauté a piece of meat so that it browns without losing its juices, how to fold beaten egg whites into a cake batter to retain their maximum volume, how to add egg yolks to a hot sauce so they will not curdle, where to put the tart in the oven so it will puff and brown, and how to chop an onion quickly. Although you will perform with different ingredients for different dishes, the same general processes are repeated over and over again. As you enlarge your repertoire, you will find that the seemingly endless babble of recipes begins to fall rather neatly into groups of theme and variations; that *homard à l'américaine* has many technical aspects in common with *coq au vin,* that *coq au vin* in turn is almost identical in technique to *boeuf bourguignon;* all of them are types of fricassees, so follow the fricassee pattern. In the sauce realm, the cream and egg-yolk sauce for a *blanquette* of veal is the same type as that for a sole in white-wine sauce, or for a *gratin* of scallops. Eventually you will rarely need recipes at all, except as reminders of ingredients you may have forgotten.

All of the techniques employed in French cooking are aimed at one goal: how does it taste? The French are seldom interested in unusual combinations or surprise presentations. With an enormous background of traditional dishes to choose from (*1000 Ways to Prepare and Serve Eggs* is the title of one French book on the subject) the Frenchman takes his greatest pleasure from a well-known dish impeccably cooked and served. A perfect *navarin* of lamb, for instance, requires a number of operations including brownings, simmerings, strainings, skimmings, and flavorings. Each of the several steps in the process, though simple to accomplish, plays a critical role, and if any is eliminated or combined with another, the texture and taste of the *navarin* suffer. One of the main reasons that pseudo-French cooking, with which we are all too familiar, falls far below good French cooking is just this matter of elimination of steps, combination of processes, or skimping on ingredients such as butter, cream — and time. "Too much trouble," "Too expensive," or "Who will know the difference" are death knells for good food.

Cooking is not a particularly difficult art, and the more you cook and learn about cooking, the more sense it makes. But like any art it requires practice and experience. The most important ingredient you can bring to it is love of cooking for its own sake.

Introduction

Bernard DeVoto was a historian, a literary and social critic, and a writer of fiction. Author of *Mark Twain's America,* editor of volumes of Twain's works, author of *Year of Decision: 1946* and other histories, for twenty years writer of the column "The Editor's Easy Chair" in *Harper's Magazine,* DeVoto was a tireless practical writer. "I believe," he once said, "that clear thinking is one of the most difficult and most desirable things in the world." The following is the opening section of the introduction to his collection of Twain's writings, *The Portable Mark Twain.* Note that he did not have to establish the subject for his readers — did not have to tell them that the big subject to which this introduction is building is Mark Twain.

THE FIRST truly American literature grew out of the tide-water culture of the early republic. It was the culture of a people who, whatever their diversity, were more homogeneous in feeling and belief than Americans as a people have ever been since them. We have come to think of the literature whose greatest names are Emerson and Poe, Thoreau and Melville, Hawthorne and Whitman, as our classic period, and in a very real sense the republic that shaped their mind was classical. It felt a strong affinity for the Roman Republic, it believed that Roman virtues and ideas had been expressed in the Constitution, it gave us a great architectural style because it identified its own emotions in the classic style. When Horatio Greenough let a toga fall from Washington's naked shoulders he was not out of tune with contemporary taste: Washington seemed a kind of consul, so did Jefferson, and in the portraits of them which our stamps and coins preserve they have a Roman look. This classical republican culture was at its most vigorous when our classic writers were growing up. But there is an element of anachronism in all literature, and while these men were themselves in full vigor American culture entered a new phase.

The culture of the early republic crossed the Alleghenies in two streams, one Southern, the other mainly New England; but they were more like each other than either was like the one which their mingling presently helped to produce. For beyond the mountains people found different landscapes, different river courses, different relationships of sky and wind and water, different conceptions of space and distance, different soils and climates — different conditions of life. Beyond still farther mountains lay Oregon and California — and they were implicit in the expanding nation as soon as the treaty that gave us Louisiana was signed — but first the United States had to incorporate the vast expanse between the eastern and the western heights of land. That area is the American heartland. Its greatest son was to call it the Egypt of the West because nature had organized it round a central river and it touched no ocean, but it came into the American consciousness as the Great Valley. When the tidewater culture came to the Great Valley it necessarily broke down: new conditions demanded adaptations, innovations, new combinations and amplifications. The new way of life that began to develop there had a different organization of feeling, a different metabolism of thought. It was no more native, no more "American," than that of the first republic, but it was different and it began to react on it.

The heartland was midcontinental and its energies were oriented toward the river at its center — and were therefore turned away from Europe, which had been a frontier of the early republic. And life in the heartland, with its mingling of stocks, its constant shifting of population, and its tremendous distances, led people in always increasing numbers to think continentally. Both facts were fundamental in the thought and feeling of the new culture.

The American littoral came only slowly, with greater slowness than the fact demanded, to realize that the nation's center of gravity was shifting westward. It tragically failed to understand one consequence of that shift, thirty years of contention between the Northeast and the South to dominate the Great Valley or at least achieve a preferential linkage with it. The failure to understand was in great part a failure to think continentally—as was made clear at last when the Civil War demonstrated that no peaceful way of resolving the contention had been found. Even now too many Americans fail to understand that war, the resolution by force, only made explicit the organization of our national life that is implicit in the geography which the Great Valley binds together. Abraham Lincoln understood our continental unity; he argued it persistently down to the outbreak of the war and from then on. And Lincoln was a distillation of the heartland culture.

Lincoln's feeling for the continentalism of the American nation was so intense that it almost transcended the transcendent facts. It was a deposit in the very cells of his bones from the soil of the Great Valley. He was, Herndon rightly says, one of the limestone men, the tall, gaunt, powerful, sallow, saturnine men who appear in quantity enough to constitute a type when the wilderness on both sides of the Ohio comes under the plow. His radical democracy was wrought from the experience of the Great Valley. In his ideas and beliefs as in the shadowed depths of his personality there is apparent a new articulation of American life. His very lineaments show it. When you turn from the Jefferson nickel to the Lincoln penny as when you turn from Jefferson's first inaugural address to any of Lincoln's state papers, in the flash of a total and immediate response you understand that you have turned from one era to a later one. You have turned from the tidewater republic to the continental empire.

Lincoln expressed a culture and brought a type to climax. Similarly, when that culture found major literary expression it did so from a rich and various, if humble, literary tradition. As always, the literary expression was the later one; the economic, social, and political impact was felt much earlier. The lag, however, was not so great as Walt Whitman thought. Whitman was sixty when in 1879 he traveled across the Great Valley to its western limit, where the Front Range walls it off. He traversed it with a steadily growing conviction that here in the flesh were the people whose society he had envisioned in so many rhapsodies, Americans who had been fused, annealed, compacted (those are his words) into a new identity. He felt that literature had not yet spoken to these prairie people, "this continental inland West," that it had not yet spoken for them, that it had not made images for their spirit.

The poet supposed that he was speaking of things still to come but he was already wrong by a full ten years. The thing had happened. And the first notification that it had happened can be dated with an exactness not often possible in the history of literature. That notification came in 1869 with the appearance of a book of humorous travel sketches by Samuel Langhorne Clemens, who, faithful to the established tradition, signed it with a pen name, Mark Twain.

Innocents Abroad was greeted with an enthusiasm that made Mark Twain a celebrity overnight, and with too much misunderstanding of a kind that was to persist throughout his career. It was a funny book and a cardinal part of its fun was its disdain of European culture. This disdain, the mere fact of making humor of such disdain, and its frequent exaggeration into burlesque all produced an effect of shock — in most ways a delightful shock but in some ways an uneasy one. Yet the point was not the provinciality of such humor, though it was frequently provincial, and not its uncouthness, though it was sometimes uncouth, but the kind of consciousness it implied. Again it is absurd to speak of this as the first American literature that was independent of European influences, for our literature had obediently divorced itself from Europe as soon as Emerson ordered it to. The humorous core of *Innocents Abroad* was not independence of Europe, but indifference to it. Thoreau and Emerson and Poe were detached from Europe but completely aware of being heirs to it, but here was a literature which had grown up in disregard of Europe—which had looked inward toward the Mississippi and not outward beyond the Atlantic. Failure to appreciate the implications of this difference was one reason, no doubt the weightiest one, why for two full generations literary critics thought of Mark Twain as no more than a clown. But the same identity, the same organization of personality, that made Lincoln the artificer of our continental unity was what made Mark Twain a great writer.

There are striking affinities between Lincoln and Mark Twain. Both spent their boyhoods in a society that was still essentially frontier; both were rivermen. Both absorbed the midcontinental heritage: fiercely equalitarian democracy, hatred of injustice and oppression, the man-to-man individualism of an expanding society. Both were deeply acquainted with melancholy and despair; both were fatalists. On the other hand, both were instinct with the humor of the common life and from their earliest years made fables of it. As humorists, both felt the basic gravity of humor; with both it was an adaptation of the mind, a reflex of the struggle to be sane; both knew, and Mark Twain said, that there is no humor in heaven. It was of such resemblances that William Dean Howells was thinking when he called Mark Twain "the Lincoln of our literature."

JAMES BALDWIN

As much of the truth as one can bear

James Baldwin is a novelist and an essayist. He is a spokesman for the Negro revolution in America. He is the author of novels, including *Go Tell It On the Mountain, Giovanni's Room,* and *Another Country;* a play, *Blues for Mister Charlie;* and several books of essays. In the following essay, he speaks not as a Negro writer but simply as a young American writer viewing the literary scene. The essay appeared on the front page of the *New York Times Book Review* — what does that suggest about the readers and about the need to establish rapport with them?

SINCE World War II, certain names in recent American literature — Hemingway, Fitzgerald, Dos Passos, Faulkner — have acquired such weight and become so sacrosanct that they have been used as touchstones to reveal the understandable, but lamentable, inadequacy of the younger literary artists. We still hear complaints, for example, that World War II failed to produce a literary harvest comparable to that which we garnered from the first. We will discuss the idiocy of this complaint later.

Let one of us, the younger, attempt to create a restless, unhappy, free-wheeling heroine and we are immediately informed that Hemingway or Fitzgerald did the same thing better — infinitely better. Should we be rash enough to make any attempt to link the lives of some men with their time,

© 1962 by The New York Times Company. Reprinted by permission of James Baldwin.

we are sternly (or kindly) advised to re-read "U.S.A." It has all, it would seem, been done, by our betters and our masters. In much the same way, not so very long ago, it appeared that American poetry was destined to perish in the chill embrace of T. S. Eliot.

Neither I, nor any of my confrères, are willing to be defined or limited in this way. Not one of us suffers from an excess of modesty, and none of what follows is written in a complaining spirit. And it is certainly not my purpose here to denigrate the achievement of the four men I have named. On the contrary, I am certain that I and that handful of younger writers I have in mind have more genuine respect for this achievement than do most of their unbearably cacophonous worshipers.

I respect Faulkner enough, for example, to be saddened by his pronouncements on the race question, to be offended by the soupy rhetoric of his Nobel Prize speech, and to resent—for *his* sake—the critical obtuseness which accepted (from the man who wrote "Light in August") such indefensibly muddy work as "Intruder in the Dust," or "Requiem for a Nun."

It is useful, furthermore, to remember in the case of Hemingway that his reputation began to be unassailable at the very instant that his work began that decline from which it never recovered—at about the time of "For Whom the Bell Tolls." Hindsight allows us to say that this boyish and romantic and inflated book marks Hemingway's abdication from the effort to understand the many-sided evil that is in the world. This is exactly the same thing as saying that he somehow gave up the effort to become a great novelist.

I myself believe that this is the effort every novelist must make, in spite of the fact that the odds are ludicrously against him, and that he can never, after all, *know.* In my mind, the effort to become a great novelist simply involves attempting to tell as much of the truth as one can bear, and then a little more. It is an effort which, by its very nature—remembering that men write the books, that time passes and energy flags, and safety beckons—is obviously doomed to failure. Success is an American word which cannot conceivably, unless it is defined in an extremely severe, ironical and painful way, have any place in the vocabulary of any artist.

The example afforded by the later development, if one can call it that, of John Dos Passos is at least equally disturbing. And I suppose that there is no longer anything to say about Fitzgerald, at least not by me, and not now. Each of these men in his own way dramatizes for me the extraordinary hazards an American artist must run. Particularly, I must say, an American artist, whose tool is the common penny of language: who must try to deal with what words hide and what they reveal.

We live in a country in which words are mostly used to cover the sleeper, not to wake him up; and, therefore, it seems to me, the adulation so cruelly proffered our elders has nothing to do with their achievement — which, I repeat, was mighty — but has to do with our impulse to look back on what we now imagine to have been a happier time. It is an adulation which has panic at the root.

I think that it is true, but I am willing to be corrected, that the previously mentioned giants have at least one thing in common: their simplicity. I do not refer to their styles (though indeed, flying in the face of both critic and layman, I might be) but to their way of looking on the world. It is the American way of looking on the world, as a place to be corrected, and in which innocence is inexplicably lost. It is this almost inexpressible pain which lends such force to some of the early Hemingway stories — including "The Killers" and to the marvelous fishing sequence in "The Sun Also Rises"; and it is also the reason that Hemingway's heroines seem so peculiarly sexless and manufactured.

It is the sorrow of Gatsby, who searches for the green light, which continually recedes before him; and he never understands that green light is there precisely in order to recede. Ben and Charley and Moorehouse and the entire cast of "U.S.A." are tricked by life in just this way; nor is there any intimation in the book that we have, all, always, lived in a world in which dreams betray, and are betrayed, where love dies, or, more unbearably, fails to die, and where innocence *must* die, if we are ever to begin that journey toward the greater innocence called wisdom.

As for the work of Faulkner, which would seem, superficially, to escape these strictures, one has only to consider his vision, running throughout his work, of the gallant South. Even when he is most appalled by the crimes of his region—by which I do not so much mean the crimes committed against Negroes as the crimes his forebears and contemporaries have committed, and do commit, against themselves—he is testing it against the vision of a failed possibility.

One hears, it seems to me, in the work of all American novelists, even including the mighty Henry James, songs of the plains, the memory of a virgin continent, mysteriously despoiled, though all dreams were to have become possible here. This did not happen. And the panic, then, to which I have referred comes out of the fact that we are now confronting the awful question of whether or not all our dreams have failed. How have we managed to become what we have, in fact, become? And if we are, as, indeed, we seem to be, so empty and so desperate, what are we to do about it? How shall we put ourselves in touch with reality?

Writers are extremely important people in a country, whether or not the country knows it. The multiple truths about a people are revealed by that people's artists—that is what the artists are for. Whoever, for example, attempts to understand the French will be forced, sooner or later, to read Balzac. And Balzac himself, in his own personality, illustrates all those vices, conundrums, delusions, ambitions, joys, all that recklessness, caution, patience, cunning, and revenge which activate his people. For, of course, he *is* those people; being French, like them, they operate as his mirror and he operates as theirs. And this is also entirely true of American writers, from James Fenimore Cooper to Henry James to William Faulkner.

Is it not possible to discern, in the features of Faulkner's Lucas, the lineaments of Fenimore Cooper's Uncas? And does not Lambert Strether of James' "The Ambassadors" come out of the loins of men who conquered a continent, destroying Uncas and enslaving Lucas, in order to build a factory which produces "unmentionable" articles—and which, in the absence of any stronger force, is now ruled by a strong-minded widow? What *is* the moral dilemma of Lambert Strether if not that, at the midnight hour, he realizes that he has, somehow, inexplicably, failed his manhood; that the "masculine sensibility," as James puts it, has failed in him? This "masculine sensibility" does not refer to erotic activity but to the responsibility that men must take upon themselves of facing and reordering reality.

Strether's triumph is that he is able to realize this, even though he knows it is too late for him to act on it. And it is James' perception of this peculiar impossibility which makes him, until today, the greatest of our novelists. For the question which he raised, ricocheting it, so to speak, off the backs of his heroines, is the question which so torments us now. The question is this: How is an American to become a man? And this is precisely the same thing as asking: How is America to become a nation? By contrast with him, the giants who came to the fore between the two world wars merely lamented the necessity.

These two strains in American fiction — nostalgia for the loss of innocence as opposed to an ironical apprehension of what such nostalgia means — have been described, not very helpfully, as the Redskin tradition as opposed to the Paleface. This has never made any sense to me. I have never read an American writer in whom the Redskin and the Paleface were not inextricably intertwined, usually, to be sure, in dreadful battle. Consider, for example, the tormented career of the author of "Tom Sawyer." Or, for that matter, the beautiful ambiguity of the author of "Leaves of Grass." And what was Hart Crane attempting to celebrate, in his indisputably Paleface fashion, in that magnificent failure which he called "The Bridge"?

It seems to me that the truth about us, as individual men and women, and as a nation, has been, and is being recorded, whether we wish to read it or not. Perhaps we cannot read it now, but the day is coming when we will have nothing else to read. The younger writers, so relentlessly and unfavorably compared to their elders, are, nevertheless, their descendants and are under the obligation to go further than their elders went. It is the only way to keep faith with them. The real difficulty is that these very same questions, that same anguish, must now be expressed in a way that more closely corresponds to our actual condition.

It is inane, for example, to compare the literary harvest of World War II with that of World War I—not only because we do not, after all, fight wars in order to produce literature, but also because the two wars had nothing in common. We did not know, when we fought the first war, what we were forced to discover—though we did not face it, and have not faced it yet—when we fought the second. Between 1917 and 1941, the ocean, inconceivably, had shrunk to the size of a swimming pool.

In 1917, we had no enemies; 1941 marks our reluctant discovery—which, again, we have not faced—that we had enemies everywhere. During World War I, we were able to be angry at the atrocities committed in the name of the Kaiser; but it was scarcely possible in World War II to be *angry* over the systematic slaughter of six million Jews; nor did our performance at Nuremberg do anything but muddy the moral and legal waters. In short, by the time of World War II, evil had entered the American Eden, and it had come to stay.

I am a preacher's son. I beg you to remember the proper name of that troubling tree in Eden: it is "the tree of the knowledge of good and evil." What is meant by the masculine sensibility is the ability to eat the fruit of that tree, and live. What is meant by the "human condition" is that, indeed, one has no choice: eat, or die. And we are slowly discovering that there are many ways to die.

The younger American writers, then, to whom we shall, one day, be most indebted—and I shall name no names, make no prophecies—are precisely those writers who are compelled to take it upon themselves to describe us to ourselves as we now are. The loneliness of those cities described in Dos Passos is greater now than it has ever been before; and these cities are more dangerous now than they were before, and their citizens are yet more unloved. And those panaceas and formulas which have so spectacularly failed Dos Passos have also failed this country, and the world. The trouble is deeper than we wished to think: the trouble is in us. And we will never remake those cities, or conquer our cruel and unbearable human isolation — we will never establish human communities — until we stare our ghastly failure in the face.

We will never understand what motivates Chinese or Cuban peasants until we ask ourselves who *we* are, and what we are doing in this lonely place. Faulkner's South, and grandfather's slaves, have vanished; the sun will never look on them again. The curtain has come down forever on Gatsby's career; there will be no more Gatsbys. And the green hills of Africa have come out of the past, and out of the imagination, into the present, the troubling world.

Societies are never able to examine, to overhaul themselves: this effort must be made by that yeast which every society cunningly and unfailingly secretes. This ferment, this disturbance, is the responsibility, and the necessity, of writers. It is, alas, the truth that to be an American writer today means mounting an unending attack on all that Americans believe themselves to hold sacred. It means fighting an astute and agile guerrilla warfare with that American complacency which so inadequately masks the American panic.

One must be willing, indeed, one must be anxious, to locate, precisely, that American morality of which we boast. And one must be willing to ask one's self what the Indian thinks of this morality, what the Cuban or the Chinese thinks of it, what the Negro thinks of it. Our own record must be read. And, finally, the air of this time and place is so heavy with rhetoric, so thick with soothing lies, that one must really do great violence to language, one must somehow disrupt the comforting beat, in order to be heard. Obviously, one must dismiss any hopes one may ever have had of winning a popularity contest. And one must take upon one's self the right to be entirely wrong — and accept penalties for penalties there will certainly be, even here.

"We work in the dark," said Henry James, "we do what we can, our doubt is our passion and our passion is our task. The rest is the madness of art." This madness, thank Heaven, is still at work among us here, and it will bring, inexorably, to the light at last the truth about our despairing young, our bewildered lovers, our defeated junkies, our demoralized young executives, our psychiatrists, and politicians, cities, towns, suburbs and inter-racial housing projects. There is a thread which unites them all, and which unites every one of us. We have been both searching and evading the terms of this union for many generations. We are the generation that must throw everything into the endeavor to remake America into what we say we want it to be. Without this endeavor, we will perish. However immoral or subversive this may sound to some, it is the writer who must always remember that morality, if it is to remain or become morality, must be perpetually examined, cracked, changed, made new. He must remember, however powerful the many who would rather forget, that life is the only touchstone and that life is dangerous, and that without the joyful acceptance of this danger, there can never be any safety for anyone, ever, anywhere.

What the writer is always trying to do is utilize the particular in order to reveal something much larger and heavier than any particular can be. Thus Dostoevsky, in "The Possessed," used a small provincial town in order to dramatize the spiritual state of Russia. His particulars were not very attractive, but he did not invent them, he simply used what there was. Our particulars are not very attractive, either, but we must use them. They will not go away because we pretend that they are not there.

Not everything that is faced can be changed; but nothing can be changed until it is faced. The principal fact that we must now face, and that a handful of writers are trying to dramatize, is that the time has now come for us to turn our backs forever on the big two-hearted river.

AGNES DE MILLE

Rhythm in my blood

Agnes de Mille is a dancer and choreographer with an
international reputation. She composed the dances for
the musicals *Oklahoma!, Bloomer Girl, Carousel,* and
Brigadoon, among others, and the ballets *Rodeo* and
Fall River Legend. She is also a professional writer,
author of many magazine articles and the books *Dance to
the Piper, And Promenade Home,* and *To a Young Dancer.*
The following essay appeared in *The Atlantic Monthly,*
which means that it was addressed to a general public
of fairly high education but that Miss de Mille had to
explain what she was about and establish a rapport
with her readers.

ARTISTS work in the belief that what lies in their hearts is
as attractive to others—great numbers of others—as to
themselves. Now obviously hearts must be in some things
similar or they could not communicate; but similarity of
expression in art is castigated with scorn, at first sight anyway—criticism which must on consideration prove as in-
valid as it is futile. For artists must repeat themselves.

In all processes of life people imitate, and so must artists.
They are influenced by their peers as by their antecedents
because this is the way of organic development. Late
Beethoven and early Schubert, for instance, are almost
indistinguishable; while Brahms took certain themes, note

for note, from Beethoven; and Shakespeare stole nearly all his plots — all the good ones certainly. Had they worked as contemporaries in the same studio, as do choreographers, with the same performers, the tie would have been closer yet. Furthermore, most choreographers, like the apprentice painters of the Renaissance, get their initial experience studying under the personal influence of a master, taking part in the actual creation of his works, and spending years — the formative years — under constant personal artistic domination. The wonder is that any individual expression develops at all.

But it does develop, and with it the deviations and mannerisms we call personal style. Usually the artist is unaware of the process, as he is unaware of his other spontaneous modes of expression. Few willingly believe the insistent repetition, the catch phrases, the special idioms we use in conversation. Who among us has recognized a first recording of his own voice? We prefer to think of ourselves in terms of universals shared by all mankind — by all the ways, in short, in which we resemble or possibly surpass others. Our neighbors, on the contrary, distinguish us by our oddities and crotchets, and it is just for this reason that a cartoon when effective strikes everyone but the subject as revealing.

If idiosyncrasies of expression constitute a key to others' understanding, they serve the artist in much the same way, as a means of self-revelation and a technique for reaching his emotional reservoir. They determine his work habits and of course the character of his expression. But whereas each worker will develop his own combination, his own formula so to speak, he will have virtually nothing to do with its choosing and can use his critical faculties only to shape and correct. The emotional key, the kindling spark, lies beyond the reach of his mind deep in instinct. When we find these habitual patterns pleasing, we say the artist has developed style; when they appeal to our taste less, we say that he is repeating himself.

But the great repeated constantly. How do we, for instance, recognize Bach in any two measures of his music? Obviously because it sounds precisely like him and no one else. It is a question, I believe, of what is basically present and not how often the devices and tricks are employed. Indeed if variety were all, one could compose with a slide rule. There is great style and lesser style, and style altogether to be condemned; but none of it has to do either with repetition or derivation.

Every worker recognizes his own devices. I can name mine easily. I cannot always control them, but I can name them: I have an affinity for diagonal movement on the stage, with figures entering at one corner and leaving at the opposite, and unless I watch myself, this pattern recurs tiresomely. Why in one corner and out the other? I am not such a fool that I don't recognize the tendency, nor so starved for invention that I cannot think of other geometric directions. But this particular arrangement moves me and releases ideas. Could it be because the first fine choreographic design I ever saw was the *Sylphides* mazurka danced by Lydia Sokolowa with the Diaghilev ballet? And when I think of her great leap and the lines of still and waiting women leaning in a kind of architectural wonder for the next cross flight, I understand. That was the path of the first comet and it blazed a mark on my brain. That track spells ecstasy. But behind this reason, there must be more.

I use a still figure, usually female, waiting on the stage, side or center, with modifying groups revolving about, always somehow suggesting the passing of time and life experience. Why does the woman waiting seem to me so emotionally pregnant? One woman standing alone on the stage while people pass until a man enters upstage behind her? Why upstage and why always behind and why the long wait? I cannot be sure, but I remember waiting for years seemingly shut away in my mother's garden. My father was absent most of that time and I longed for him to come home to release me from the spell. Possibly the answer is somewhere here.

Why is my use of circles open or closed a constant? The avoidance of symmetrical design with the exception of the circle, my acute difficulty with all symmetrical design even including square-dance pattern which one might think was my native language? My repeated use of three female figures, a trilogy which because of plurality takes on symbolic force? And the falling patterns—the falling to earth, the swooning back, the resurrection, the running away always to return to a focal point—seem also to be insistent; and more important, more gross and unbearable, the breaking of all lyric line with a joke, as though I could not trust emotional development but must escape with a wisecrack.

It must be obvious even to people not familiar with dancing that these relations are individual, that they are to some degree sexual, and that they reflect a special personality pattern. I speak of my own work because I have a right to, but these observations apply to everyone. Consider, for instance, some of the recurring idioms of Balanchine: the single male figure embroiled with two to six females, one of whom either blinds or strangles him; the entanglement of either male or female bodies in endless ropes or chains (the lines are seldom made up of both men and women); the repetitive use of the grand reverence or imperial court bow as part of the texture of movement; the immaculate discipline of traditional gesture; the metrical, machine-like arrangement of school positions as unadorned as the use of unmodified scales in a musical composition; the insistence on two-dimensional symmetrical design; the superb but classic relation to music. One might build an interesting picture of Balanchine, the man, from these points of style. They are as natural to him as his sniff.

The characteristics of Jerome Robbins are very different. There is above all his free-limbed and virile use of the body, a complete spontaneous release as in sports, an exuberance, a total employment of all energies. Whether the gesture is gay or anguished, all resources are put into play and the strength and vigor of the movement communicates with the gusto of an athlete's. This in part may explain his enormous popularity with all audiences. The gesture is manly, it is keen and bold, and it is complete. Briefly it is exhilarating, and it brings to the spirit the satisfaction that a yawn or a stretch brings to the muscles. Women choreographers are less released, their movement often blocked or broken, or modified by reticences, not shyness of content but carefulness in physical effort. The difference is equivalent to that between a man and a woman throwing or jumping. Her gesture may be exact and serviceable; his will be total. Robbins enhances this quality by quoting literally from acrobatics or by using stunts. His skill in rhythmic invention is the greatest in the business, according to the composer Trude Rittmann, who has worked with all of us. Robbins is besot by rhythm, visual and bodily rhythms as well as auditory, and when he gets hold of a gesture he continues inventing out of the core of the matter until he has built an entire design and must wait for the composer to catch up. His rhythms will then work in counterpoint to the musical pattern. It is thought that if he had turned his attention to music, he might have been a first-class composer. Whereas Balanchine's rhythmic sense is spatial and linked to the music, Robbins' is independent. I, on the other hand, am totally derivative and lean and grow on melody. I cannot move without melody. May there not here be revealed a subtle sexual distinction? The men work free and on their own. The woman must wait for the lead.

But Robbins' most easily recognized trait is, praise heaven, his humor. In its grossest aspects, it takes the form of straight gags — very good ones, but bald and outrageous. In its more sophisticated manifestations, he introduces surprising and impertinent conclusions into his pattern, deliberately leading one on to expect a certain resolution and then insolently offering another, untraditional and slightly rude, though always logical because he is never foolish. He jokes with rhythms, with space, with relations of bodies, with light, with silence, with sound. These are all elements of style.

The grosser emotional fixtures of theme and content are plainly manifest — fixtures such as, in the case of Robbins, a preoccupation with childhood and games, with the bewilderment of growing up, with the anguish of choice. The unexpected, the joke, in this field seems to turn back on the choreographer and sit hard; each love story splits into three or more people; each romance spells destruction or transience; all repeats over and over. There is no resolution. In short, life turns out not to be a joke.

For my part, I seem to be obsessed by an almost Henry Jamesian inability for hero and heroine to come together happily, and by that other bedeviling theme, the woman as hunter. These are easily read. But the impregnation of abstract pattern with personality adjustments is, I find, far more subtle and more interesting. A great deal has been written about the kinesthetic transference between audience and dancer in the actual muscular technique; the field of spatial aesthetics remains, however, almost unexplored.

We know much about emotional symbols. They have a history and a science, iconography. Those used by the medieval and Renaissance painters were understood by the scholars and artists of the time — but, more wonderful, they mean to us today spontaneously just what they meant then; they seem to be permanent. We dream, Jung tells us, in the terms and symbols of classic mythology. Moreover, primitives shut away from classic learning dream in the same terms. Is it not also likely then that certain space relations, rhythms, and stresses have psychological significance, that some of these patterns are universal and the key to emotional response, that their deviations and modifications can be meaningful to the artist in terms of his own life experience and that these overtones are grasped by the spectator without conscious analysis?

Doctors are aware of this and utilize the knowledge in diagnosis. The significance of children's manipulation of space in writing and drawing is carefully studied, and the insane are observed for their relation to and use of walls, floor, doorways, heights, and so forth. Obviously these matters are basic to our well-being as land and air animals. And as plants will turn to sunlight or rocks or moisture according to their nature, so we bend toward or escape from spatial arrangements according to our emotional needs. In the diseased mind, the reactions are overwhelmingly overt. But look around any restaurant and see how few sane people will sit at a center table unless the sides are filled up. Yet formerly the king always dined dead center and many times in public.

The individual as a personality then has his own code in space and rhythm. It is evolved from his life history and from his race memory or, as Jung calls it, the collective unconscious. It is just the manipulation of these suggestions through time-space that is the material of choreography.

Take, for example, a simple daily gesture like walking forward and shaking hands. There are in this, first, the use of a separate limb common to most vertebrates, the upright position of the spine and head characteristic of man, the instinctively recognized expression of friendliness shared by all species as opposed to the instinctive expressions of fear and distrust. With animals, when approaching a friend, the hair lies flat, the ears are relaxed though alert, and all enlargements and ferocious distentions subside; breathing is normal. So with man. Heart, pulse, and lungs are easy, the eyes alert but neither distended to see danger nor con-tracted to pinpoint a target; the mouth is closed or smiling because no unusual demands will be made on hearing (to hear extraordinarily in times of acute danger, the mouth is opened and breathing suspends). And since no unusual effort will be demanded, the muscles neither brace nor tremble. The sum total of all this will be spelled out in the rhythm and position of the reaching hand.

But let there occur the slightest rebuff and see now what happens; hackles rise, hair bristles, lips curl to bare incisors, hearts pound, lungs fill, and on the instant all muscles pre-pare for attack. In ordinary intercourse, this naturally is not visible on full scale. But it needs only the slight widening of the pupil or nostril, the barest flicker of fingertip, to give the signal; the enemy has been recognized and addressed. Further subtle and meaningful modifications take over when the passage alters by the tension of a specific situation — when, for instance, someone who is often frightened of encounter meets a friend, or one who is never frightened meets someone not to be trusted, or two trusting friends meet under dreadful conditions, and so ad infinitum. Within each of these circumstances the body becomes a totally different chemical organization and yet retains the stamp of its own life habits.

It is the actor's art to mimic exactly with a full awareness of all the overtones and significances. The dancer, on the other hand, explodes the gesture to its components and reassembles them into a symbol that has connotations of what lies around and behind the fact, while the implications of rhythm and spatial design add further comment. Of course the choreographer is no more troubled by all this than is the businessman by the enormous anthropological heritage he puts into play every time he casually tips his hat.

Coleridge says of portraiture: "A good artist must imitate that which is within the thing, that which is active through form and figure, and discourses to us by symbols . . . the universal in the individual or the individuality itself—the glance and the exponent of the indwelling power. . . . Hence a good portrait is the abstract of the personal; it is not the likeness for actual comparison, but for recollection." Every gesture is a portrait. Behind it lie the histories of the race and the individual as well as the comment of the artist.

When I, as an artist, am moved I must respond in my own instinctive way; and because I am a choreographer, I respond through my instinctive gestures. I may come into the pattern with conviction and the excitement of fresh experience, but this will reflect a personality habit. It cannot be otherwise. Somehow, as in the grooves in a gramophone record, the cutting edge of my emotion follows a track played deep into the subconscious.

There is a further personal identification in choreography because most choreographers compose on their own bodies. Certain recurring steps can be explained simply by the fact that the choreographer performs these steps well and has a tendency to use them when demonstrating. Martha Graham has a kick and a particular skip that have stood her in good stead for twenty years. The explanation is simply that her left leg kicks straight up in a split, 180 degrees—a very spectacular feat. The right does not; hence the single-legged pattern. (It has been very interesting to observe over the years that Graham pupils who began by imitating her mannerisms have gradually eliminated the physical idiosyncrasies and personal accent and maintained the great style unblemished. In *Diversion of Angels* and *Canticle for Innocent Comedians,* Graham's personal gesture has been purified of all subjective tricks and stands in the keeping of her disciples as impersonal and abstract as the ballet code. It is overwhelmingly beautiful.) I am right-legged and right-footed, and most of the sustaining and balancing work in my choreography is done on the left leg; many of my dancers have complained bitterly. A dancer with short legs jumps in one manner, whereas a dancer with longer ones performs the same kind of jumps in quite another. So with composing. And identical pattern problems take on the modification of the composer's physique as well as his character adjustment, for it is always the choreographer who has to start the moving, and naturally he does it his way. If there were no instrument on which a song-writer could work except on his own voice, unquestionably his vocal restrictions would shape the melodic line.

The choreographer is also influenced by his performers. If I were to work, let us say, with a soloist whose arms and back were the strongest in the dance world and whose phrasing of legato lifts the most beautiful, but whose footwork, on the other hand, and allegro were weaker, quite obviously my composing style would adjust to his needs. Were I to compose with a man of enormous elevation and brilliant *batterie* but less dramatic force, my approach would then be necessarily different. And it must be noted that one works with the dancers at hand. One cannot summon from outer space a dream body capable of anything—or even exactly what one wishes. In the matter of one's own body one has obviously even less choice and must make do.

It is difficult for the individual to evaluate his own strengths and characteristics, and the theatre is strewn with lives ruined by unwarranted determinations to sing, or write, or act. No guarantee goes with desire, and there is unhappily just enough genuine talent neglected to confuse the issue. Nevertheless, granting a modicum of true ability, one must not be afraid to fail now and then. It all depends on the reason why.

One may, of course, fail because one has chosen the wrong kind of work.

One may fail because one has no discipline either in work or the handling of emotional problems.

One may fail because one wishes to fail—a hard tendency to detect, but a history of avoidable catastrophe indicates a need for medical help. One may fail temporarily because of grief, harassment, or exhaustion and, in the theatre, from lack of time. And then one may fail in trying new and unknown ways of expression. A creative life without failure is unthinkable. All physical growth and emotional change involve discomfort and a good bit of highly unattractive transition. Consider any adolescent, for example, taken at face value and with no thought of what is to come.

This fear of defeat haunts the creative worker uncomfortably, and there are fat days when all of us long to be let alone. But the first moment we permit ourselves to feel safe, the first moment we save ourselves from exposure, we are in danger of retreating from the outposts. We can be quite sure that this particular job need not be done, for, in all probability, it will have been done before.

"One must risk one's career every six months," says Elia Kazan, "in order to stay alive and effective in one's work."

But although work will never be safe, it may happily sometimes be easy and quick. Very frequently the best work is the easiest. But the rhapsodic release comes only infrequently and the professional must learn to compose at will—to employ aesthetic aphrodisiacs. For a young artist, this is perhaps the hardest task. Each person must learn his own path through the labyrinth of escape and idleness. Anne Lindbergh speaks of a technique of "acquiring grace": "Most people are aware of periods in their lives when they seem to be 'in grace' and other periods when they feel 'out of grace.' . . . In the first happy condition, one seems to carry all one's tasks before one lightly, as if borne along on a great tide; and in the opposite state one can hardly tie a shoe-string. It is true that a large part of life consists of tying the shoe-string, whether one is in grace or not."

To translate this into terms of the working artist, the state of "grace" or inspiration occurs when an idea is both clearly perceived and deeply felt, when circumstances do not block realization, and when technique waits ready and almost unconsciously available. The last is the controllable factor, a technique ready and available at the needed moment. Behind this lies a life's ordering.

Jerome Robbins works himself into a lather of excitement the three weeks preceding any big job on studies, all of which, he explains, may very well be discarded once the dancers are assembled but without which he cannot begin. These preliminary exercises furnish him with momentum and conviction. They are a warming-up process. Hanya Holm, on the other hand, never prepares this way. She studies and thinks, but when she walks into the studio, no plan has been determined on. It is between her and the dancers and God, she says. But God, I have found, cannot be held to a schedule, and any kind of composition that involves a finishing time — and this is the essence of all theatre — makes definite demands on inspiration. Inspiration has to be on tap as long as the components of design are living bodies paid by the hour.

But we may be grateful that very seldom are circumstances propitious and that the work fights through hard and slow. The moment one knows how, one begins to die a little. Living is a form of not being sure, of not knowing what next or how. And the artist before all others never entirely knows. He guesses. And he may be wrong. But then how does one know whom to befriend or, for that matter, to marry? One can't go through life on hands and knees. One leaps in the dark. For this reason creative technique reduces itself basically to a recognition and befriending of one's self. "Who am I?" the artist asks, and he devotes his entire career to answering. There is one clue: what moves him is his. What amuses or frightens or pleases him becomes by virtue of his emotional participation a part of his personality and history; conversely what neither moves nor involves him, what brings him no joy, can be reckoned as spurious. An artist begins to go wrong exactly at the point where he begins to pretend. But it is difficult sometimes to accept the truth. He has to learn who he in fact is, not who he would like to be, nor even who it would be expedient or profitable to be.

He may think he cannot afford this risk, but it is equally evident he cannot afford hackneyed success. For this is no success. And everyone instantly recognizes what has happened. The breath of life has gone; the workshop has become a morgue.

The real failing, the killing off, is not in taking risks but in choosing some work beneath his capacities and in doing it in a slick and routine fashion purely for recompense. This hurts the whole field of work, dirties and dulls down the audience, and destroys the individual. In the disreputable suburbs of each art form flourish great fortunes made just this way. I do not for one moment wish to imply that first-class work does not also bring in money. God is good, and it frequently does. But let us be sure in our hearts, no first-class job was ever achieved without a good deal in view besides the check.

The folks who think only of money may cynically pretend they do not care, but their stomach ulcers and their alcoholism prove they do most dreadfully. It is not so much a matter of what work is done but how it is done. It is vital to everyone to know that work is necessary and done to the best of ability whether making soap operas or washing floors, and it is only when the dust is swept under the rug that the process of disintegration sets in.

Far better than succeeding regularly is a good tough falling-short of a challenge. All work — one's own and everyone else's — benefits from this effort, successful or not, just as all science benefits from each difficult experiment — even the ones that seem not directly to bring results.

Louis Horst said recently at a testimonial banquet tendered him by the dancers of New York that he wished to thank all the dedicated and devoted artists with whom he had had the privilege of achievement; and he wished also to thank those who had tried and failed, because without them, the great could not have gone so far.

It is not for the individual to demand a certificate of quality before starting. He cannot and he may not. He has to work on faith. And he must listen only to his conscience, which will be stern enough in truth. He must listen to no other voices. For to listen is to be lost — to listen to critic, or friend, or business interest. He can pray only that his tastes and passions will be common to many. But he must suit himself first, himself before everyone else. He must, in other words, marry the girl of his heart despite the family or he will bed down for life with a wench not of his choosing.

ELIA KAZAN

Writers and motion pictures

Elia Kazan is a widely known and admired director of
plays and motion pictures. Among the plays he has
directed are *The Skin of Our Teeth, All My Sons,
A Streetcar Named Desire, Death of a Salesman, Tea and
Sympathy, Cat on a Hot Tin Roof, JB,* and *Sweet Bird
of Youth.* His movies include *A Tree Grows in Brooklyn,
A Streetcar Named Desire, Viva Zapata!, On the
Waterfront,* and *Wild River.* The following essay was
used as an introduction to the published version of
the movie *A Face in the Crowd,* but it is better judged
as a magazine article, addressed to a general literate
audience.

I ARRIVED in Hollywood in 1944 to make my first motion
picture, *A Tree Grows in Brooklyn.* I went from the train to
the hotel and then I checked in with my producer, Louis
Lighton. He was a fine man, an old-timer, a fine producer,
too. His eyesight was failing and I found him bent close
over his desk peering through a very large magnifying glass.
He was working on the script. He had before him Betty
Smith's novel, as well as several earlier versions of the
screenplay. These were being cannibalized—as they say at
plane repair shops—in a search for usable parts. Laboriously
and with practiced craftsmanship, the producer was putting
the incidents together into sequences, arranging these for
climax, and shaping the whole into what he always called

three "acts." Bud Lighton knew what he was doing: he'd done it since the days of the silents.

The screenplay was credited to Tess Slesinger and Frank Davis, but in all the nine months I was in Hollywood on this project, I never met these two people. Years later in New York, I heard of Miss Slesinger's death. I still hadn't met her. Another few years passed, and one night at a party a strange man came up and introduced himself. It was Frank Davis.

I was fresh from the theatre, and this separation of the writers from the director—and from their own work—came as a shock to me. I was to learn that it was regular practice.

I remember my first day at lunch in the Twentieth Century Fox commissary. I was told that Mr. Zanuck ate in state, flanked by his producers, behind the closed doors of the executive dining room. I didn't care about them. To me, the figures of glamour were the famous directors—gods! There they were, ranged along the best wall, looking out over the enormous dining room, each at his reserved table with his favorite waitress, also reserved. The center tables were taken by the stars. They were surrounded by their favorites and sycophants: make-up men, hairdressers, stand-ins, agents, girl or boy friends. At other prominent tables sat the big men of the back lot, the cameramen. Each had his heads of departments, his gaffers and key grips and so on: a Homeric catalogue.

Only after several weeks did I notice and explore a sorry group at a remote table. Their isolation was so evident that it seemed planned. There was no mixing with this group, no table-hopping to their table. They seemed out of place. Their dress was tamer. Few had the fashionable sun tan that a Beverly Hills success carries right to his grave. They laughed in a hysterical way, giddy or bitter. The writers. . . .

Some of them were admitted hacks and some were unadmitted hacks. Some were top screen writers. There would be an occasional Pulitzer Prize playwright or a famous novelist who had come out to do one screen assignment. Every last one of them seemed embarrassed to be there, and the embarrassment expressed itself in a bitter wit. They specialized in long sagas about the idiocy of the motion-picture business. There was a never-ending competition of appalling anecdote. They razzed everything and anybody — including themselves. A wealth of talent spent itself in mockery. My education continued on the set of *Tree*. Since I was a total stranger to film, Lighton assigned me one of Hollywood's best cameramen, Leon Shamroy. I was to stage the scenes "as if they were happening in life" and Leon would decide how to photograph them. He would get onto film various angles that could subsequently be cut together to make an effective cinematic narration. Leon was a new experience to me. As I say, I'd come from Broadway, where the writer was God and his lines were sacred by contract. Now I'm sure that Leon read the script, or most of it, before he started on the picture, but I know he didn't look at the day's scenes before coming to work each morning. This wasn't negligence: it was policy. There was a superstition that to look at the literary foliage would blur one's sense of the essential action.

When I came on the set in the morning, he was usually there, a victim of sleep (too much or too little) and ready for the ministrations of the set porter. In those halcyon days, each set had its porter. In a daily ritual, Leon was presented with coffee, a Danish, the Hollywood *Daily Variety,* and the Hollywood *Reporter*. While he read, I would earnestly rehearse the actors. In time, Leon would lower his *Reporter* and ask, "Well, what's the garbage for today?" The garbage was the dialogue. If he had a criticism, it was always the same one: "What do you need all those words for?" On his benign days, he didn't say "garbage." He said "nonsense."

The writers were in a humiliating position. The motion-picture makers insisted on referring to themselves as an industry. An industry aspires to efficiency. They were supplying fifty-odd pictures per major studio per year to the market. They tried to supervise the manufacture of scripts by methods that worked splendidly in the automobile and heavy appliance industries. Their system, with variations, went something like this: —

An "original property" (a novel, a play, a "story idea") was bought outright. By this act, a studio acquired material and at the same time got rid of a potential troublemaker, the "original author." The next step was an executive conference about the property and, usually, the casting of the stars. The original property was then turned over to a "construction man." His job was to "lick the story." In other words, he was to bring the material into digestible shape and length, twist it to fit the stars and to eliminate unacceptable elements. These last included elements banned by the Code, elements which might offend any section of the world audience, unentertaining elements such as unhappy endings or messages ("Leave them to Western Union!"). There was a word that governed what went out: the word "offbeat." This covered anything, really, that hadn't been done before, that hadn't been, as the marketing experts say, pretested. The construction man, to put it simply, was supposed to outline a hit. (For some reason, at this time, Middle Europeans were highly regarded for this job. Their knowledge of our language and country was slight, but they were thought to be hell on structure.) After the construction man, a "dialogue man" was brought in. (The verb "to dialogue" was added to the writers' glossary of Hollywood words.) After the man who dialogued it, there frequently followed a "polish man." The script was getting close. (They hoped.) There was a good chance that an "additional dialogue man" would spend a few weeks on the job. His instructions might be very simple, as, "Put thirty laughs in it."

What was wrong with hiring a specialist in each field? It should have been efficient.

Trouble was, the final shooting script was so often preposterous. Characters went out of character. Plot threads got snarled. Climaxes made no sense because the preparation for them had got lost somewhere on the assembly line. If it was a "B" picture, they usually shot it anyway. But if it was a "big" picture, the producer, like Lighton, would find himself late at night compiling a *last* final shooting script out of bits and pieces of all the previous versions. More often it was the director who did this. Or sometimes a brand-new writer was called in. The Screen Writers Guild put in a lot of time ruling on which writers were entitled to what screen credit for a picture that none of them could altogether recognize.

It was all pretty confusing, as I said, to a director fresh from the theatre. The theatre was Eugene O'Neill and Sidney Howard and Robert Sherwood and S. N. Behrman and Thornton Wilder and Clifford Odets and twenty others. The least, newest, greenest playwright shared the aura and the rights that the giants had earned. The rest of us — actors, directors, and so on — knew that our function was to bring to life the plays they wrote.

But, I was told, pictures are different. . . . Film is a pictorial medium. The strip of celluloid ought to tell the story with the sound track silent. There are crucial artistic choices that can't possibly be anticipated in a script. They have to be made hour by hour on the set and in the cutting room. A director stages plays; he *makes* pictures.

This was all true, and I must say that I took to it rather readily. I was disinclined to quarrel with a line of reasoning which thrust power and pre-eminence upon the director.

I was a good while longer learning certain other facts. I learned them tripping up on inadequate scripts — including some that I vigorously helped to shape. I can state them with painful brevity: —

There can't be a fine picture without a fine script.

There can't be a fine script without a first-class writer.

A first-class writer won't do first-class work unless he feels that the picture is *his.*

I doubt if the writer's place in pictures will — or should — ever be exactly the same as in the theatre, but I've been thinking a lot lately about what happened in the theatre. It's relevant and salutary.

Take 1900–1920. The theatre flourished all over the country. It had no competition. The box office boomed. The top original fare it had to offer was *The Girl of the Golden West.* Its bow to culture was fusty productions of Shakespeare. Either way, the plays were treated as showcases for stars. The business was in the hands of the managers and the actor-managers. The writers were nowhere. They were hacks who turned out new vehicles each season, to order. A playwright had about as little pride in his work, as little recognition for it, as little freedom, as a screen writer in Hollywood in the palmy days. And his output was, to put it charitably, not any better.

Came the moving pictures. At first they were written off as a fad. Then they began to compete for audiences, and they grew until they threatened to take over. The theatre had to be better or go under. It got better. It got so spectacularly better so fast that in 1920–1930 you wouldn't have recognized it. Perhaps it was an accident that Eugene O'Neill appeared at that moment—but it was no accident that in that moment of strange competition, the theatre made room for him. Because it was disrupted and hard pressed, it made room for his experiments, his unheard-of subjects, his passion, his power. There was room for him to grow to his full stature. And there was freedom for the talents that came after his. For the first time, American writers turned to the theatre with anticipation and seriousness, knowing it could use the best they could give.

Well, now it's 1957 and television is the "industry." It's a giant—and a growing giant. It's fated to be much bigger than pictures ever were. Even now, it's overwhelming. We've all seen that. Television has shaken up the whole picture business. It's our turn now. We in pictures have got to be better or go under.

When TV appeared, the motion-picture people put up a struggle. They didn't give up easily. First they pretended that it wasn't there. Then they tried to combat it with every conceivable technical novelty. They tried big screens in all sorts of ratios of width to height. They tried the third dimension, with and without goggles. They tried multiple sound sources and bigger budgets. As I write, the novelty is long long long pictures. They tried just about everything except the real novelty: three-dimensional material, new and better stories.

There are signs that they are being forced to that. It was hard to miss the meaning of the most recent Academy Awards. In 1954, *From Here to Eternity;* 1955, *On the Waterfront;* 1956, *Marty.* Of these, only the first came from a major studio. All three used ordinary old-fashioned screens. All three were shot in black and white. And different as they were, each of them was plainly, undeniably, offbeat. People simply didn't care what size the screen was. They went to see those pictures because they had life in them.

The writers rejoiced in a recognition that went beyond their awards; and, notice, in each case the writer carried through from start to finish, working actively with the director. James Jones had written a hot novel out of his war experience. Daniel Taradash made the material his own, turned it into a fine screenplay, and worked closely with Fred Zinneman, the director. Budd Schulberg did an original screenplay out of long research and conviction and feeling, consulting with me often as he wrote, and standing by during much of the shooting. Paddy Chayevsky expanded his own television sketch into a picture and was consulted by Delbert Mann as it was being shot.

To get back to the picturemakers, they're in trouble. The box-office barometer dipped down, recovered, dropped again. Picture houses are closing, going dark. There is a rumor that one of the big studio lots is to be sold for a real-estate development. In such moments of confusion and panic, executive imaginations make unaccustomed flights. It has begun to occur to them that the writer—that eccentric, ornery, odd, unreliable, unreconstructed, independent fellow—is the only one who can give them real novelty.

The first sign that the old order was changing came in an odd but characteristic way: there was a certain loosening of the industry's self-imposed censorship code. There were departures from the frantic and crippling rule that *you must please everybody, you can't offend anybody.* An older law was operating at the box office: if you try to please everybody, you don't please anybody.

At the same time, the unwritten taboos began to be relaxed. The superstition about offbeat material took a new turn. There seemed to be some mysterious plus in the offbeat. Warily, story departments were instructed to look for subjects with this peculiar quality.

So now the writers—the fellows who used to sit in that caustic clump in the farthest corner of the studio commissary—are being brought forward. A number have been moved "up" to nonwriting jobs. They have been made producers and/or directors. Since it would seem obvious that writers are needed as writers, this may sound as inscrutably silly as some other Hollywood behavior—but it is at least a fumbling recognition that writers "have something" that's needed now. More reasonably, books and other stories that used to be thought unsuitable for pictures are being bought. In a surprising number of cases, the original author is being asked to make his own screen version. Above all, writers are being invited, cajoled, and very well paid to write original and serious pictures. This last is the big step and the big hope.

Another sign of change is the growing number of small independent units being financed by the big studios and operating with a freedom that was unimaginable ten years ago. The mood is "Let them try." I'm one of the ones who's trying. I've formed my own company, Newtown Productions. I like being my own boss. I make my own pictures the way I want to make them. Also, I make my own mistakes. One of the things I've done is to upset the traditional balance and make the writer more important than the stars. I don't think it's a mistake.

I think we have a wonderful chance right now. The breakdown of the old standardized picture-making has made room for creative people. It is a boon to anyone who has something personal and strong to say. For art is nothing if it is not personal. It can't be homogenized. By its nature, it must disturb, stir up, enlighten, and "offend."

I'd like to make one last point about the writers, because it's important. The Academy Award winners, Dan Taradash and Budd Schulberg and Paddy Chayevsky, don't sneer at pictures. They don't think that screen writing is beneath them or that it's somehow an inferior form. The first time I met Budd, he had published three important and successful novels, but he said to me, "God, I'd like to write a really good picture some day." I heard Paddy use almost the same words back in 1951 when he was a young TV writer. They have both done it.

I think that Budd has done it again in *A Face in the Crowd,* which we are now completing. We have made it together, every step of the way. I never worked more closely with a writer in the theatre.

For as the theatre once freed itself from stale routines, so now pictures are beginning to make room for the best that a writer can bring to them. It follows that for the first time American writers are turning seriously to pictures.

What happens next may be as exciting as what happened in the twenties in the theatre.

Charlie Chaplin

Brooks Atkinson is a reporter, English teacher, and columnist but is best known as the dean of Broadway theater critics. Since 1925, he has been one of the most influential critics in America. He is also a professional writer in a broader sense. His news reports from Moscow during World War II won a Pulitzer Prize. He is the author of *Henry Thoreau: Cosmic Yankee* and an editor of the works of Thoreau and Emerson. He is represented here by a brief, informal, reminiscent essay which appeared in his regular column in the *New York Times.*

TO BE genuinely critical one must be in part detached. No matter how congenial the subject, one must be objective enough to retain some general perspective. Toward Charlie Chaplin, however, I am wholly idolatrous. Nothing said here will be half so judicial as the two pungent and enthusiastic bulletins Frank Nugent has posted in honor of the current *Modern Times.* But Mr. Nugent, who has exclusive rights to all screen pabulum in this newspaper, has given me permission this morning to prattle away about the beloved vagabond whose tottering image I first saw on a wrinkled screen more than twenty years ago. On Saturday evenings some itinerant impresario used to show films in the local hall of our Massachusetts town to the rag-time accompaniment of a facetious piano. All the boys used to go, racing noisily up the wooden stairs to the balcony in the hope of getting into the first row of seats. The colored and comic slide, "Ladies will kindly remove their hats," was the signal that at last the show was on. It lasted until almost ten o'clock, leaving just time enough to run to the butter-and-egg store for the family provisions before the crotchety manager locked the door for the night.

In those days there was no such thing as a bad movie show. Every one enjoyed every film every Saturday night. But one night cross-eyed Ben Turpin, who was a familiar figure, appeared in the company of a ragged little tramp, who was new to us, and they fled the cops and floundered over the landscape in an epic style that was more hilarious than anything we had ever seen before. The laughter was titanic. No one knew the name of the clown who was making Ben Turpin look like old Sober-sides, for it was not the fashion then to pay much attention to the names of screen performers. But for some inexplicable reason his image was vivid. When it next appeared in a film entitled *The Janitor* he was already an old friend who improved upon acquaintance, and Charlie Chaplin was an easy name to remember, particularly when we began to see it everywhere on bulletin boards and in store windows. From that time on we made it our business to see every Chaplin picture that appeared, and for the next few years they came out with grateful rapidity, although they were likely to be much too short for our taste. To the best of my knowledge I have seen every Chaplin film at least once, including an obscure Keystone comedy made before he assembled the costume and created the character of the tramp. To judge by the revivals that occasionally turn up in the "grind houses" off Broadway he has never been a better actor than he is today. There was some pretty crude stuff in those early films, although we all liked it well enough at the time.

To an idolator he can do no wrong. Some of the films have been better than others, and at least one of them, *The Idle Class,* was indisputably bad. Especially in those early, rushing days some of the gags were malodorously stale, for Charlie had to learn his business amid the helter-skelter of rapid producing. But the character he gradually created out of his imagination and his genius for pantomime is now so perfectly wrought that the merits of the films are of subordinate importance. Like Puck, Ariel and Mickey Mouse, Charlie Chaplin is unearthly—a figure in the dance, a masquerade. In well-balanced plays that arrive at an emotional conclusion, like *Shoulder Arms* and *The Kid,* the character is doubtless most satisfying and useful. But the joy, pathos and sentiment a Chaplin film arouses are chiefly evocations of character, unfettered and free; they are not to be imprisoned in a plot. The most we can hope for is a story pattern that does not confine the agile pantomimic dance of the little man with the hard hat and mustache.

Those of us who have been sitting at Charlie's knee, lo! these many years, have been uncomfortably aware of his restless longing for profundity. He has the clown's respect for intellect. *Modern Times* begins ominously with a sociological prologue which indicates that the little tramp is about to hand down a judgment on mankind. Whereupon you see him at work in an inhuman factory, gradually going mad from the monotony of labor at the moving belt. If you have an eager eye for social comment, you may see in some of the other episodes a suggestion that Charlie broods o' nights. But if he is offering *Modern Times* as social philosophy it is plain that he has hardly passed his entrance examinations, his comment is so trivial. As a matter of practical fact, the "modern times" of the title are only the dour background of an indifferent and hostile world that comically exaggerates the unworldliness of the little tramp. To be fully articulate he has always needed hostility—ferocious foremen, brutish police, villainous thugs; and the industrial tyranny of factory discipline, savage machinery and unemployment are an excellent environment to set off the pathos and comedy of the little tramp who does not belong. Like the scene in which he unwittingly carries a red flag at the head of a parade of bellicose strikers, the social significance of the new film is more technique than philosophy.

As an actor he has never been more brilliant. He is the master of pantomime who found in the silent screen the perfect medium for his genius. In these modern times of the audible screen he still realizes that the little tramp will lose immortality if he speaks in the tongue of common men. At the age of forty-six Charlie's roller-skating is full of exuberance and ecstasy; in the scenes of joy his tottering clown's gait is on tiptoe with lyric rapture. Put him in an austere line of ordinary men, as in a jail yard, where he spends a good deal of time, and the buoyancy of his spirit makes him instantly distinguished. He cannot be assimilated. Charlie is the footloose vagrant who has the instincts of a gentleman; he is courteous, elaborately proper, kind, chivalrous, generous and his manners are instinctively elegant. Even his vulgarity is daintily acted. His career as an actor has been marked by a steady refinement in the art of the character he created. In the course of two decades every man has to revise or discard many things he once believed, for only the true things endure. One of the durables is Charlie Chaplin. I have never had to change my mind about the funny little tramp who scampered across a screen that Saturday night in a rapt town hall.

ERICH FROMM

Is love an art?

Erich Fromm is a highly respected psychologist and
social critic, the author of *Escape from Freedom, The
Sane Society, Psychology and Culture,* and many other
books. Like all social scientists, he has had to
wrestle with the problem of jargon, that is, the
problem of how to explain to a general public things
which he is used to discussing with other social
scientists in a particular professional language. How
well he succeeds can be judged by the following, which
is the opening chapter of his book *The Art of Loving.*

IS LOVE an art? Then it requires knowledge and effort. Or
is love a pleasant sensation, which to experience is a matter
of chance, something one "falls into" if one is lucky? This
little book is based on the former premise, while undoubtedly the majority of people today believe in the latter.
Not that people think that love is not important. They are
starved for it; they watch endless numbers of films about
happy and unhappy love stories, they listen to hundreds of
trashy songs about love — yet hardly anyone thinks that there
is anything that needs to be learned about love.

This peculiar attitude is based on several premises which
either singly or combined tend to uphold it. Most people see
the problem of love primarily as that of *being loved,* rather
than that of *loving,* of one's capacity to love. Hence the problem to them is how to be loved, how to be lovable. In pursuit

of this aim they follow several paths. One, which is especially used by men, is to be successful, to be as powerful and rich as the social margin of one's position permits. Another, used especially by women, is to make oneself attractive, by cultivating one's body, dress, etc. Other ways of making oneself attractive, used both by men and women, are to develop pleasant manners, interesting conversation, to be helpful, modest, inoffensive. Many of the ways to make oneself lovable are the same as those used to make oneself successful, "to win friends and influence people." As a matter of fact, what most people in our culture mean by being lovable is essentially a mixture between being popular and having sex appeal.

A second premise behind the attitude that there is nothing to be learned about love is the assumption that the problem of love is the problem of an *object,* not the problem of a *faculty.* People think that to *love* is simple, but that to find the right object to love—or to be loved by—is difficult. This attitude has several reasons rooted in the development of modern society. One reason is the great change which occurred in the twentieth century with respect to the choice of a "love object." In the Victorian age, as in many traditional cultures, love was mostly not a spontaneous personal experience which then might lead to marriage. On the contrary, marriage was contracted by convention—either by the respective families, or by a marriage broker, or without the help of such intermediaries; it was concluded on the basis of social considerations, and love was supposed to develop once the marriage had been concluded. In the last few generations the concept of romantic love has become almost universal in the Western world. In the United States, while considerations of a conventional nature are not entirely absent, to a vast extent people are in search of "romantic love," of the personal experience of love which then should lead to marriage. This new concept of freedom in love must have greatly enhanced the importance of the *object* as against the importance of the *function.*

Closely related to this factor is another feature characteristic of contemporary culture. Our whole culture is based on the appetite for buying, on the idea of a mutually favorable exchange. Modern man's happiness consists in the thrill of looking at the shop windows, and in buying all that he can afford to buy, either for cash or on installments. He (or she) looks at people in a similar way. For the man an attractive girl — and for the woman an attractive man — are the prizes they are after. "Attractive" usually means a nice package of qualities which are popular and sought after on the personality market. What specifically makes a person attractive depends on the fashion of the time, physically as well as mentally. During the twenties, a drinking and smoking girl, tough and sexy, was attractive; today the fashion demands more domesticity and coyness. At the end of the nineteenth and the beginning of this century, a man had to be aggressive and ambitious — today he has to be social and tolerant — in order to be an attractive "package." At any rate, the sense of falling in love develops usually only with regard to such human commodities as are within reach of one's own possibilities for exchange. I am out for a bargain; the object should be desirable from the standpoint of its social value, and at the same time should want me, considering my overt and hidden assets and potentialities. Two persons thus fall in love when they feel they have found the best object available on the market, considering the limitations of their own exchange values. Often, as in buying real estate, the hidden potentialities which can be developed play a considerable role in this bargain. In a culture in which the marketing orientation prevails, and in which material success is the outstanding value, there is little reason to be surprised that human love relations follow the same pattern of exchange which governs the commodity and the labor market.

The third error leading to the assumption that there is nothing to be learned about love lies in the confusion between the initial experience of *"falling"* in love, and the permanent state of *being* in love, or as we might better say, of "standing" in love. If two people who have been strangers, as all of us are, suddenly let the wall between them break down, and feel close, feel one, this moment of oneness is one of the most exhilarating, most exciting experiences in life. It is all the more wonderful and miraculous

Marginal annotations (handwritten):
love is an exchange of peoples valuable traits of attractiveness + worth. an exchange one for another
people take early intimate feelings about love stopping without learn

for persons who have been shut off, isolated, without love. This miracle of sudden intimacy is often facilitated if it is combined with, or initiated by, sexual attraction and consummation. However, this type of love is by its very nature not lasting. The two persons become well acquainted, their intimacy loses more and more its miraculous character, until their antagonism, their disappointments, their mutual boredom kill whatever is left of the initial excitement. Yet, in the beginning they do not know all this: in fact, they take the intensity of the infatuation, this being "crazy" about each other, for proof of the intensity of their love, while it may only prove the degree of their preceding loneliness.

This attitude—that nothing is easier than to love—has continued to be the prevalent idea about love in spite of the overwhelming evidence to the contrary. There is hardly any activity, any enterprise, which is started with such tremendous hopes and expectations, and yet, which fails so regularly, as love. If this were the case with any other activity, people would be eager to know the reasons for the failure, and to learn how one could do better—or they would give up the activity. Since the latter is impossible in the case of love, there seems to be only one adequate way to overcome the failure of love—to examine the reasons for this failure, and to proceed to study the meaning of love.

The first step to take is to become aware that *love is an art,* just as living is an art; if we want to learn how to love we must proceed in the same way we have to proceed if we want to learn any other art, say music, painting, carpentry, or the art of medicine or engineering.

What are the necessary steps in learning any art?

The process of learning an art can be divided conveniently into two parts: one, the mastery of the theory; the other, the mastery of the practice. If I want to learn the art of medicine, I must first know the facts about the human body, and about various diseases. When I have all this theoretical knowledge, I am by no means competent in the art of medicine. I shall become a master in this art only after a great deal of practice, until eventually the results of my theoretical knowledge and the results of my practice are blended into one — my intuition, the essence of the mastery of any art. But, aside from learning the theory and practice, there is a third factor necessary to becoming a master in any art — the mastery of the art must be a matter of ultimate concern; there must be nothing else in the world more important than the art. This holds true for music, for medicine, for carpentry — and for love. And, maybe, here lies the answer to the question of why people in our culture try so rarely to learn this art, in spite of their obvious failures: in spite of the deep-seated craving for love, almost everything else is considered to be more important than love: success, prestige, money, power — almost all our energy is used for the learning of how to achieve these aims, and almost none to learn the art of loving.

Could it be that only those things are considered worthy of being learned with which one can earn money or prestige, and that love, which "only" profits the soul, but is profitless in the modern sense, is a luxury we have no right to spend much energy on? However this may be, the following discussion will treat the art of loving in the sense of the foregoing divisions: first I shall discuss the theory of love — and this will comprise the greater part of the book; and secondly I shall discuss the practice of love — little as can be *said* about practice in this, as in any other field.

CLIFFORD GEERTZ

The transition to humanity

Clifford Geertz is a professor of anthropology at the
University of Chicago, specializing in studies of
Southeast Asian cultures. The following essay was
originally a radio talk, delivered on the Voice of
America to peoples of other countries as part of a
series of talks on developments in the field of
anthropology. Notice that Geertz has chosen to strike
a balance, neither talking down to his audience nor
speaking only to other social scientists but appealing
to thoughtful listeners among the general public.

THE QUESTION of the relationship of man to the other
animals has been a persisting one in the human sciences.
Since Darwin, it has hardly been doubted that there is such
a relationship. But concerning its nature, and particularly its
closeness, there has been very much more debate, not all of
it enlightening. Some students, especially those in the biological sciences — zoölogy, palaeontology, anatomy and
physiology — have tended to stress the kinship between man
and what we are pleased to call the lower animals. They see
evolution as a relatively unbroken flow of biological
process, and they tend to view man as but one of the more
interesting forms life has taken, along with dinosaurs, white
mice and dolphins. What strikes them is continuity, the
pervasive unity of the organic world, the unconditioned

From *Horizons of Anthropology,* edited by Sol Tax. Copyright © 1964 by
Aldine Publishing Company. All rights reserved.

generality of the principles in terms of which it is formed. However, students in the social sciences—psychologists, sociologists, political scientists—while not denying man's animal nature have tended to view him as unique, as being different, as they often put it, not just in "degree" but in "kind." Man is the toolmaking, the talking, the symbolizing animal. Only he laughs; only he knows that we will die; only he disdains to mate with his mother and sister; only he contrives those visions of other worlds to live in which Santayana called religions, or bakes those mudpies of the mind which Cyril Connolly called art. He has, the argument continues, not just mentality but consciousness, not just needs but values, not just fears but conscience, not just a past but a history. Only he, it concludes in grand summation, has culture.

The reconciliation of these two points of view has not been easy, particularly in a field such as anthropology, which, in the United States at least, has always had a foot in both camps. On the one hand, anthropologists have been the main students of human physical evolution, tracing the stages by which modern man emerged out of a general primate background. On the other, they have been the students par excellence of culture, even when they were not entirely certain what they meant by that term. Unlike some biological scientists, they could not ignore man's cultural life as belonging "over on the Arts side," beyond the confines of Science altogether. Unlike some social scientists, they could not dismiss his physical history as irrelevant to an understanding of his present condition. As a result, the problem of the origin of culture, no matter how often ignored as unimportant or derided as insoluble, has continually come pressing back to the center of our attention as, piece by piece, the story of the physical evolution of *Homo sapiens* has been put together. It is the peculiar genius of such an eclectic discipline as American anthropology that the triumphs of one branch of it expose the failures of the others; and in such a way the science is built.

For the past half century or so, the reigning solution of the origin-of-culture problem has been what might be called the "critical point" theory. This term, which I take from the recently deceased dean of American anthropology, Alfred Kroeber, postulates that the development of the capacity for acquiring culture was a sudden, all-or-none, quantum-leap type of occurrence in the phylogeny of the primates. At some specific moment in the history of hominidization — i.e., the "humanization" of one branch of the primate line — a portentous, but in genetic or anatomical terms probably quite minor, organic alteration took place. This change, presumably in cortical structure, enabled an animal whose parents had not been competent, in Kroeber's words, "to communicate, to learn and to teach, to generalize from the endless chain of discrete feelings and attitudes" to become competent. With him culture began and, once begun, set upon its own course so as to grow wholly independently of the further organic evolution of man. The whole process of the creation of modern man's capacity for producing and using culture was conceptualized as one of a marginal quantitative change giving rise to a radical qualitative difference. Kroeber used the simile of the freezing of water, which can be reduced degree by degree without any loss in fluidity until suddenly it solidifies at 0° C. Another anthropologist compared the process to that of a taxiing plane as it accelerates along the ground toward that tremulous instant when it is launched into flight. A physical anthropologist, critical of the notion, referred to it drily as the appointment to rank view of the appearance of man, "as if he had suddenly been promoted from colonel to brigadier general." Man's humanity, like the flare of a struck match, leaped into existence.

There were three major considerations which led to and supported this general view. First, there was the tremendous apparent gap between the mental abilities of man and his closest living relatives, the great apes. Man can talk, can symbolize, can fabricate tools, etc.; no other contemporary animal can even approximate such accomplishments. One primatologist couple even undertook the heroic experiment of raising a chimpanzee in their household as though it were an adopted sibling to their natural daughter, giving it, in a rough sort of way, the same care and education given to the human child. But though the chimp learned a good many rather unusual things for a chimp to learn—how to operate a spray gun, how to pry the lids off of tin cans with a screwdriver, and, at one glorious point, how to pull an imaginary toy around by an imaginary string—it never even began to learn to talk. And, unable to talk, it was soon left far behind by its less agile but more loquacious human sister who proceeded onward, one presumes, to spin complicated theories about the uniqueness of the human condition.

Second, language, symbolization, abstraction, etc., seemed, on purely logical grounds, to be all-or-none, yes-or-no matters. One either spoke or did not; made tools or did not; imagined demons or did not. Half-religions, half-arts, half-languages did not seem even conceivable, for the essential process which lay behind them—i.e., the imposition of an arbitrary framework of symbolic meaning upon reality—was not the sort of activity of which there were partial versions. The progress from simple reflex activity, through conditioned responses and complex sign behavior, to symbolic thought was seen as a series of jumps, not an ascending continuum. Between the perception of the natural relationship of dark clouds to rain and the establishment of the arbitrary relationship of dark clouds to hopelessness there were, so it was thought, no intermediate stages.

And, third, there was the more delicate problem of what is usually called "the psychic unity of mankind." This has reference to the proposition—today not seriously questioned by any reputable anthropologist—which asserts that there are no important differences in the nature of the thought process among the various living races of mankind. If one assumes that culture appeared full-blown at some instant of time at a period before racial differentiation began, then this proposition becomes true virtually by deduction. To raise the question as to whether there might be historical differences in the ability to acquire culture among different species of hominids—i.e., among the various sorts of "men," living and extinct—seemed to raise it with respect to different races of modern men. And as the empirical evidence against such differences among the various groups of *Homo sapiens* was, and is, overwhelming, the hypothesis seemed disproved on the face of it. Thus comparative psychology, semantics, and ethnology converged to support the critical point theory of the origin of culture.

One branch of anthropology, however, did not so converge — human palaeontology, i.e., the study of human evolution by means of the discovery and analysis of fossil remains. Ever since that strange Dutch physician, Eugene DuBois, found the skull cap of *Pithecanthropus erectus,* the "erect ape-man," in a Javanese river bed in 1891, historical physical anthropology has been steadily piling up evidence that makes the drawing of a sharp line between man and non-man on an anatomical basis increasingly difficult. Despite some halfhearted attempts to establish a "cerebral Rubicon" — a critical brain size at which the ability to behave in a properly human manner springs full-grown into existence like Athena from the brow of Zeus — the findings of human palaeontologists have, bit by fossil bit, smoothed the curve of the descent of man to the point where flat assertions about what is human and what is not human have come to have a painfully arbitrary air about them. Whether or not human minds or souls come in degrees, human bodies most assuredly do.

The most disturbing fossil finds in this connection have been the various sorts of australopithecine "man-apes" which have been coming out of southern and eastern Africa since Raymond Dart dug the first one up out of the Transvaal in 1924. Certainly the most momentous discoveries in the history of human palaeontology, these fossils, which date anywhere from three-quarters of a million to a million and three-quarters years ago, show a striking mosaic of primitive and advanced morphological characteristics, in which the most outstanding features are a pelvis and leg formation strikingly similar to that of modern man and a cranial capacity hardly larger than that of living apes. The initial tendency was to regard this puzzling conjunction in one animal of a "manlike" bipedal locomotive system and an "apelike" brain as indicating that the australopithecines represented an aberrant and ill-fated line of development separate from both the human and the great ape lines — better to be a thoroughgoing ape than half a man, as Ernest Hooton once put it. But the present consensus is that they represent the oldest known forms in the evolutionary process which eventually produced modern man out of some generally simian stock. In these bizarre half-men our own full humanity is rooted.

F. Clark Howell will discuss the significance of the australopithecines from the point of view of human phylogeny in the next chapter; my interest in them here is in their implications for the critical point theory of the origin of culture. These more or less erect, small-brained proto-men, their hands freed from locomotion, manufactured tools and probably hunted small animals—or at least some of them did so. But that they could have had a developed culture comparable to that of, say, the Australian aborigine or possessed language in the modern sense of the term with a brain about a third the size of our own seems wholly unlikely. In the australopithecine we seem to have, therefore, a kind of "man" who evidently was capable of acquiring some elements of culture—simple toolmaking, sporadic hunting, and perhaps some system of communication more advanced than that of contemporary apes and less advanced than that of true speech—but not others, a state of affairs which casts something of a shadow on the critical point theory. What seemed presumptively unlikely, or even logically impossible, turns out to have been empirically true— like man himself, the capacity for culture emerged gradually, continuously, step by step, over a quite extended period of time.

But the situation is even more desperate. Because if the australopithecines had an elementary form of culture (what one anthropologist has called "proto-culture") with a brain one-third the size of that of modern man, then it follows that the greater part of human cortical expansion has followed, *not* preceded, the "beginning" of culture. In the critical point view man was considered more or less complete, neurologically at least, before the growth of culture commenced, because the biological capacity for culture was an all-or-none thing. Once achieved it was achieved entirely; all else was a mere adding on of new customs and developing of older ones. Organic evolution proceeded up to a certain point and then, the cerebral Rubicon crossed, cultural evolution took over, a process in itself autonomous and not dependent upon or productive of further nervous system alterations. The fact that this is apparently not the case, that cultural development was underway well before organic development ceased, is of fundamental significance for our view of the nature of man. He becomes, now, not just the producer of culture but, in a specifically biological sense, its product.

This is true because the pattern-of-selection pressures during the terminal phases of the evolution of the human animal was partly determined by the initial phases of human cultural development, not simply by natural environmental factors alone. A reliance upon tool manufacture, for example, puts a premium both on manual dexterity and on foresight. Within a population of australopithecines an individual somewhat better endowed with these characteristics would have had a selective advantage over an individual somewhat less well endowed. Hunting small animals with primitive weapons involves, among other things, great patience and persistence. The individual with more of these sober virtues would have an advantage over a flightier individual with less of them. All these various abilities, skills, dispositions, or whatever, are, of course, dependent in turn upon nervous system development. And so the introduction of tool manufacture and hunting must have acted to shift selection pressures so as to favor the rapid growth of the forebrain, as, in all likelihood, did the advances in social organization, communication, and moral regulation which, there is reason to believe, also occurred during this period of overlap between cultural and biological change.

Much of the work in this area is, of course, still speculative, and we are just beginning to ask the questions rather than to answer them. The systematic study of primate behavior under natural conditions which DeVore described, and which is having such an impact on our interpretations of the social life of early man, is, save for a few isolated exceptions, scarcely a decade old, for example. The fossil record itself is now expanding at such a fantastic rate and dating procedures are becoming so rapidly refined that only the foolhardy would attempt to set out definitive opinions on particular matters. But, details, evidence, and specific hypotheses aside, the essential point is that the innate, generic constitution of modern man (what, in a simpler day, used to be called "human nature") now appears to be both a cultural and a biological product. "It is probably more correct," the physical anthropologist Sherwood Washburn has written, "to think of much of our [physical] structure as a result of culture rather than to think of men anatomically like ourselves slowly discovering culture." The slogan "man makes himself" now comes to have a more literal meaning than originally supposed.

The ice age, with its rapid and radical variations in climate, land formations, and vegetation, has long been recognized to be a period in which conditions were ideal for the speedy and efficient evolutionary development of man. Now it seems also to have been a period in which a cultural environment increasingly supplemented the natural environment in the selection process so as to further accelerate the rate of human evolution to an unprecedented speed. It appears not to have been merely a time of receding brow ridges and shrinking jaws, but a time in which were forged nearly all those characteristics of man's existence which are most graphically human: his thoroughly encephalated nervous system, his incest-taboo-based social structure, and his capacity to create and use symbols. The fact that these distinctive features of humanity emerged together in complex interaction with one another rather than serially, as for so long supposed, is a fact of exceptional importance in the interpretation of human mentality, because it suggests that man's nervous system does not merely enable him to acquire culture, it positively demands that he do so if it is going to function at all. Rather than culture acting only to supplement, develop, and extend organically based capacities genetically prior to it, it would seem to be ingredient to those capacities themselves. A cultureless human being would probably turn out to be not an intrinsically talented though unfulfilled ape, but a wholly mindless and consequently unworkable monstrosity. Like the cabbage it so much resembles, the *Homo sapiens* brain, having arisen within the framework of human culture, would not be viable outside of it.

The general implications of this revised view of the transition to humanity are many, only a few of which can be touched upon here. On the one hand, it has forced a reinvestigation and reformulation of the theoretical considerations which supported the critical point theory in the first place. The argument from comparative primate psychology, for example, it is now apparent, established not the uniqueness of modern man, but rather the distinctiveness of the whole five- to twenty-five-million year hominid line of which he is but the culminating and, it so happens, the only living representative, but which includes a large number of different kinds of extinct animals, all of them much "closer" to man than is any living ape. The fact that chimpanzees do not talk is both interesting and important, but to draw from that fact the conclusion that speech is an all-or-nothing phenomenon is rather like assuming that, since the giraffe is the only living quadruped with such a long neck, he must have achieved it by a sort of quantum stretch. The great apes may be man's closest living relatives, but "close" is, to commit a pun, a relative term. Given a realistic time scale they are not actually so close at all, the last common ancestor being at the very least fifty thousand centuries back in what geologists call the Pliocene, and perhaps even further back than that.

As for the logical argument, that too has come to be questioned. The rapidly increasing interest in communication as a general process which has marked disciplines from engineering to ethnology in the last decade or two has, on the one hand, reduced speech to but one — admittedly highly flexible and efficient — mechanism for the transmission of meanings among many, and, on the other hand, provided a theoretical framework in terms of which series of graded steps leading up to true speech can be conceived. This work cannot be reviewed here, but as an example one linguist has compared eight different systems of communication ranging from bee dancing, fish courtship and bird singing through gibbon calls, instrumental music and human language. Rather than pivoting his entire analysis around the simple, and by now somewhat overburdened, sign-*vs.*-symbol distinction, he distinguishes thirteen design features of language and attempts in terms of them to analyze the difference between human and subhuman communication more precisely and to construct a possible course from the gradual development of true speech out of proto-speech during the ice age. This kind of work, too, is only in its infancy. But the day seems to be coming to an end when the only thing that could usefully be said about the origins of language was that all humans equally possess it and all nonhumans equally do not.

Finally, the established fact that there are no significant differences in innate mental capacity among the living races of man is not contradicted, but if anything supported and deepened by the postulation of differences in the capacity to acquire culture among different forms of presapiens men. The physical divergence of the human races is, of course, a very recent matter, beginning perhaps only fifty thousand years or so ago, or, by the most conservative estimates, less than one hundredth of the length of the whole hominid, i.e., man-forming, line. Thus mankind has not only spent the overwhelming proportion of its history in an altogether common evolutionary process, but this period now seems to have been precisely the one during which the fundamental features of its humanity were forged. Modern races are just that: modern. They represent very late, and very secondary, adaptation in skin color, facial structure, etc. — probably due mainly to climatic differences — as *Homo sapiens* dispersed throughout the world toward the close of the glacial period. These adaptations are thus entirely subsequent to the basic formative processes of neural and anatomical development which occurred between the founding of the hominid line and the emergence, fifty to one-hundred-fifty millennia ago, of *Homo sapiens*. Mentally, man was made in the ice age, and the really decisive shaping force in producing his uniqueness — the interaction of the initial phases of cultural development and the culminating ones of biological transformation — is part of the common background of all modern races. Thus, the view that the capacity for carrying culture, rather than bursting into full flower at a single point, was hammered out in old stone age toolshops over an extended period of time, far from undermining the doctrine of psychic unity explains and specifies it. It gives it a realistic historical grounding it previously rather lacked.

But even more important than the revision or reinterpretation of older theories which the synchronous, rather than the sequential, view of the relationship between the evolution of human anatomy and the birth of human culture necessitates, is its implications for a novel way of thinking about culture itself. If man grew up, so to speak, within the context of a developing cultural environment, then that environment must needs be viewed not as a mere extrasomatic extension, a sort of artificial amplification, of already given innate capacities, but as ingredient to the existence of those capacities themselves. The apparent fact that the final stages of the biological evolution of man occurred after the initial stages of the growth of culture implies, as I have already noted, that "basic," "pure," or "unconditioned" human nature, in the sense of the innate constitution of man, is so functionally incomplete as to be unworkable. Tools, hunting, family organization, and later, art, religion, and a primitive form of "science," molded man somatically, and they are therefore necessary not merely to his survival but to his existential realization. It is true that without men there would be no cultural forms. But it is also true that without cultural forms there would be no men.

The symbolic network of belief, expression, and value within which we live provides for us the mechanisms for ordered behavior which in lower animals are genetically built in to their bodies but which in ourselves are not. The uniqueness of man has often been expressed in terms of how much and how many different things he is capable of learning. And, although chimpanzees who learn to play with imaginary toys may give us some pause, this is true enough. But what is of perhaps even more fundamental theoretical importance is how much there is for man to learn. Without the guiding patterns of human culture, man's intellectual life would be but the buzzing, booming confusion that William James called it; cognition in man depends upon the existence of objective, external symbolic models of reality in a way no ape's does. Emotionally, the case is the same. Without the guidance of the public images of sentiment found in ritual, myth, and art we would, quite literally, not know how to feel. Like the expanded forebrain itself, ideas and emotions are cultural artifacts in man.

What this heralds, I think, is a fundamental revision in the theory of culture itself. We are going, in the next few decades, to look at culture patterns less and less in terms of the way in which they constrain human nature, and more and more in the way in which, for better or for worse, they actualize it; less and less as an accumulation of ingenious devices to extend pre-existing innate capacities, and more and more as part and parcel of those capacities themselves; less and less as a superorganic cake of custom, and more and more as, in a vivid phrase of the late Clyde Kluckhohn's, designs for living. Man is the only living animal who needs such designs for he is the only living animal whose evolutionary history has been such that his physical being has been significantly shaped by their existence and is, therefore, irrevocably predicated upon them. As the full import of this fact becomes recognized, the tension between the view of man as but a talented animal and the view of him as an unaccountably unique one should evaporate, along with the theoretical misconceptions which gave rise to it.

CHARLES E. SILBERMAN

Give slum children a chance: a radical proposal

Charles E. Silberman is an economist and one of the editors of *Fortune* magazine. Here, he turns his attention to an educational problem and speaks to a wide general audience. The essay was designed to be part of a book, *Crisis in Black and White,* in which it subsequently appeared, but as a magazine article it had to be self-explanatory and self-contained. Notice the evidence in the opening that Silberman is conscious of this problem.

HORACE Mann called education "the great equalizer of the conditions of men . . . the balance wheel of the social machinery."

The wheel is out of balance. As the one institution with which every Negro and white slum child comes into intensive and prolonged contact, the public school offers the greatest opportunity to dissolve the cultural barrier that helps block their advance. But the opportunity is being muffed: no city in the United States has even begun to face up to the problem involved in educating the Negro or white slum youngster.

The root of the problem educationally is that the slum child does not learn to read properly in the first two grades. Whether because of this reading disability alone, or because of difficulty in handling abstract concepts that stem from independent causes, the slum child falls further and further behind after the third grade; the gap widens, and his IQ actually declines. His failure to read properly affects a lot more than his school work. It has a profound impact on how he regards himself and consequently on how he regards school. Poor reading skill at the start is the major cause of school dropouts and subsequent unemployment.

No informed person can believe any longer that the poor—or the Negroes specifically—are congenitally slow or illiterate. Yet we have had almost no success in combating this most crippling of a child's handicaps. Even the most well-intentioned and well-financed special program for the "culturally deprived child" serves to help only a small upper crust. New York City, for example, spends some $200 a year *more* per child in slum schools than in white middle-class schools. Yet with it all, third-grade pupils in the schools of central Harlem are one year behind grade level in academic performance; by the sixth grade, they have fallen nearly two years behind, and by eighth grade, two and a half years. And some cities aren't even making an effort. Chicago, for example, appropriates 20 per cent *less* per child in Negro schools than in white middle-class schools.

The reason we have failed is that we start much too late, after the damage is already done. Instruction in the first grade of our public schools takes it for granted that a child has completed a reading-readiness program in the kindergarten year. Yet only a small fraction of Negro or lower-class white youngsters attend kindergarten. Compulsory kindergarten undoubtedly would improve matters, but the basic problem would remain. That problem, stated simply, is that the environment in which lower-class Negro and white children grow up does not provide the intellectual and sensory stimulus they so desperately need. The result is that youngsters from impoverished backgrounds enter school lacking a great many skills which the teachers and the curriculum take for granted, and which most middle-class children have acquired as a matter of course.

The slum youngsters, for example, may lack the sense of auditory discrimination—the ability to distinguish very subtle differences and nuances in sound—that is essential to reading. The noise level in a household in which a half-dozen people are living in two rooms tends to be so high that the child is forced to learn how *not* to listen; he develops the ability to wall himself off from his surroundings. Hence he fails to develop an ability to distinguish between relevant and irrelevant sounds, and to screen out the irrelevant. If, for instance, a truck rumbles by while the teacher is talking, the lower-class pupil hears only one big jumble of sound; the middle-class pupil has the ability to screen out the irrelevant noise of the truck and listen only to the teacher.

More important, the lower-class child has not had the experience of having adults correct his pronunciation; correction of baby speech and of mistakes in syntax or grammar is one crucial way in which the middle-class child learns the ability to distinguish subtle nuances of sound and language—"b" as opposed to "p," for example. In the case of the lower-class Negro youngster, particularly in families recently moved from the South, the problem is compounded several times over by the fact that the phonic system of the language he speaks is quite different from the system of the language which the teacher speaks and which the reading primers use.

The lower-class child, moreover, tends to have a poor attention span and to have great difficulty following the teacher's orders. The reason is that he generally comes from a nonverbal household: adults speak in short sentences, if indeed they speak at all, and when they give orders to the child, it is usually in monosyllables—"get this," "bring that." The child has never been obliged to listen to several lengthy sentences spoken consecutively. And the speech he does hear tends to be of a very simple sort from the standpoint of grammar and syntax. In school, the middle-class teacher who rambles on for several sentences might just as well be talking another language. The nonverbal atmosphere of the home also means that lower-class children have a limited perception of the world about them: they do not know that objects have names (table, wall, book), or that the same object may have several names (an apple is fruit, red, round, juicy). They also have very little concept of size or time.

The lower-class youngsters are poorly motivated, because they have had little experience in receiving approval for success in a task or disapproval for failure; but school is organized on the assumption that children expect approval for success. And since the parents, because of their general nonverbal orientation, do not ask the youngsters about school, the children have no way of knowing that the parents *do* very much want and expect success. For much the same reason, these children do not conceive of an adult as a person of whom you ask questions and from whom you get answers—yet school is based on the assumption that children who don't understand will ask. The middle-class mother, by contrast, is engaged in almost constant dialogue with her child. The slum child's home is characterized by a general sparsity of objects: there are few toys, few pictures, few books, few magazines, few of anything except people and noise. In one group of Negro children whom Dr. Martin Deutsch, director of the Institute of Developmental Studies of New York Medical College, has studied, 50 per cent said they did not have a pencil or pen at home, and about as many said there were no books or magazines. Their experiences outside the home are equally narrow; 65 per cent had never gone beyond a twenty-five block radius.

Given this poverty of experience, it is almost inevitable that the slum child will fail when he enters school. He simply has not been prepared to produce what the school demands, and by and large the school makes no attempt to adjust its curriculum to the realities of what its children actually know, as opposed to what they are *assumed* to know.

So far, I have stressed the slum youngsters' failure to acquire a specific set of skills—auditory discrimination, sense of timing, etc.—which are prerequisite to learning how to read. The problem cuts far deeper than that. An impressive body of research in the psychology of cognition and perception as well as in the neurophysiology of the brain has made it clear that exercise of the mind early in life is essential for its later development. The human being is born with less than one third of the adult brain capacity, and there is tremendous growth of the cortex after birth. The way in which the cortex and, indeed, the whole nervous system develop is directly affected by the environment. Hence, mental alertness and in particular the ability to handle abstractions depend physiologically on a broad diversity of experience in the environment of early childhood.

"We know now," says Professor Jerome Bruner, director of Harvard's Center for Cognitive Studies, "that the early challenges of problems to be mastered, of stresses to be overcome, are the preconditions of attaining some measure of our full potentiality as human beings. The child is father to the man in a manner that may be irreversibly one-directional, for to make up for a bland impoverishment of experience early in life may be too great an obstacle for most organisms." As Bruner puts it, "supply creates its own demand"; in the phrase of the great Swiss child psychologist Jean Piaget, "the more a child has seen and heard, the more he wants to see and hear."

The problems Negro and other slum youngsters have in learning are no different in kind, therefore, and hardly different in degree, from those of any children coming from a culture of poverty. Thus, the analysis that Deutsch, J. McV. Hunt, and others have made of the reasons for the failure of lower-class children in school are virtually identical with the diagnoses Israeli educators have made of the reasons for the academic failures of the so-called "Oriental Jews"—children of immigrants to Israel from Arabic countries in North Africa (Morocco, Algeria, Egypt) and the Middle East (Iraq, Yemen, Kurdestan). A sizable gap is evident when these youngsters start school: they score, on average, sixteen points lower on IQ tests than children coming from a Western European background. And the gap widens as they go through school; by age thirteen, the IQ differential is twenty-two points. Until remedial measures were taken, few went to high school, which is not compulsory, and hardly any to the university. Yet there could be no conclusion drawn about inherent inferiority; for a thousand years, the flowering of Jewish culture and learning was in Arabic countries. Studies by Israeli educators have pointed to the same reasons for these youngsters' poor academic performance: an impoverishment of environment—a lack of stimulation, particularly of the verbal sort, in the early years — which must be compensated for in some way if it is to be overcome.

Nothing less than a radical reorganization of American elementary education is necessary, therefore, if the schools are to begin to discharge their obligation to teach the Negro and white slum youngsters. To reverse the effects of a starved environment, the schools must begin admitting children at the age of three or four, instead of at five or six. The nursery school holds the key to the future — but a very different kind of nursery school from the one most Americans are familiar with.

It is between the ages of three and six that the battle is won or lost. "The two-and-a-half and three-year-olds are almost universally curious and friendly," says Dr. Ronald Koegler, a neuropsychiatrist at UCLA who is experimenting with a Montessori nursery program for culturally deprived children, "but by the age of six, the children are already different. The culturally deprived have already been deadened by their environment and are already so far behind the middle-class child that all the best elementary education will not be sufficient for them to catch up." Dr. Koegler may be exaggerating somewhat, but the point he is making is basic: the schools which wait until kindergarten or first grade will need to employ many, many more resources to do what they might do with comparative ease for children at age three and four.

By all odds the most important experiment in nursery education for Negro and white slum children is a research and demonstration project directed by Martin Deutsch in ten New York City public schools and five day-care centers. Deutsch's ultimate objective is to develop a standardized curriculum and a set of teaching techniques that can be used in similar programs anywhere in the country. (Some thirty cities are setting up, or talking about setting up, nursery programs for the culturally deprived, more or less modeled on the Deutsch experiment.) The curriculum is designed to teach the youngsters the verbal and perceptual skills they need in order to learn to read, and also to bolster their sense of self. There is a great deal of emphasis on teaching labeling—getting across the notion, first, that every object has a name, and, second, the more sophisticated concept that objects may have a number of different labels, each referring to different attributes. A teacher may use puppets or other replicas of people, animals, and objects to illustrate the story she is reading, to drive home the relation between people and things. Much use is made, also, of toys: stuffed animals, dolls, peg boards, color cones, to teach color, shape, and size. Auditory discrimination is taught through a tape recorder, in which background noise is used to mask a relevant sound; the level of the background noise is gradually stepped up, to enhance the child's discrimination. To help develop a sense of self, the rooms contain a great many mirrors; many children have never seen themselves in one. One of Deutsch's most successful techniques has been to take a photograph of each child and give a copy to the child and to the parent; 85 per cent of the youngsters had never seen a picture of themselves. The pictures were then used to construct a book about the class.

The physical arrangements of the classroom are planned carefully. The emphasis is on order, beauty, and clarity—on balancing color, physical objects, and space. This is important, Deutsch feels, because there is so little beauty and so little structure in the children's own lives. They respond amazingly to beauty. (Children will typically comment, "I wish I could live in this classroom," and older brothers or sisters in the same school will express envy at the younger child being in such an attractive room.) Each room is divided into a number of self-contained sections: a reading section with books, as well as tape recorders children can use on their own to play back a favorite story; a music section, with phonograph and records; an activity section with blocks and other toys involving motor skills and coordination. The sections are quite distinct—clarity is necessary, in Deutsch's view—but not rigid; they can be rearranged whenever desired. Each child has his own cubby to provide a sense of privacy and personal possession, both of which are difficult to find in a slum home.

It is not enough just to work with the children. Deutsch tries to work with the parents too—to win their trust, which is essential if the program is to succeed, and to give them some instruction in how to help their children. Once the former is done, the latter is relatively easy: once they have been persuaded that this is a genuine attempt to help their children, not a venture in brainwashing, the parents (or rather, the mothers—55 per cent of the youngsters come from broken homes) are eager to get instruction. Deutsch and his staff suggest that the parents encourage the child to talk at the dinner table, especially about school, a completely novel experience to a great many parents; that they give him toys, praise his success—in short, let the child know that the parent wants him to succeed in school and is interested in what he does. This has enormous impact on the children's verbal ability, for they begin talking about school when they get home, instead of remaining mute; and it has profound effect on increasing motivation.

The youngsters in Deutsch's experimental classes show significant improvements in IQ test scores. The more profound effects may be less measurable, but they are striking to anyone who spends even a few weeks in one of the classrooms observing the children; they change under the observer's eye. Kindergarten teachers who receive youngsters exposed to even as little as six months of Deutsch's experimental program are almost speechless with enthusiasm. In all their years of teaching, they say, they have never had slum youngsters enter as well-equipped intellectually, as alert, as interested, or as well-behaved.

My proposal to extend public education down to the nursery level is not nearly as extreme as it sounds. Israel, with a standard of living only about one third that of the United States, has already adopted such a policy, and is in the process of establishing nurseries for the Oriental Jews as the means of acculturating its new immigrants in a single generation. The government has formally adopted a policy of preferential treatment, called "state protection." Compensatory education begins at the prenatal level, when amateur social workers visit the pregnant mother and the father; among other things, they teach the parents how to play with the children, and leave a set of toys which the government lends the family for a period of a year or so.

The government is rapidly establishing free nursery schools so that the Oriental youngsters can begin school at three; the curriculum closely resembles the one Martin Deutsch is developing.

Help does not stop at that point, however. The Israeli educators have tried to isolate the critical points in intellectual development. The first is the nursery-school years; the second is the first and second grades, when the children learn to read. The Israelis are convinced that anyone, even the mentally retarded, can be taught to read. The problem, as Dr. Moshe Smilansky, Pedagogical Adviser to the Minister of Education, puts it, is simply one of adapting the method of instruction to the state of development in which the child comes to school. Three years of intensive work have convinced the Israelis that 80 to 85 per cent of the Oriental youngsters can be brought up to the expected reading level.

The third critical point at which Israel's Oriental youngsters need help is the junior-high period (ages twelve to fourteen); they receive up to eleven hours of additional instruction a week, in order to help them adjust to the more complex curriculum they begin to receive, and to help them prepare for high school. In addition to the extra instruction given to all the Oriental youngsters, the government has adopted a separate program for the most academically talented: the top 25 per cent. The object, quite explicitly, is to encourage the development of an intellectual elite among the Oriental students — to create a group that will go through high school and the university without difficulty and then move into positions of responsibility in government, in business management, and in the army, thereby demonstrating to the rest of the Oriental community as well as to the Western Jewish community that Orientals *do* have the capacity to move to the top of Israeli society.

One reason the Israelis have been so successful is that they have far greater administrative flexibility than we do in America; the director of research operates out of the office of the Minister of Education, so his research results can be immediately translated into administrative policy. The main reason for success, however, is the commitment to the program of "state protection" at all levels of government. The officials in charge of the program (though needless to say, not all the teachers in the field) really believe that there is no inherent difference in intelligence between Oriental and Western youngsters—and that in any case IQ scores are meaningless as a guide to a child's potential.

This notion is crucial if any program is to succeed in the United States. The traditional American approach has been to see the child as a more or less fixed, static entity that has been determined by genetic environment. Hence the emphasis on IQ: you have to measure what the child is before you can decide what to teach him, and how. The Israeli educators—and people like Deutsch, Bruner, Professor O. K. Moore of Rutgers, and Professor J. McV. Hunt of the University of Illinois, in the United States, as well as Montessori before them—see the child instead as an "open system." They are interested less in what the child *is* than in what he can *become,* and their goal is to provide whatever materials and techniques are needed to develop his intellectual abilities to the fullest. This is a far cry from the so-called "life adjustment" approach so popular in the United States a while ago; indeed, it is its very opposite, since life adjustment assumed irreversibility of a child's nature. The Israelis reject the idea that there is a point at which it is too late to help a child, though they agree that help is far more effective if begun in the nursery years. And they assume that intellectual development is a major source of mental health; children who receive an infusion of competence from the very beginning—who learn "I can" at the start of school—will tend to be stable, well-adjusted individuals as adults.

The Israeli example is by no means the only one. The first demonstration of the value of early childhood education in reversing the effects of poverty occurred nearly sixty years ago, when the Casa dei Bambini was established in a Roman tenement by Dr. Maria Montessori, one of the towering figures in the history of education, and one who is just beginning to be appreciated. Something of a Montessori revival has occurred in the United States in recent years, and several experiments using her methods are in process.

The Montessori approach may be particularly relevant to our own time for a number of reasons. It emphasizes what psychologists call *intrinsic* motivation — harnessing the child's innate curiosity and delight in discovery. Each child is free, therefore, to examine and work with whatever interests him, for as long as it interests him, from the materials that are available. What is available is determined by the Montessori concept of "prepared environment," which places great stress on training the sensory processes: cognition is enhanced by providing appropriate stimuli to *all* the senses.

The chief advantage of the Montessori approach, in the opinion of J. McV. Hunt, is that "it gives the individual child an opportunity to find the circumstances which match his own particular stage of development." It has the corollary advantage of making learning fun, whereas the conventional American approach to kindergarten and elementary education manages to establish remarkably early the notion that learning is unpleasant. ("Let's stop playing with the blocks now, children; it's time to learn our letters.")

As in Israel, help for our underprivileged cannot stop with creation of a nursery program, though such a program is crucial. The cultural distance between the school and the community, and the disorganization of Negro and slum life, mean that a great many lower-class youngsters will need extra help all the way through school, and especially in the early grades. It may be useful, for example, to provide them with texts that offer a better bridge between their own lives and the rich world of Western civilization than, say, the almost universal "Dick, Jane, and Sally" series of reading primers. Unfortunately the first experiment in creating an "integrated" series of reading primers — *Play with Jimmy, Fun with David,* and *Laugh with Larry,* written by staff members of the Detroit Public Schools, moves in precisely the wrong direction. The books show a well-scrubbed Negro family in the same sort of antiseptic suburban environment that Dick, Jane, and Sally play in, and the level of prose almost makes the Dick, Jane, and Sally readers sound like poetry. (The Detroit readers use a much smaller vocabulary; the Detroit experts made tape recordings of Negro children's speech, and discovered that their vocabulary contains only about half as many words as white children's.) There is some reason to assume, however, that what these youngsters need is stimulus to the imagination—some evidence that reading is a means of escaping the confines of the slum for something more exciting than a backyard barbecue or a trip to the supermarket.

Current dogma, of course, condemns any program of compensatory education, no matter how massive, as a return to "separate but equal," hence an expression of prejudice. But one group of Negro leaders, headed by Professor Kenneth Clark and the Reverend Eugene Callender, has already had the courage to face up to the realities of the education problem in central Harlem. Their views are expressed in a report issued by Harlem Youth Opportunities Unlimited, Inc. (HARYOU), a group set up with funds from the President's Committee on Juvenile Delinquency and Youth Crime.

The authors mince no words about their belief in integration and their distrust of many of the measures taken so far. But their main proposition is "that this vicious cycle of educational inefficiency and social pathology can be broken only by instituting an educational program of excellence in the schools of deprived communities," and their most important recommendation is a proposal to establish compensatory nursery programs for all Harlem children. In the long run, they argue, excellence requires an end to segregation. But in the short run—"during that period required to obtain more adaptive, democratic, nonsegregated schools for all children"—compensatory education is necessary, for 50 per cent of the junior-high-school students need massive remedial work if they are to be brought up to grade level.

Integration is a moral imperative—the greatest moral imperative of our time. It is essential not so much for Negroes as for whites, who must learn to live in the great world in which they are the minority. But merely throwing white and black students into the same classroom without regard to differences in knowledge and academic performance does not constitute integration in any meaningful sense. How are we to achieve meaningful integration—

which leads to genuine contact, to real communication, and to understanding of each group by the other?

The only honest answer is that genuine integration will not be possible until the schools in Negro neighborhoods, and the schools in white slum areas as well, are brought up to the level of the very best in the city — until the schools do their job so well that children's educational performance will no longer reflect their income, or their social status, or their ethnic group, or their color.

To say this is not to suggest indefinite postponement, but to demand that the public schools stop dithering with projects and demonstrations and turn immediately to the most pressing task. Neither the large cities nor the nation as a whole can afford a public-school system which fails to educate between 50 and 80 per cent of its Negro and white slum students.

Suppositions or hypotheses; their uses and their value

In nineteenth-century England, Thomas Henry Huxley
was the great champion of the scientific method, which
he advocated not only for the advancement of science
but as a moral and intellectual discipline of the
utmost importance in daily life. He was an eminent
scientist himself, in the field of comparative anatomy,
but was also a popularizer, in the best sense of
that word, preaching the scientific attitude in a great
outpouring of books, articles, and public lectures.
The following essay is from his *Science Primers* of
1885. In it you can see the great scientist explaining
scientific method to the general public—a problem in
tact as well as in vocabulary.

WHEN our means of observation of any natural fact fail to
carry us beyond a certain point, it is perfectly legitimate,
and often extremely useful, to make a supposition as to
what we should see, if we could carry direct observation a
step further. A supposition of this kind is what is called a
hypothesis, and the value of any hypothesis depends upon the
extent to which reasoning upon the assumption that it is
true, enables us to explain or account for the phenomena
with which it is concerned.

Thus, if a person is standing close behind you, and you
suddenly feel a blow on your back, you have no direct evi-

From *Science Primers,* "Introductory." New York: D. Appleton, 1885.

dence of the cause of the blow; and if you two were alone, you could not possibly obtain any; but you immediately suppose that this person has struck you. Now that is a hypothesis, and it is a legitimate hypothesis, first, because it explains the fact; and secondly, because no other explanation is probable; probable meaning in accordance with the ordinary course of nature. If your companion declared that you fancied you felt a blow, or that some invisible spirit struck you, you would probably decline to accept his explanation of the fact. You would say that both the hypotheses by which he professed to explain the phenomenon were extremely improbable; or in other words, that in the ordinary course of nature fancies of this kind do not occur, nor spirits strike blows. In fact, his hypotheses would be illegitimate, and yours would be legitimate; and, in all probability, you would act upon your own. In daily life, nine-tenths of our actions are based upon suppositions or hypotheses, and our success or failure in practical affairs depends upon the legitimacy of these hypotheses. You believe a man on the hypothesis that he is always truthful; you give him pecuniary credit on the hypothesis that he is solvent.

Thus, everybody invents, and, indeed, is compelled to invent, hypotheses in order to account for phenomena of the cause of which he has no direct evidence; and they are just as legitimate and necessary in science as in common life. Only the scientific reasoner must be careful to remember that which is sometimes forgotten in daily life, that a hypothesis must be regarded as a means and not as an end; that we may cherish it so long as it helps us to explain the order of nature; but that we are bound to throw it away without hesitation as soon as it is shown to be inconsistent with any part of that order.

J. B. S. HALDANE

On being
the right size

J. B. S. Haldane is, in the tradition of Huxley, a
scientist who speaks to the general public. He was the
first geneticist to map a human chromosome and the
first to measure the mutation rate of a human gene.
"A scientist," he has said, "if he can do so, should
help to render science intelligible to ordinary
people." In the following essay, notice the problem for
the reader posed by the ending, in which Haldane
unexpectedly shifts the subject from biology to
political science; it makes an interesting problem in
the uses of analogy — also a problem in the writer's
obligations to his readers.

THE MOST obvious differences between different animals
are differences of size, but for some reason the zoologists
have paid singularly little attention to them. In a large textbook of zoology before me I find no indication that the
eagle is larger than the sparrow, or the hippopotamus bigger
than the hare, though some grudging admissions are made
in the case of the mouse and the whale. But yet it is easy to
show that a hare could not be as large as a hippopotamus, or
a whale as small as a herring. For every type of animal there
is a most convenient size, and a large change in size inevitably carries with it a change of form.

Let us take the most obvious of possible cases, and consider a giant man sixty feet high—about the height of Giant Pope and Giant Pagan in the illustrated *Pilgrim's Progress* of my childhood. These monsters were not only ten times as high as Christian, but ten times as wide and ten times as thick, so that their total weight was a thousand times his, or about eighty to ninety tons. Unfortunately the cross sections of their bones were only a hundred times those of Christian, so that every square inch of giant bone had to support ten times the weight borne by a square inch of human bone. As the human thigh-bone breaks under about ten times the human weight, Pope and Pagan would have broken their thighs every time they took a step. This was doubtless why they were sitting down in the picture I remember. But it lessens one's respect for Christian and Jack the Giant Killer.

To turn to zoology, suppose that a gazelle, a graceful little creature with long thin legs, is to become large; it will break its bones unless it does one of two things. It may make its legs short and thick, like the rhinoceros, so that every pound of weight has still about the same area of bone to support it. Or it can compress its body and stretch out its legs obliquely to gain stability, like the giraffe. I mention these two beasts because they happen to belong to the same order as the gazelle, and both are quite successful mechanically, being remarkably fast runners.

Gravity, a mere nuisance to Christian, was a terror to Pope, Pagan, and Despair. To the mouse and any smaller animal it presents practically no dangers. You can drop a mouse down a thousand-yard mine shaft; and, on arriving at the bottom, it gets a slight shock and walks away, provided that the ground is fairly soft. A rat is killed, a man is broken, a horse splashes. For the resistance presented to movement by the air is proportional to the surface of the moving object. Divide an animal's length, breadth, and height each by ten; its weight is reduced to a thousandth, but its surface only to a hundredth. So the resistance to falling in the case of the small animal is relatively ten times greater than the driving force.

An insect, therefore, is not afraid of gravity; it can fall without danger, and can cling to the ceiling with remarkably little trouble. It can go in for elegant and fantastic forms of support like that of the daddy-long-legs. But there is a force which is as formidable to an insect as gravitation to a mammal. This is surface tension. A man coming out of a bath carries with him a film of water of about one-fiftieth of an inch in thickness. This weighs roughly a pound. A wet mouse has to carry about its own weight of water. A wet fly has to lift many times its own weight and, as every one knows, a fly once wetted by water or any other liquid is in a very serious position indeed. An insect going for a drink is in as great danger as a man leaning out over a precipice in search of food. If it once falls into the grip of the surface tension of the water—that is to say, gets wet—it is likely to remain so until it drowns. A few insects, such as water-beetles, contrive to be unwettable; the majority keep well away from their drink by means of a long proboscis.

Of course tall land animals have other difficulties. They have to pump their blood to greater heights than a man and, therefore, require a larger blood pressure and tougher blood-vessels. A great many men die from burst arteries, especially in the brain, and this danger is presumably still greater for an elephant or a giraffe. But animals of all kinds find difficulties in size for the following reason. A typical small animal, say a microscopic worm or rotifer, has a smooth skin through which all the oxygen it requires can soak in, a straight gut with sufficient surface to absorb its food, and a simple kidney. Increase its dimensions tenfold in every direction, and its weight is increased a thousand times, so that if it is to use its muscles as efficiently as its miniature counterpart, it will need a thousand times as much food and oxygen per day and will excrete a thousand times as much of waste products.

Now if its shape is unaltered its surface will be increased only a hundredfold, and ten times as much oxygen must enter per minute through each square millimetre of skin, ten times as much food through each square millimetre of intestine. When a limit is reached to their absorptive powers their surface has to be increased by some special device.

For example, a part of the skin may be drawn out into tufts to make gills or pushed in to make lungs, thus increasing the oxygen-absorbing surface in proportion to the animal's bulk. A man, for example, has a hundred square yards of lung. Similarly, the gut, instead of being smooth and straight, becomes coiled and develops a velvety surface, and other organs increase in complication. The higher animals are not larger than the lower because they are more complicated. They are more complicated because they are larger. Just the same is true of plants. The simplest plants, such as the green algae growing in stagnant water or on the bark of trees, are mere round cells. The higher plants increase their surface by putting out leaves and roots. Comparative anatomy is largely the story of the struggle to increase surface in proportion to volume.

Some of the methods of increasing the surface are useful up to a point, but not capable of a very wide adaptation. For example, while vertebrates carry the oxygen from the gills or lungs all over the body in the blood, insects take air directly to every part of their body by tiny blind tubes called tracheae which open to the surface at many different points. Now, although by their breathing movements they can renew the air in the outer part of the tracheal system, the oxygen has to penetrate the finer branches by means of diffusion. Gases can diffuse easily through very small distances, not many times larger than the average length travelled by a gas molecule between collisions with other molecules. But when such vast journeys—from the point of view of a molecule—as a quarter of an inch have to be made, the process becomes slow. So the portions of an insect's body more than a quarter of an inch from the air would always be short of oxygen. In consequence hardly any insects are much more than half an inch thick. Land crabs are built on the same general plan as insects, but are much clumsier. Yet like ourselves they carry oxygen around in their blood, and are therefore able to grow far larger than any insects. If the insects had hit on a plan for driving air through their tissues instead of letting it soak in, they might well have become as large as lobsters, though other considerations would have prevented them from becoming as large as man.

Exactly the same difficulties attach to flying. It is an elementary principle of aeronautics that the minimum speed needed to keep an aeroplane of a given shape in the air varies as the square root of its length. If its linear dimensions are increased four times, it must fly twice as fast. Now the power needed for the minimum speed increases more rapidly than the weight of the machine. So the larger aeroplane, which weighs sixty-four times as much as the smaller, needs one hundred and twenty-eight times its horsepower to keep up. Applying the same principles to the birds, we find that the limit to their size is soon reached. An angel whose muslces developed no more power weight for weight than those of an eagle or a pigeon would require a breast projecting for about four feet to house the muscles engaged in working its wings, while to economize in weight, its legs would have to be reduced to mere stilts. Actually a large bird such as an eagle or kite does not keep in the air mainly by moving its wings. It is generally to be seen soaring, that is to say balanced on a rising column of air. And even soaring becomes more and more difficult with increasing size. Were this not the case eagles might be as large as tigers and as formidable to man as hostile aeroplanes.

But it is time that we passed to some of the advantages of size. One of the most obvious is that it enables one to keep warm. All warm-blooded animals at rest lose the same amount of heat from a unit area of skin, for which purpose they need a food-supply proportional to their surface and not to their weight. Five thousand mice weigh as much as a man. Their combined surface and food or oxygen consumption are about seventeen times a man's. In fact a mouse eats about one quarter its own weight of food every day, which is mainly used in keeping it warm. For the same reason small animals cannot live in cold countries. In the arctic regions there are no reptiles or amphibians, and no small mammals. The smallest mammal in Spitzbergen is the fox. The small birds fly away in the winter, while the insects die, though their eggs can survive six months or more of frost. The most successful mammals are bears, seals, and walruses.

Similarly, the eye is a rather inefficient organ until it reaches a large size. The back of the human eye on which an image of the outside world is thrown, and which corresponds to the film of a camera, is composed of a mosaic of 'rods and cones' whose diameter is little more than a length of an average light wave. Each eye has about half a million, and for two objects to be distinguishable their images must fall on separate rods or cones. It is obvious that with fewer but larger rods and cones we should see less distinctly. If they were twice as broad two points would have to be twice as far apart before we could distinguish them at a given distance. But if their size were diminished and their number increased we should see no better. For it is impossible to form a definite image smaller than a wave-length of light. Hence a mouse's eye is not a small-scale model of a human eye. Its rods and cones are not much smaller than ours, and therefore there are far fewer of them. A mouse could not distinguish one human face from another six feet away. In order that they should be of any use at all the eyes of small animals have to be much larger in proportion to their bodies than our own. Large animals on the other hand only require relatively small eyes, and those of the whale and elephant are little larger than our own.

For rather more recondite reasons the same general principle holds true of the brain. If we compare the brain-weights of a set of very similar animals such as the cat, cheetah, leopard, and tiger, we find that as we quadruple the body-weight the brain-weight is only doubled. The larger animal with proportionately larger bones can economize on brain, eyes, and certain other organs.

Such are a very few of the considerations which show that for every type of animal there is an optimum size. Yet although Galileo demonstrated the contrary more than three hundred years ago, people still believe that if a flea were as large as a man it could jump a thousand feet into the air. As a matter of fact the height to which an animal can jump is more nearly independent of its size than proportional to it. A flea can jump about two feet, a man about five. To jump a given height, if we neglect the resistance of the air, requires an expenditure of energy proportional to the jumper's weight. But if the jumping muscles form a constant fraction of the animal's body, the energy developed per ounce of muscle is independent of the size, provided it can be developed quickly enough in the small animal. As a matter of fact an insect's muscles, although they can contract more quickly than our own, appear to be less efficient; as otherwise a flea or grasshopper could rise six feet into the air. And just as there is a best size for every animal, so the same is true for every human institution. In the Greek type of democracy all the citizens could listen to a series of orators and vote directly on questions of legislation. Hence their philosophers held that a small city was the largest possible democratic state. The English invention of representative government made a democratic nation possible, and the possibility was first realized in the United States, and later elsewhere. With the development of broadcasting it has once more become possible for every citizen to listen to the political views of representative orators, and the future may perhaps see the return of the national state to the Greek form of democracy. Even the referendum has been made possible only by the institution of daily newspapers.

To the biologist the problem of socialism appears largely as a problem of size. The extreme socialists desire to run every nation as a single business concern. I do not suppose that Henry Ford would find much difficulty in running Andorra or Luxembourg on a socialistic basis. He has already more men on his pay-roll than their population. It is conceivable that a syndicate of Fords, if we could find them, would make Belgium Ltd. or Denmark Inc. pay their way. But while nationalization of certain industries is an obvious possibility in the largest of states, I find it no easier to picture a completely socialized British Empire or United States than an elephant turning somersaults or a hippopotamus jumping a hedge.

OLIVER P. PEARSON

The metabolism of
hummingbirds

Oliver P. Pearson is an eminent zoologist associated
with the Museum of Vertebrate Zoology of the University
of California at Berkeley. His special field is the
natural history of the Peruvian Andes; his special
skill as a writer is, in the tradition of Huxley, the
explanation of scientific knowledge to the general
public. The following essay appeared in *Scientific
American,* which is devoted to explaining scientific
developments to a literate general audience.

THE LIVING rate of an animal depends on its size: the
smaller the animal, the faster it lives. This does not necessarily mean that its life span is shorter (a man is smaller
than a horse), but pound for pound the more diminutive
animal eats more food, consumes more oxygen, produces
more energy—in short, has a higher rate of metabolism.
Each gram of mouse tissue, for example, metabolizes much
faster and uses much more oxygen per minute than each
gram of an elephant's tissues. If the elephant's cells were to
live at the pace set by mouse cells, the ponderous animal
would be unable to dissipate the resulting heat rapidly
enough. It would perish within a few minutes from overheating.
 Life has been compared to the flame of a candle. The
candle's wax combines with oxygen from the air and produces heat and carbon dioxide. The rate at which the flame

From *Scientific American,* Volume 188, January 1953, pp. 69–72. Used by
permission.

burns can be measured by any of these four factors: its consumption of wax or oxygen or its production of heat or carbon dioxide. Similarly, one can measure how "alive" an animal is, how intense are its life processes, by determining how fast it consumes food or oxygen or how fast it produces heat or carbon dioxide. For practical reasons the easiest and most satisfactory yardstick is oxygen consumption. Such measurements have been made on a host of animals from protozoa to mice to elephants.

We are interested here in the small end of the scale. Among the warm-blooded animals about the smallest is the hummingbird — some species of hummingbirds weigh no more than a dime. As we should expect, the hummingbird has the highest rate of metabolism of any bird or mammal. In a resting hummingbird each gram of tissue metabolizes 15 times as fast as a gram of pigeon and more than 100 times as fast as a gram of elephant. When the metabolism rates of various animals are plotted on a chart, the curve goes up steeply at the small-animal end, and it indicates that at 2.5 grams the rate of metabolism would be infinitely rapid. No bird or mammal so small could exist without resorting to some metabolic legerdemain unknown to its larger relatives, for it simply could not eat fast enough to avoid starvation.

The hummingbird wins the honor of living at a rate faster than any other animal at the cost of an enormous food consumption. The bird must devote much of its day to gathering food, mainly nectar and insects. But what happens at night? Hummingbirds are not adapted for night feeding. If their intense metabolism continued undiminished through the night, as it does in other birds, they would be in danger of starving to death before morning.

The trick by which hummingbirds avoid overnight starvation was disclosed by means of a continuous record of their oxygen consumption over a 24-hour period. Each hummingbird was confined in a bell jar with a food supply in a vial. During the afternoon the bird alternately perched and hovered in front of its feeding vial. For an hour before nightfall it indulged in intensive feeding, and much flying and wing-buzzing. During that hour it consumed 24 cubic centimeters of oxygen per gram of body weight. Then the bird settled down for the night. Twenty minutes later its rate of metabolism had dropped to eight cubic centimeters per gram per hour. By the middle of the night the bird was living at a metabolism level only one fifteenth as rapid as the daytime rate.

Now this is the level at which certain mammals hibernate. The hummingbird at night showed many signs of hibernation. It was completely torpid, practically insensible, scarcely able to move, and when it did stir, it moved as though congealed. Its body temperature had dropped to that of the surrounding air—75 degrees Fahrenheit. Hibernation, then, is the metabolic magic by which hummingbirds stretch their food stores from dusk to dawn. Before daybreak the bird's body spontaneously returns to its normal temperature and high metabolic rate. By early morning it is again warm, awake, ready to dart off in search of food.

That hummingbirds behave in the same way in nature as they did in my bell jars was proved by examining them in their natural roosts. One hummingbird of the Anna species was watched while it settled down to sleep at dusk on a tree branch. When I returned to it at 3 a.m., it was completely torpid and allowed itself to be picked off like a ripe fruit. Most hummingbirds live in the tropics. A few are found in the high Andes, where temperatures fall so low at night that the birds would probably freeze to death if they stayed in the open air; there they retreat at night into caves.

We know of no other bird that hibernates overnight like the hummingbird. Bats, which are not birds but mammals, do the trick in reverse: they forage by night and slow to torpor by day.

The metabolic profit which a hummingbird gains by nocturnal hibernation can be measured by comparing it with a tiny mammal of about the same size—the shrew *Sorex cinereus*. When they are awake and going about their business in the bell jar, the shrew and the hummingbird have about the same rate of oxygen consumption. But the shrew cannot hibernate. It must keep busy most of the night feeding itself. [On a chart] we can see what this means in terms of energy expenditure. The total amount of energy each animal must spend in 24 hours to keep each gram of its tissue alive is represented by the area between the animal's hour-to-hour energy line and the base line. Almost the entire area between the line for the shrew and that for the hummingbird represents the metabolic profit the hummingbird gains by hibernating at night.

When the hummingbird is not sleeping, it is eating, and it does this entirely on the wing. How strenuous is it for a bird to fly? Hummingbirds can hover in a small space, and this attribute makes them ideal subjects for investigation in laboratory confinement.

A bird is put into the bell jar, and the jar is entirely submerged in a large tank of water to ensure a constant temperature. The bird sits quietly on its perch while a continuous record of its rate of metabolism is being made on a smoked drum. After 10 or 15 minutes the bird becomes hungry, flies up to the feed vial suspended near the top of the bell jar, hovers there while feeding, then returns to the perch. The observer times the flight with a stop watch. From the continuous metabolic record he can easily calculate the comparative rates of metabolism during rest and flight.

On the average a small hummingbird consumes somewhere around 80 cubic centimeters of oxygen per gram per hour while hovering. This is about six times its resting rate. The British physiologist A. V. Hill once calculated that a man walking at five miles per hour uses six and a half times as much oxygen as he does when standing still. It is reasonable to say, therefore, that a hummingbird works as hard when it hovers as a man does when he walks rapidly.

James L. G. Fitzpatrick, an engineer associated with the Institute of Aeronautical Sciences in New York, has calculated that hovering hummingbirds consume about 726 British thermal units of energy per pound per hour. This figure, interestingly enough, is very close to the energy consumption of a modern helicopter — 750 B.T.U. per pound per hour.

How much energy does a hummingbird spend when flying about? We do not know exactly, but probably it takes somewhat less work than hovering. Like an airplane, a bird probably gains some lift from its forward motion and thus does not have to spend so much energy to stay aloft. At very slow speeds the lift would be negligible, and at very high speeds it would be more than offset by resistance. Between these extremes, however, there is probably a speed range in which birds use less energy to fly forward than they do to hover in one place.

Our laboratory findings may have a bearing on a puzzle which has long mystified ornithologists. The ruby-throated hummingbird spends its summers in the eastern U.S. and its winters in Central America. How does it get across the Gulf of Mexico in its annual migrations? One school holds that it must fly around the shoreline, arguing that it is ridiculous to think that this tiny bird, with its exceedingly high rate of metabolism, could carry enough fuel to make a nonstop flight across the Gulf. On the other hand, many people have repeatedly seen flights of hummers head out over the Gulf, and they insist the birds must be able to make the trip, for they would not set out on a flight which was certain to be fatal.

In the face of two such unthinkable alternatives, any laboratory answer may seem foolish. But we can at least attempt a calculation, if only for the amusement of playing with the figures.

Let us assume that the hummingbirds cruise at 50 m.p.h., the speed at which they have been timed by automobiles. At this speed they might consume 80 cubic centimeters of oxygen per gram per hour. A three-gram ruby-throated hummingbird (the average weight) would burn 240 cubic centimeters of oxygen per hour, and in doing so would release 1.17 calories of heat. Now we can assume that the bird might carry one gram of fat as reserve fuel, for a fat bird of this species is about one gram heavier than a lean one. One gram of fat yields nine calories. Consequently the bird could fly 7.7 hours on its fat (9 divided by 1.17). At 50 m.p.h., this would carry it 385 miles. Impressive though the figure is, it does not get the hummingbird to shore. The shortest distance across the Gulf is more than 500 miles.

It may be argued that because of the crudity of some of our assumptions, we still have not thrown much light on the subject in dispute. Perhaps we have contributed only more heat, but if so, at least it can be measured in calories.

RACHEL L. CARSON

The long snowfall

Rachel L. Carson was a biologist of the United States
Fish and Wildlife Service. She was for many years
the editor of the bulletins published by that bureau
and also a well-known writer, author of *Under the
Sea Wind, The Edge of the Sea,* and *Silent Spring,*
besides *The Sea Around Us* (of which the following is
one chapter). Like Huxley, Haldane, and Pearson, she
combined expert scientific knowledge with the ability
to explain to the general public what scientists have
discovered. She is especially admired for the vividness
and drama of her presentation of scientific fact.

EVERY part of the earth or air or sea has an atmosphere
peculiarly its own, a quality or characteristic that sets it
apart from all others. When I think of the floor of the deep
sea, the single, overwhelming fact that possesses my imagination is the accumulation of sediments. I see always the
steady, unremitting, downward drift of materials from
above, flake upon flake, layer upon layer — drift that has
continued for hundreds of millions of years, that will go on
as long as there are seas and continents.

For the sediments are the materials of the most stupendous 'snowfall' the earth has ever seen. It began when the
first rains fell on the barren rocks and set in motion the
forces of erosion. It was accelerated when living creatures

developed in the surface waters and the discarded little shells of lime or silica that had encased them in life began to drift downward to the bottom. Silently, endlessly, with the deliberation of earth processes that can afford to be slow because they have so much time for completion, the accumulation of the sediments has proceeded. So little in a year, or in a human lifetime, but so enormous an amount in the life of earth and sea.

The rains, the eroding away of the earth, the rush of sediment-laden waters have continued, with varying pulse and tempo, throughout all of geologic time. In addition to the silt load of every river that finds its way to the sea, there are other materials that compose the sediments. Volcanic dust, blown perhaps half way around the earth in the upper atmosphere, comes eventually to rest on the ocean, drifts in the currents, becomes waterlogged, and sinks. Sands from coastal deserts are carried seaward on off-shore winds, fall to the sea, and sink. Gravel, pebbles, small boulders, and shells are carried by icebergs and drift ice, to be released to the water when the ice melts. Fragments of iron, nickel, and other meteoric debris that enter the earth's atmosphere over the sea—these, too, become flakes of the great snowfall. But most widely distributed of all are the billions upon billions of tiny shells and skeletons, the limy or silicious remains of all the minute creatures that once lived in the upper waters.

The sediments are a sort of epic poem of the earth. When we are wise enough, perhaps we can read in them all of past history. For all is written here. In the nature of the materials that compose them and in the arrangement of their successive layers the sediments reflect all that has happened in the waters above them and on the surrounding lands. The dramatic and the catastrophic in earth history have left their trace in the sediments—the outpourings of volcanoes, the advance and retreat of the ice, the searing aridity of desert lands, the sweeping destruction of floods.

The book of the sediments has been opened only within the lifetime of the present generation of scientists, with the most exciting progress in collecting and deciphering samples made since 1945. Early oceanographers could scrape up surface layers of sediment from the sea bottom with dredges.

But what was needed was an instrument, operated on the principle of an apple corer, that could be driven vertically into the bottom to remove a long sample or 'core' in which the order of the different layers was undisturbed. Such an instrument was invented by Dr. C. S. Piggot in 1935, and with the aid of this 'gun' he obtained a series of cores across the deep Atlantic from Newfoundland to Ireland. These cores averaged about 10 feet long. A piston core sampler, developed by the Swedish oceanographer Kullenberg about 10 years later, now takes undisturbed cores 70 feet long. The rate of sedimentation in the different parts of the ocean is not definitely known, but it is very slow; certainly such a sample represents millions of years of geologic history.

Another ingenious method for studying the sediments has been used by Professor W. Maurice Ewing of Columbia University and the Woods Hole Oceanographic Institution. Professor Ewing found that he could measure the thickness of the carpeting layer of sediments that overlies the rock of the ocean floor by exploding depth charges and recording their echoes; one echo is received from the top of the sediment layer (the apparent bottom of the sea), another from the 'bottom below the bottom' or the true rock floor. The carrying and use of explosives at sea is hazardous and cannot be attempted by all vessels, but this method was used by the Swedish *Albatross* as well as by the *Atlantis* in its exploration of the Atlantic Ridge. Ewing on the *Atlantis* also used a seismic refraction technique by which sound waves are made to travel horizontally through the rock layers of the ocean floor, providing information about the nature of the rock.

Before these techniques were developed, we could only guess at the thickness of the sediment blanket over the floor of the sea. We might have expected the amount to be vast, if we thought back through the ages of gentle, unending fall—one sand grain at a time, one fragile shell after another, here a shark's tooth, there a meteorite fragment—but the whole continuing persistently, relentlessly, endlessly. It is, of course, a process similar to that which has built up the layers of rock that help to make our mountains, for they, too, were once soft sediments under the shallow seas that have overflowed the continents from time to time. The sediments eventually became consolidated and cemented and, as the seas retreated again, gave the continents their thick, covering layers of sedimentary rocks—layers which we can see uplifted, tilted, compressed, and broken by the vast earth movements. And we know that in places the sedimentary rocks are many thousands of feet thick. Yet most people felt a shock of surprise and wonder when Hans Pettersson, leader of the Swedish Deep Sea Expedition, announced that the *Albatross* measurements taken in the open Atlantic basin showed sediment layers as much as 12,000 feet thick.

If more than two miles of sediments have been deposited on the floor of the Atlantic, an interesting question arises: has the rocky floor sagged a corresponding distance under the terrific weight of the sediments? Geologists hold conflicting opinions. The recently discovered Pacific sea mounts may offer one piece of evidence that it has. If they are, as their discoverer called them, 'drowned ancient islands,' then they may have reached their present stand a mile or so below sea level through the sinking of the ocean floor. Hess believed the islands had been formed so long ago that coral animals had not yet evolved; otherwise the corals would presumably have settled on the flat, planed surfaces of the sea mounts and built them up as fast as their bases sank. In any event, it is hard to see how they could have been worn down so far below 'wave base' unless the crust of the earth sagged under its load.

One thing seems probable—the sediments have been unevenly distributed both in place and time. In contrast to the 12,000-foot thickness found in parts of the Atlantic, the Swedish oceanographers never found sediments thicker than 1000 feet in the Pacific or in the Indian Ocean. Perhaps a deep layer of lava, from ancient submarine eruptions on a stupendous scale, underlies the upper layers of the sediments in these places and intercepts the sound waves.

Interesting variations in the thickness of the sediment layer on the Atlantic Ridge and the approaches to the Ridge from the American side were reported by Ewing. As the bottom contours became less even and began to slope up into the foothills of the Ridge, the sediments thickened, as though piling up into mammoth drifts 1000 to 2000 feet deep against the slopes of the hills. Farther up in the mountains of the Ridge, where there are many level terraces from a few to a score of miles wide, the sediments were even deeper, measuring up to 3000 feet. But along the backbone of the Ridge, on the steep slopes and peaks and pinnacles, the bare rock emerged, swept clean of sediments.

Reflecting on these differences in thickness and distribution, our minds return inevitably to the simile of the long snowfall. We may think of the abyssal snowstorm in terms of a bleak and blizzard-ridden arctic tundra. Long days of storm visit this place, when driving snow fills the air; then a lull comes in the blizzard, and the snowfall is light. In the snowfall of the sediments, also, there is an alternation of light and heavy falls. The heavy falls correspond to the periods of mountain building on the continents, when the lands are lifted high and the rain rushes down their slopes, carrying mud and rock fragments to the sea; the light falls mark the lulls between the mountain-building periods, when the continents are flat and erosion is slowed. And again, on our imaginary tundra, the winds blow the snow into deep drifts, filling in all the valleys between the ridges, piling the snow up and up until the contours of the land are obliterated, but scouring the ridges clear. In the drifting sediments on the floor of the ocean we see the work of the 'winds,' which may be the deep ocean currents, distributing the sediments according to laws of their own, not as yet grasped by human minds.

We have known the general pattern of the sediment carpet, however, for a good many years. Around the foundations of the continents, in the deep waters off the borders of the continental slopes, are the muds of terrestrial origin. There are muds of many colors—blue, green, red, black, and white—apparently varying with climatic changes as well as with the dominant soils and rocks of the lands of their origin. Farther at sea are the oozes of predominantly marine origin—the remains of the trillions of tiny sea creatures. Over great areas of the temperate oceans the sea floor is largely covered with the remains of unicellular creatures known as foraminifera, of which the most abundant genus is Globigerina. The shells of Globigerina may be recognized in very ancient sediments as well as in modern ones, but over the ages the species have varied. Knowing this, we can date approximately the deposits in which they occur. But always they have been simple animals, living in an intricately sculptured shell of carbonate of lime, the whole so small you would need a microscope to see its details. After the fashion of unicellular beings, the individual Globigerina normally did not die, but by the division of its substance became two. At each division, the old shell was abandoned, and two new ones were formed. In warm, lime-rich seas these tiny creatures have always multiplied prodigiously, and so, although each is so minute, their innumerable shells blanket millions of square miles of ocean bottom, and to a depth of thousands of feet.

In the great depths of the ocean, however, the immense pressures and the high carbon-dioxide content of deep water dissolve much of the lime long before it reaches the bottom and return it to the great chemical reservoir of the sea. Silica is more resistant to solution. It is one of the curious paradoxes of the ocean that the bulk of the organic remains that reach the great depths intact belong to unicellular creatures seemingly of the most delicate construction. The radiolarians remind us irresistibly of snow flakes, as infinitely varied in pattern, as lacy, and as intricately made. Yet because their shells are fashioned of silica instead of carbonate of lime, they can descend unchanged into the abyssal depths. So there are broad bands of radiolarian ooze in the deep tropical waters of the North Pacific, underlying the surface zones where the living radiolarians occur most numerously.

Two other kinds of organic sediments are named for the creatures whose remains compose them. Diatoms, the microscopic plant life of the sea, flourish most abundantly in cold waters. There is a broad belt of diatom ooze on the floor of the Antarctic Ocean, outside the zone of glacial debris dropped by the ice pack. There is another across the North Pacific, along the chain of great deeps that run from Alaska to Japan. Both are zones where nutrient-laden water wells up from the depths, sustaining a rich growth of plants. The diatoms, like the radiolaria, are encased in silicious coverings—small, boxlike cases of varied shape and meticulously etched design.

Then, in relatively shallow parts of the open Atlantic, there are patches of ooze composed of the remains of delicate swimming snails, called pteropods. These winged mollusks, possessing transparent shells of great beauty, are here and there incredibly abundant. Pteropod ooze is the characteristic bottom deposit in the vicinity of Bermuda, and a large patch occurs in the South Atlantic.

Mysterious and eerie are the immense areas, especially in the North Pacific, carpeted with a soft, red sediment in which there are no organic remains except sharks' teeth and the ear bones of whales. This red clay occurs at great depths. Perhaps all the materials of the other sediments are dissolved before they can reach this zone of immense pressures and glacial cold.

The reading of the story contained in the sediments has only begun. When more cores are collected and examined we shall certainly decipher many exciting chapters. Geologists have pointed out that a series of cores from the Mediterranean might settle several controversial problems concerning the history of the ocean and of the lands around the Mediterranean basin. For example, somewhere in the layers of sediment under this sea there must be evidence, in a sharply defined layer of sand, of the time when the deserts of the Sahara were formed and the hot, dry winds began to skim off the shifting surface layers and carry them seaward. Long cores recently obtained in the western Mediterranean off Algeria have given a record of volcanic activity extending back through thousands of years, and including great prehistoric eruptions of which we know nothing.

The Atlantic cores taken more than a decade ago by Piggot from the cable ship *Lord Kelvin* have been thoroughly studied by geologists. From their analysis it is possible to look back into the past 10,000 years or so and to sense the pulse of the earth's climatic rhythms; for the cores were composed of layers of cold-water globigerina faunas (and hence glacial stage sediments), alternating with globigerina ooze characteristic of warmer waters. From the clues furnished by these cores we can visualize inter-glacial stages when there were periods of mild climates, with warm water overlying the sea bottom and warmth-loving creatures living in the ocean. Between these periods the sea grew chill. Clouds gathered, the snows fell, and on the North American continent the great ice sheets grew and the ice mountains moved out to the coast. The glaciers reached the sea along a wide front; there they produced icebergs by the thousand. The slow-moving, majestic processions of the bergs passed out to sea, and because of the coldness of much of the earth they penetrated farther south than any but stray bergs do today. When finally they melted, they relinquished their loads of silt and sand and gravel and rock fragments that had become frozen into their under surfaces as they made their grinding way over the land. And so a layer of glacial sediment came to overlie the normal globigerina ooze, and the record of an Ice Age was inscribed.

Then the sea grew warmer again, the glaciers melted and retreated, and once more the warmer-water species of Globigerina lived in the sea—lived and died and drifted down to build another layer of globigerina ooze, this time over the clays and gravels from the glaciers. And the record of warmth and mildness was again written in the sediments. From the Piggot cores it has been possible to reconstruct four different periods of the advance of the ice, separated by periods of warm climate.

It is interesting to think that even now, in our own lifetime, the flakes of a new snow storm are falling, falling, one by one, out there on the ocean floor. The billions of Globigerina are drifting down, writing their unequivocal record that this, our present world, is on the whole a world of mild and temperate climate. Who will read their record, ten thousand years from now?

The water-ouzel

John Muir was a wild romantic naturalist whose field
was the mountains and glaciers of the Amerian West.
The first to describe living glaciers in the California
mountains, he was also a leader of the conservation
movement that established our national parks. He is
best known as a writer who knew wild nature intimately
and reported it in a highly personal, highly
enthusiastic style. "The Water-Ouzel" is one chapter
of his book *Mountains of California*.

THE WATERFALLS of the Sierra are frequented by only
one bird,—the ouzel or water thrush (*Cinclus Mexicanus,
Sw.*). He is a singularly joyous and lovable little fellow,
about the size of a robin, clad in a plain waterproof suit of
bluish gray, with a tinge of chocolate on the head and
shoulders. In form he is about as smoothly plump and compact as a pebble that has been whirled in a pot-hole, the
flowing contour of his body being interrupted only by his
strong feet and bill, the crisp wing-tips, and the up-slanted
wren-like tail.

Among all the countless waterfalls I have met in the
course of ten years' exploration in the Sierra, whether
among the icy peaks, or warm foothills, or in the profound
yosemitic cañons of the middle region, not one was found
without its ouzel. No cañon is too cold for this little bird,

From *Mountains of California* by John Muir, by permission of Appleton-
Century. Copyright, Revised Edition, 1911 by the Century Company,
renewed, 1938.

none too lonely, provided it be rich in falling water. Find a fall, or cascade, or rushing rapid, anywhere upon a clear stream, and there you will surely find its complementary ouzel, flitting about in the spray, diving in foaming eddies, whirling like a leaf among beaten foam bells; ever vigorous and enthusiastic, yet self-contained, and neither seeking nor shunning your company.

If disturbed while dipping about in the margin shallows, he either sets off with a rapid whir to some other feeding-ground up or down the stream, or alights on some half-submerged rock or snag out in the current, and immediately begins to nod and courtesy like a wren, turning his head from side to side with many other odd dainty movements that never fail to fix the attention of the observer.

He is the mountain streams' own darling, the humming-bird of blooming waters, loving rocky ripple slopes and sheets of foam as a bee loves flowers, as a lark loves sunshine and meadows. Among all the mountain birds, none has cheered me so much in my lonely wanderings,—none so unfailingly. For both in winter and summer he sings, sweetly, cheerily, independent alike of sunshine and of love, requiring no other inspiration than the stream on which he dwells. While water sings, so must he, in heat or cold, calm or storm, ever attuning his voice in sure accord; low in the drought of summer and the drought of winter, but never silent.

During the golden days of Indian summer, after most of the snow has been melted, and the mountain streams have become feeble,—a succession of silent pools, linked together by shallow, transparent currents and strips of silvery lacework,—then the song of the ouzel is at its lowest ebb. But as soon as the winter clouds have bloomed, and the mountain treasuries are once more replenished with snow, the voices of the streams and ouzels increase in strength and richness until the flood season of early summer. Then the torrents chant their noblest anthems, and then is the flood-time of our songster's melody. As for weather, dark days and sun days are the same to him. The voices of most song birds, however joyous, suffer a long winter eclipse; but the ouzel sings on through all the seasons and every kind of storm. Indeed, no storm can be more violent than those of the waterfalls in the midst of which he delights to dwell. However dark and boisterous the weather, snowing, blowing, or cloudy, all the same he sings, and with never a note of sadness. No need of spring sunshine to thaw *his* song, for it never freezes. Never shall you hear anything wintery from *his* warm breast; no pinched cheeping, no wavering notes between sorrow and joy; his mellow, fluty voice is ever tuned to downright gladness, as free from dejection as cock-crowing.

It is pitiful to see wee frost-pinched sparrows on cold mornings in the mountain groves shaking the snow from their feathers, and hopping about as if anxious to be cheery, then hastening back to their hidings out of the wind, puffing out their breast feathers over their toes, and subsiding among the leaves, cold and breakfastless, while the snow continues to fall, and there is no sign of clearing. But the ouzel never calls forth a single touch of pity; not because he is strong to endure, but rather because he seems to live a charmed life beyond the reach of every influence that makes endurance necessary.

One wild winter morning, when Yosemite Valley was swept its length from west to east by a cordial snowstorm, I sallied forth to see what I might learn and enjoy. A sort of gray, gloaming-like darkness filled the valley, the huge walls were out of sight, all ordinary sounds were smothered, and even the loudest booming of the falls was at times buried beneath the roar of the heavy-laden blast. The loose snow was already over five feet deep on the meadows, making extended walks impossible without the aid of snowshoes. I found no great difficulty, however, in making my way to a certain ripple on the river where one of my ouzels lived. He was at home, busily gleaning his breakfast among the pebbles of a shallow portion of the margin, apparently unaware of anything extraordinary in the weather. Presently he flew out to a stone against which the icy current was beating, and turning his back to the wind, sang as delightfully as a lark in springtime.

After spending an hour or two with my favorite, I made my way across the valley, boring and wallowing through the drifts, to learn as definitely as possible how the other birds were spending their time. The Yosemite birds are easily found during the winter because all of them excepting the ouzel are restricted to the sunny north side of the valley, the south side being constantly eclipsed by the great frosty shadow of the wall. And because the Indian Cañon groves, from their peculiar exposure, are the warmest, the birds congregate there, more especially in severe weather.

I found most of the robins cowering on the lee side of the larger branches where the snow could not fall upon them, while two or three of the more enterprising were making desperate efforts to reach the mistletoe berries by clinging nervously to the under side of the snow-crowned masses, back downward, like woodpeckers. Every now and then they would dislodge some of the loose fringes of the snow-crown, which would come sifting down on them and send them screaming back to camp, where they would subside among their companions with a shiver, muttering in low, querulous chatter like hungry children.

Some of the sparrows were busy at the feet of the larger trees gleaning seeds and benumbed insects, joined now and then by a robin weary of his unsuccessful attempts upon the snow-covered berries. The brave woodpeckers were clinging to the snowless sides of the larger boles and over-arching branches of the camp trees, making short flights from side to side of the grove, pecking now and then at the acorns they had stored in the bark, and chattering aimlessly as if unable to keep still, yet evidently putting in the time in a very dull way, like storm-bound travelers at a country tavern. The hardy nuthatches were threading the open furrows of the trunks in their usual industrious manner, and uttering their quaint notes, evidently less distressed than their neighbors. The Steller jays were, of course, making more noisy stir than all the other birds combined; ever coming and going with loud bluster, screaming as if each had a lump of melting sludge in his throat, and taking good care to improve the favorable opportunity afforded by the storm to steal from the acorn stores of the woodpeckers. I also noticed one solitary gray eagle braving the storm on the top of a tall pine stump just outside the main grove. He was standing bolt upright with his back to the wind, a tuft of snow piled on his square shoulders, a monument of passive endurance. Thus every snow-bound bird seemed more or less uncomfortable if not in positive distress. The storm was reflected in every gesture, and not one cheerful note, not to say song, came from a single bill; their cowering, joyless endurance offering a striking contrast to the spontaneous, irrepressible gladness of the ouzel, who could no more help exhaling sweet song than a rose sweet fragrance. He *must* sing, though the heavens fall. I remember noticing the distress of a pair of robins during the violent earthquake of the year 1872, when the pines of the Valley, with strange movements, flapped and waved their branches, and beetling rock brows came thundering down to the meadows in tremendous avalanches. It did not occur to me in the midst of the excitement of other observations to look for the ouzels, but I doubt not they were singing straight on through it all, regarding the terrible rock thunder as fearlessly as they do the booming of the waterfalls.

What may be regarded as the separate songs of the ouzel are exceedingly difficult of description, because they are so variable and at the same time so confluent. Though I have been acquainted with my favorite ten years, and during most of this time have heard him sing nearly every day, I still detect notes and strains that seem new to me. Nearly all of his music is sweet and tender, lapsing from his round breast like water over the smooth lip of a pool, then breaking farther on into a sparkling foam of melodious notes, which glow with subdued enthusiasm, yet without expressing much of the strong, gushing ecstasy of the bobolink or skylark.

The more striking strains are perfect arabesques of melody, composed of a few full, round, mellow notes, embroidered with delicate trills which fade and melt in long slender cadences. In a general way his music is that of the streams refined and spiritualized. The deep booming notes of the falls are in it, the trills of rapids, the gurgling of margin eddies, the low whispering of level reaches, and the sweet tinkle of separate drops oozing from the ends of mosses and falling into tranquil pools.

The ouzel never sings in chorus with other birds, nor with his kind, but only with the streams. And like flowers that bloom beneath the surface of the ground, some of our favorite's best song-blossoms never rise above the surface of the heavier music of the water. I have often observed him singing in the midst of beaten spray, his music completely buried beneath the water's roar; yet I knew he was surely singing by his gestures and the movements of his bill.

His food, as far as I have noticed, consists of all kinds of water insects, which in summer are chiefly procured along shallow margins. Here he wades about ducking his head under water and deftly turning over pebbles and fallen leaves with his bill, seldom choosing to go into deep water where he has to use his wings in diving.

He seems to be especially fond of the larvae of mosquitoes, found in abundance attached to the bottom of smooth rock channels where the current is shallow. When feeding in such places he wades upstream, and often while his head is under water the swift current is deflected upward along the glossy curves of his neck and shoulders, in the form of a clear, crystalline shell, which fairly incloses him like a bell-glass, the shell being broken and re-formed as he lifts and dips his head; while ever and anon he sidles out to where the too powerful current carries him off his feet; then he dexterously rises on the wing and goes gleaning again in shallower places.

But during the winter, when the stream banks are embossed in snow, and the streams themselves are chilled nearly to the freezing-point, so that the snow falling into them in stormy weather is not wholly dissolved, but forms a thin, blue sludge, thus rendering the current opaque — then he seeks the deeper portions of the main rivers, where he may dive to clear water beneath the sludge. Or he repairs to some open lake or millpond, at the bottom of which he feeds in safety.

When thus compelled to betake himself to a lake, he does not plunge into it at once like a duck, but always alights in the first place upon some rock or fallen pine along the shore. Then flying out thirty or forty yards, more or less, according to the character of the bottom, he alights with a dainty glint on the surface, swims about, looks down, finally makes up his mind, and disappears with a sharp stroke of his wings. After feeding for two or three minutes, he suddenly reappears, showers the water from his wings with one vigorous shake, and rises abruptly into the air as if pushed up from beneath, comes back to his perch, sings a few minutes, and goes out to dive again; thus coming and going, singing and diving at the same place for hours.

The ouzel is usually found singly; rarely in pairs, excepting during the breeding-season, and *very* rarely in threes or fours. I once observed three thus spending a winter morning in company, upon a small glacier lake, on the Upper Merced, about seventy-five hundred feet above the level of the sea. A storm had occurred during the night, but the morning sun shone unclouded, and the shadowy lake, gleaming darkly in its setting of fresh snow, lay smooth and motionless as a mirror. My camp chanced to be within a few feet of the water's edge, opposite a fallen pine, some of the branches of which leaned out over the lake. Here my three dearly welcome visitors took up their station, and at once began to embroider the frosty air with their delicious melody, doubly delightful to me that particular morning, as I had been somewhat apprehensive of danger in breaking my way down through the snow-choked cañons to the lowlands.

The portion of the lake bottom selected for a feeding-ground lies at a depth of fifteen or twenty feet below the surface, and is covered with a short growth of algae and other aquatic plants,—facts I had previously determined while sailing over it on a raft. After alighting on the glassy surface, they occasionally indulged in a little play, chasing one another round about in small circles; then all three would suddenly dive together, and then come ashore and sing.

The ouzel seldom swims more than a few yards on the surface, for, not being web-footed, he makes rather slow progress, but by means of his strong, crisp wings he swims, or rather flies, with celerity under the surface, often to considerable distances. But it is in withstanding the force of heavy rapids that his strength of wing in this respect is most strikingly manifested. The following may be regarded as a fair illustration of his power of sub-aquatic flight. One stormy morning in winter when the Merced River was blue and green with unmelted snow, I observed one of my ouzels perched on a snag out in the midst of a swift-rushing rapid, singing cheerily, as if everything was just to his mind; and while I stood on the bank admiring him, he suddenly plunged into the sludgy current, leaving his song abruptly broken off. After feeding a minute or two at the bottom, and when one would suppose that he must inevitably be swept far downstream, he emerged just where he went down, alighted on the same snag, showered the water beads from his feathers, and continued his unfinished song, seemingly in tranquil ease as if it had suffered no interruption.

The ouzel alone of all birds dares to enter a white torrent. And though strictly terrestrial in structure, no other is so inseparably related to water, not even the duck, or the bold ocean albatross, or the stormy petrel. For ducks go ashore as soon as they finish feeding in undisturbed places, and very often make long flights overland from lake to lake or field to field. The same is true of most other aquatic birds. But the ouzel, born on the brink of a stream, or on a snag or boulder in the midst of it, seldom leaves it for a single moment. For, notwithstanding he is often on the wing, he never flies overland, but whirs with rapid, quail-like beat above the stream, tracing all its windings. Even when the stream is quite small, say from five to ten feet wide, he seldom shortens his flight by crossing a bend, however abrupt it may be; and even when disturbed by meeting some one on the bank, he prefers to fly over one's head, to dodging out over the ground. When, therefore, his flight along a crooked stream is viewed end-wise, it appears most strikingly wavered — a description on the air of every curve with lightning-like rapidity.

The vertical curves and angles of the most precipitous torrents he traces with the same rigid fidelity, swooping down the inclines of cascades, dropping sheer over dizzy falls amid the spray, and ascending with the same fearlessness and ease, seldom seeking to lessen the steepness of the acclivity by beginning to ascend before reaching the base of the fall. No matter though it may be several hundred feet in height he holds straight on, as if about to dash headlong into the throng of booming rockets, then darts abruptly upward, and, after alighting at the top of the precipice to rest a moment, proceeds to feed and sing. His flight is solid and impetuous, without any intermission of wing-beats,— one homogeneous buzz like that of a laden bee on its way home. And while thus buzzing freely from fall to fall, he is frequently heard giving utterance to a long outdrawn train of unmodulated notes, in no way connected with his song, but corresponding closely with his flight in sustained vigor.

Were the flights of all the ouzels in the Sierra traced on a chart, they would indicate the direction of the flow of the entire system of ancient glaciers, from about the period of the breaking up of the ice sheet until near the close of the glacial winter; because the streams which the ouzels so rigidly follow are, with the unimportant exceptions of a few side tributaries, all flowing in channels eroded for them out of the solid flank of the range by the vanished glaciers,— the streams tracing the ancient glaciers, the ouzels tracing the streams. Nor do we find so complete compliance to glacial conditions in the life of any other mountain bird, or animal of any kind. Bears frequently accept the pathways laid down by glaciers as the easiest to travel; but they often leave them and cross over from cañon to cañon. So also, most of the birds trace the moraines to some extent, because the forests are growing on them. But they wander far, crossing the cañons from grove to grove, and draw exceedingly angular and complicated courses.

The ouzel's nest is one of the most extraordinary pieces of bird architecture I ever saw, odd and novel in design, perfectly fresh and beautiful, and in every way worthy of the genius of the little builder. It is about a foot in diameter, round and bossy in outline, with a neatly arched opening near the bottom, somewhat like an old-fashioned brick oven, or Hottentot's hut. It is built almost exclusively of green and yellow mosses, chiefly the beautiful fronded hypnum that covers the rocks and old drift-logs in the vicinity of waterfalls. These are deftly interwoven, and felted together into a charming little hut; and so situated that many of the outer mosses continue to flourish as if they had not been plucked. A few fine, silky-stemmed grasses are occasionally found interwoven with the mosses, but, with the exception of a thin layer lining the floor, their presence seems accidental, as they are of a species found growing with the mosses and are probably plucked with them. The site chosen for this curious mansion is usually some little rock shelf within reach of the lighter particles of the spray of a waterfall, so that its walls are kept green and growing, at least during the time of high water.

No harsh lines are presented by any portion of the nest as seen in place, but when removed from its shelf, the back and bottom, and sometimes a portion of the top, is found quite sharply angular, because it is made to conform to the surface of the rock upon which and against which it is built, the little architect always taking advantage of slight crevices and protuberances that may chance to offer, to render his structure stable by means of a kind of gripping and dovetailing.

In choosing a building-spot, concealment does not seem to be taken into consideration; yet notwithstanding the nest is large and guilelessly exposed to view, it is far from being easily detected, chiefly because it swells forward like any other bulging moss cushion growing naturally in such situations. This is more especially the case where the nest is kept fresh by being well sprinkled. Sometimes these romantic little huts have their beauty enhanced by rock ferns and grasses that spring up around the mossy walls, or in front of the doorsill, dripping with crystal beads.

Furthermore, at certain hours of the day, when the sunshine is poured down at the required angle, the whole mass of the spray enveloping the fairy establishment is brilliantly irised; and it is through so glorious a rainbow atmosphere as this that some of our blessed ouzels obtain their first peep at the world.

Ouzels seem so completely part and parcel of the streams they inhabit, they scarce suggest any other origin than the streams themselves; and one might almost be pardoned in fancying they come direct from the living waters, like flowers from the ground. At least, from whatever cause, it never occurred to me to look for their nests until more than a year after I had made the acquaintance of the birds themselves, although I found one the very day on which I began the search. In making my way from Yosemite to the glaciers at the heads of the Merced and Tuolumne Rivers, I camped in a particularly wild and romantic portion of the Nevada cañon where in previous excursions I had never failed to enjoy the company of my favorites, who were attracted here, no doubt, by the safe nesting-places in the shelving rocks, and by the abundance of food and falling water. The river, for miles above and below, consists of a succession of small falls from ten to sixty feet in height, connected by flat, plume-like cascades that go flashing from fall to fall, free and almost channelless, over waving folds of glacier-polished granite.

On the south side of one of the falls, that portion of the precipice bathed by the spray presents a series of little shelves and tablets caused by the development of planes of cleavage in the granite, and by the consequent fall of masses through the action of the water. "Now, here," said I, "of all places, is the most charming spot for an ouzel's nest." Then carefully scanning the fretted face of the precipice through the spray, I at length noticed a yellowish moss cushion, growing on the edge of a level tablet within five or six feet of the outer folds of the fall. But apart from the fact of its being situated where one acquainted with the lives of ouzels would fancy an ouzel's nest ought to be, there was nothing in its appearance visible at first sight, to distinguish it from other bosses of rock-moss similarly situated with reference to perennial spray; and it was not until I had scrutinized it again and again, and had removed my shoes and stockings and crept along the face of the rock within eight or ten feet of it, that I could decide certainly whether it was a nest or a natural growth.

In these moss huts three or four eggs are laid, white like foam bubbles; and well may the little birds hatched from them sing water songs, for they hear them all their lives, and even before they are born.

I have often observed the young just out of the nest making their odd gestures, and seeming in every way as much at home as their experienced parents, like young bees on their first excursions to the flower fields. No amount of familiarity with people and their ways seems to change them in the least. To all appearance their behavior is just the same on seeing a man for the first time, as when they have seen him frequently. On the lower reaches of the rivers where mills are built, they sing on through the din of the machinery, and all the noisy confusion of dogs, cattle, and workmen. On one occasion, while a wood-chopper was at work on the river-bank, I observed one cheerily singing within reach of the flying chips. Nor does any kind of unwonted disturbance put him in bad humor, or frighten him out of calm self-possession. In passing through a narrow gorge, I once drove one ahead of me from rapid to rapid, disturbing him four times in quick succession where he could not very well fly past me on account of the narrowness of the channel. Most birds under similar circumstances fancy themselves pursued, and become suspiciously uneasy; but, instead of growing nervous about it, he made his usual dippings, and sang one of his most tranquil strains. When observed within a few yards their eyes are seen to express remarkable gentleness and intelligence; but they seldom allow so near a view unless one wears clothing of about the same color as the rocks and trees, and knows how to sit still. On one occasion, while rambling along the shore of a mountain lake, where the birds, at least those born that season, had never seen a man, I sat down to rest on a large stone close to the water's edge, upon which it seemed the ouzels and sandpipers were in the habit of alighting when they came to feed on that part of the shore, and some of the other birds also, when they came down to wash or drink. In a few minutes, along came a whirring ouzel and alighted on the stone beside me, within reach of my hand. Then suddenly observing me, he stooped nervously as if about to fly on the instant, but as I remained as motionless as the stone, he gained confidence, and looked me steadily in the face for about a minute, then flew quietly to the outlet and began to sing. Next came a sandpiper and gazed at me with much the same guileless expression of eye as the ouzel. Lastly, down with a swoop came a Steller's jay out of a fir tree, probably with the intention of moistening his noisy throat. But instead of sitting confidingly as my other visitors had done, he rushed off at once, nearly tumbling heels over head into the lake in his suspicious confusion, and with loud screams roused the neighborhood.

Love for song-birds, with their sweet human voices, appears to be more common and unfailing than love for flowers. Every one loves flowers to some extent, at least in life's fresh morning, attracted by them as instinctively as hummingbirds and bees. Even the young Digger Indians have sufficient love for the brightest of those found growing on the mountains to gather them and braid them as decorations for the hair. And I was glad to discover, through the few Indians that could be induced to talk on the subject, that they have names for the wild rose and the lily, and other conspicuous flowers, whether available as food or otherwise. Most men, however, whether savage or civilized, become apathetic toward all plants that have no other apparent use than the use of beauty. But fortunately one's first instinctive love of song-birds is never wholly obliterated, no matter what the influences upon our lives may be. I have often been delighted to see a pure, spiritual glow come into the countenances of hard business men and old miners, when a song-bird chanced to alight near them. Nevertheless, the little mouthful of meat that swells out the breasts of some song-birds is too often the cause of their death. Larks and robins in particular are brought to market in hundreds. But fortunately the ouzel has no enemy so eager to eat his little body as to follow him into the mountain solitudes. I never knew him to be chased even by hawks.

An acquaintance of mine, a sort of foothill mountaineer, had a pet cat, a great, dozy, overgrown creature, about as broad-shouldered as a lynx. During the winter, while the snow lay deep, the mountaineer sat in his lonely cabin among the pines smoking his pipe and wearing the dull time away. Tom was his sole companion, sharing his bed, and sitting beside him on a stool with much the same drowsy expression of eye as his master. The good-natured bachelor was content with his hard fare of soda bread and bacon, but Tom, the only creature in the world acknowledging dependence on him, must needs be provided with fresh meat. Accordingly he bestirred himself to contrive squirrel traps, and waded the snowy woods with his gun, making sad havoc among the few winter birds, sparing neither robin, sparrow, nor tiny nuthatch, and the pleasure of seeing Tom eat and grow fat was his great reward.

One cold afternoon, while hunting along the river-bank, he noticed a plain-feathered little bird skipping about in the shallows, and immediately raised his gun. But just then the confiding songster began to sing, and after listening to his summery melody the charmed hunter turned away, saying, "Bless your little heart, I can't shoot you, not even for Tom."

Even so far north as icy Alaska, I have found my glad singer. When I was exploring the glaciers between Mount Fairweather and the Stickeen River, one cold day in November, after trying in vain to force a way through the innumerable icebergs of Sum Dum Bay to the great glaciers at the head of it, I was weary and baffled and sat resting in my canoe convinced at last that I would have to leave this part of my work for another year. Then I began to plan my escape to open water before the young ice which was beginning to form should shut me in. While I thus lingered drifting with the bergs, in the midst of these gloomy forebodings and all the terrible glacial desolation and grandeur, I suddenly heard the well-known whir of an ouzel's wings, and, looking up, saw my little comforter coming straight across the ice from the shore. In a second or two he was with me, flying three times round my head with a happy salute, as if saying, "Cheer up, old friend; you see I'm here, and all's well." Then he flew back to the shore, alighted on the topmost jag of a stranded iceberg, and began to nod and bow as though he were on one of his favorite boulders in the midst of a sunny Sierra cascade.

The species is distributed all along the mountain-ranges of the Pacific Coast from Alaska to Mexico, and east to the Rocky Mountains. Nevertheless, it is as yet comparatively little known. Audubon and Wilson did not meet it. Swainson was, I believe, the first naturalist to describe a specimen from Mexico. Specimens were shortly afterward procured by Drummond near the sources of the Athabasca

River, between the fifty-fourth and fifty-sixth parallels; and it has been collected by nearly all of the numerous exploring expeditions undertaken of late through our Western States and Territories; for it never fails to engage the attention of naturalists in a very particular manner.

Such, then, is our little cinclus, beloved of every one who is so fortunate as to know him. Tracing on strong wing every curve of the most precipitous torrents from one extremity of the Sierra to the other; not fearing to follow them through their darkest gorges and coldest snow-tunnels; acquainted with every waterfall, echoing their divine music; and throughout the whole of their beautiful lives interpreting all that we in our unbelief call terrible in the utterances of torrents and storms, as only varied expressions of God's eternal love.

HENRY DAVID THOREAU

Concord river

Henry David Thoreau is best known for the book in which
he described his two-year sojourn in a small house
beside Walden Pond. He was also a fierce social critic,
a lecturer, and a writer of books on travel in New
England. "Concord River" is the first chapter of *A Week
on the Concord and Merrimack Rivers,* a book in which
Thoreau combines the description of his trip with his
thoughts on a great many subjects — a book which flows
as gently as the river he here describes.

THE MUSKETAQUID, or Grass-ground River, though
probably as old as the Nile or Euphrates, did not begin to
have a place in civilized history until the fame of its grassy
meadows and its fish attracted settlers out of England in
1635, when it received the other but kindred name of CON-
CORD from the first plantation on its banks, which appears
to have been commenced in a spirit of peace and harmony.
It will be Grass-ground River as long as grass grows and
water runs here; it will be Concord River only while men
lead peaceable lives on its banks. To an extinct race it was
grass-ground, where they hunted and fished; and it is still
perennial grass-ground to Concord farmers, who own the
Great Meadows, and get the hay from year to year. "One
branch of it," according to the historian of Concord, for I
love to quote so good authority, "rises in the south part of
Hopkinton, and another from a pond and a large cedar-

From *A Week on the Concord and Merrimack Rivers,* Riverside edition. Boston: Houghton Mifflin Company, 1893.

swamp in Westborough," and flowing between Hopkinton and Southborough, through Framingham, and between Sudbury and Wayland, where it is sometimes called Sudbury River, it enters Concord at the south part of the town, and after receiving the North or Assabeth River, which has its source a little farther to the north and west, goes out at the northeast angle, and flowing between Bedford and Carlisle, and through Billerica, empties into the Merrimack at Lowell. In Concord, it is in summer from four to fifteen feet deep, and from one hundred to three hundred feet wide, but in the spring freshets, when it overflows its banks, it is in some places nearly a mile wide. Between Sudbury and Wayland the meadows acquire their greatest breadth, and when covered with water, they form a handsome chain of shallow vernal lakes, resorted to by numerous gulls and ducks. Just above Sherman's Bridge, between these towns, is the largest expanse; and when the wind blows freshly in a raw March day, heaving up the surface into dark and sober billows or regular swells, skirted as it is in the distance with alder-swamps and smoke-like maples, it looks like a smaller Lake Huron, and is very pleasant and exciting for a landsman to row or sail over. The farm-houses along the Sudbury shore, which rises gently to a considerable height, command fine water prospects at this season. The shore is more flat on the Wayland side, and this town is the greatest loser by the flood. Its farmers tell me that thousands of acres are flooded now, since the dams have been erected, where they remember to have seen the white honeysuckle or clover growing once, and they could go dry with shoes only in summer. Now there is nothing but blue-joint and sedge and cut-grass there, standing in water all the year round. For a long time, they made the most of the driest season to get their hay, working sometimes till nine o'clock at night, sedulously paring with their scythes in the twilight round the hummocks left by the ice; but now it is not worth the getting when they can come at it, and they look sadly round to their wood-lots and upland as a last resource.

It is worth the while to make a voyage up this stream, if you go no farther than Sudbury, only to see how much country there is in the rear of us: great hills, and a hundred brooks, and farm-houses, and barns, and haystacks, you never saw before, and men everywhere; Sudbury, that is *Southborough* men, and Wayland, and Nine-Acre-Corner men, and Bound Rock, where four towns bound on a rock in the river, Lincoln, Wayland, Sudbury, Concord. Many waves are there agitated by the wind, keeping nature fresh, the spray blowing in your face, reeds and rushes waving; ducks by the hundred, all uneasy in the surf, in the raw wind, just ready to rise, and now going off with a clatter and a whistling like riggers straight for Labrador, flying against the stiff gale with reefed wings, or else circling round first, with all their paddles briskly moving, just over the surf, to reconnoitre you before they leave these parts; gulls wheeling overhead, muskrats swimming for dear life, wet and cold, with no fire to warm them by that you know of, their labored homes rising here and there like haystacks; and countless mice and moles and winged titmice along the sunny, windy shore; cranberries tossed on the waves and heaving up on the beach, their little red skiffs beating about among the alders;—such healthy natural tumult as proves the last day is not yet at hand. And there stand all around the alders, and birches, and oaks, and maples full of glee and sap, holding in their buds until the waters subside. You shall perhaps run aground on Cranberry Island, only some spires of last year's pipe-grass above water to show where the danger is, and get as good a freezing there as anywhere on the Northwest Coast. I never voyaged so far in all my life. You shall see men you never heard of before, whose names you don't know, going away down through the meadows with long ducking-guns, with water-tight boots wading through the fowl-meadow grass, on bleak, wintry, distant shores, with guns at half-cock; and they shall see teal, blue-winged, green-winged, shelldrakes, whistlers, black ducks, ospreys, and many other wild and noble sights before night, such as they who sit in parlors never dream of. You shall see rude and sturdy, experienced and wise men, keeping their castles, or teaming up their summer's wood, or chopping alone in the woods; men fuller of talk and rare adventure in the sun and wind and rain, than a chestnut is of meat, who were out not only in '75 and 1812, but have been out every day of their lives; greater men than Homer, or Chaucer, or Shakespeare, only they never got time to say so; they never took to the way of writing. Look at their fields, and imagine what they might write, if ever they should put pen to paper. Or what have they not written on the face of the earth already, clearing, and burning, and scratching, and harrowing, and ploughing, and subsoiling, in and in, and out and out, and over and over, again and again, erasing what they had already written for want of parchment.

As yesterday and the historical ages are past, as the work of to-day is present, so some flitting perspectives and demi-experiences of the life that is in nature are in time veritably future, or rather outside to time, perennial, young, divine, in the wind and rain which never die.

The respectable folks,—
Where dwell they?
They whisper in the oaks,
And they sigh in the hay;
Summer and winter, night and day,
Out on the meadow, there dwell they.
They never die,
Nor snivel nor cry,
Nor ask our pity
With a wet eye.
A sound estate they ever mend,
To every asker readily lend;
To the ocean wealth,
To the meadow health,
To Time his length,
To the rocks strength,
To the stars light,
To the weary night,
To the busy day,
To the idle play;
And so their good cheer never ends,
For all are their debtors, and all their friends.

Concord River is remarkable for the gentleness of its current, which is scarcely perceptible, and some have referred to its influence the proverbial moderation of the inhabitants of Concord, as exhibited in the Revolution, and on later occasions. It has been proposed that the town should adopt for its coat of arms a field verdant, with the Concord circling nine times round. I have read that a descent of an eighth of an inch in a mile is sufficient to produce a flow. Our river has, probably, very near the smallest allowance. The story is current, at any rate, though I believe that strict history will not bear it out, that the only bridge ever carried away on the main branch, within the limits of the town, was driven upstream by the wind. But wherever it makes a sudden bend it is shallower and swifter, and asserts its title to be called a river. Compared with the other tributaries of the Merrimack, it appears to have been properly named Musketaquid, or Meadow River, by the Indians. For the most part, it creeps through broad meadows, adorned with scattered oaks, where the cranberry is found in abundance, covering the ground like a moss-bed. A row of sunken dwarf willows borders the stream on one or both sides, while at a greater distance the meadow is skirted with maples, alders, and other fluviatile trees, overrun with the grape-vine, which bears fruit in its season, purple, red, white, and other grapes. Still farther from the stream, on the edge of the firm land, are seen the gray and white dwellings of the inhabitants. According to the valuation of 1831, there were in Concord two thousand one hundred and eleven acres, or about one seventh of the whole territory in meadow; this standing next in the list after pasturage and unimproved lands, and, judging from the returns of previous years, the meadow is not reclaimed so fast as the woods are cleared.

Let us here read what old Johnson says of these meadows in his "Wonder-Working Providence," which gives the account of New England from 1628 to 1652, and see how matters looked to him. He says of the Twelfth Church of Christ gathered at Concord: "This town is seated upon a fair fresh river, whose rivulets are filled with fresh marsh, and her streams with fish, it being a branch of that large river of Merrimack. Allwifes and shad in their season come up to this town, but salmon and dace cannot come up, by reason of the rocky falls, which causeth their meadows to lie much covered with water, the which these people, together with their neighbor town, have several times essayed to cut through but cannot, yet it may be turned another way with an hundred pound charge as it appeared." As to their farming he says: "Having laid out their estate upon cattle at 5 to 20 pound a cow, when they came to winter them with inland hay, and feed upon such wild fother as was never cut before, they could not hold out the winter, but, ordinarily the first or second year after their coming up to a new plantation, many of their cattle died." And this from the same author: "Of the Planting of the 19th Church in the Mattachusets' Government, called Sudbury:" "This year [does he mean 1654?] the town and church of Christ at Sudbury began to have the first foundation stones laid, taking up her station in the inland country, as her elder sister Concord had formerly done, lying further up the same river, being furnished with great plenty of fresh marsh, but, it lying very low is much indamaged with land floods, insomuch that when the summer proves wet they lose part of their hay; yet are they so sufficiently provided that they take in cattle of other towns to winter."

The sluggish artery of the Concord meadows steals thus unobserved through the town, without a murmur or a pulse-beat, its general course from southwest to northeast, and its length about fifty miles; a huge volume of matter, ceaselessly rolling through the plains and valleys of the substantial earth with the moccasined tread of an Indian warrior, making haste from the high places of the earth to its ancient reservoir. The murmurs of many a famous river on the other side of the globe reach even to us here, as to more distant dwellers on its banks; many a poet's stream, floating the helms and shields of heroes on its bosom. The Xanthus or Scamander is not a mere dry channel and bed of a mountain torrent, but fed by the ever-flowing springs of fame: —

"And thou Simois, that as an arrowe, clere
Through Troy rennest, aie downward to the sea;" —

and I trust that I may be allowed to associate our muddy but much abused Concord River with the most famous in history.

"Sure there are poets which did never dream
Upon Parnassus, nor did taste the stream
Of Helicon; we therefore may suppose
Those made not poets, but the poets those."

The Mississippi, the Ganges, and the Nile, those journeying atoms from the Rocky Mountains, the Himmaleh, and Mountains of the Moon, have a kind of personal importance in the annals of the world. The heavens are not yet drained over their sources, but the Mountains of the Moon still send their annual tribute to the Pasha without fail, as they did to the Pharaohs, though he must collect the rest of his revenue at the point of the sword. Rivers must have been the guides which conducted the footsteps of the first travelers. They are the constant lure, when they flow by our doors, to distant enterprise and adventure; and, by a natural impulse, the dwellers on their banks will at length accompany their currents to the lowlands of the globe, or explore at their invitation the interior of continents. They are the natural highways of all nations, not only leveling the ground and removing obstacles from the path of the traveler, quenching his thirst and bearing him on their bosoms, but conducting him through the most interesting scenery, the most populous portions of the globe, and where the animal and vegetable kingdoms attain their greatest perfection.

I had often stood on the banks of the Concord, watching the lapse of the current, an emblem of all progress, following the same law with the system, with time, and all that is made; the weeds at the bottom gently bending down the stream, shaken by the watery wind, still planted where their seeds had sunk, but erelong to die and go down likewise; the shining pebbles, not yet anxious to better their condition, the chips and weeds, and occasional logs and stems of trees that floated past, fulfilling their fate, were objects of singular interest to me, and at last I resolved to launch myself on its bosom and float whither it would bear me.

ROBERT C. COSBEY

Thoreau at work: the writing of "Ktaadn"

The author of the following essay is out of place
in this company. I can think of no excuse for his
presence except that he seems to have stumbled across
some interesting information about Henry David
Thoreau's method of working.

HENRY D. Thoreau has long been respected as a master
of the high art of creating sentences, but as a writer he has
often been described as skilled *only* in the construction of
sentences, not in the handling of larger units. It accords
with long-held preconceptions about Transcendentalism
that Thoreau should be thought of as catching gleams of
inspiration, working them into sparse, lucid sentences, and
then throwing the sentences into rather carelessly organized
essays and books.

But Thoreau's transcendentalism was not inconsistent
with a thoroughgoing craftsmanship, and modern scholars
have established the fact that he worked carefully and skillfully from beginning to end of the artistic process. The most
conclusive study, James Lyndon Shanley's *The Making of
Walden* (Chicago 1957), analyzes the painstaking steps by
which Thoreau's most important book was developed. It is
also interesting to observe how Thoreau wrote lesser works
than *Walden,* and it is now possible to trace several steps in

Used by permission of the *Bulletin of the New York Public Library,* Volume
65, No. 1, January 1961.

the writing of one in particular, the account of Thoreau's first adventure in the Maine woods, the essay "Ktaadn."

The story of the writing of "Ktaadn" begins with a personal experience, an excursion which Thoreau made into the Maine wilderness in September 1846. The Penobscot River had flooded in the spring of that year, doing much property damage, and a timber merchant of Bangor, George Augustus Thatcher (husband of Thoreau's cousin Rebecca), was about to go up-river to oversee the repairing of one of his dams. Apparently he invited his cousin Henry to accompany him, and cousin Henry in turn persuaded Thatcher and two other men from Bangor to push on up the river, above the dam, and climb Mount Katahdin.

Thoreau went to Bangor by train and boat, then with his cousin proceeded by horse and buggy up the Penobscot for two days to Mattawamkeag, where they joined the others. They all hiked for a day and a half through the woods to the farthest log cabin, and there engaged two men as guides and boatsmen. They traversed rivers and lakes for two days in a bateau, Thoreau observing with great interest the boatsmen in action. Next they ascended Mount Katahdin, Thoreau taking charge here as the most experienced mountain climber of the group. Finally, they returned by bateau and buggy to Bangor, and thence Thoreau returned to Concord and Walden Pond, having been absent from his Walden cabin just ten days.

During the excursion, he took the first step in recording his experience, entering in a slim notebook, day by day, observations about each day's activities. (The book was his current journal; it also contains entries on other subjects, made at Walden before and after the trip to Maine. Still unpublished, the journal is housed in the Berg Collection of The New York Public Library.)

His daily notes are for the most part simply lists of what he did and saw, forming the starkest kind of narrative. For example, among the notes for September 5th is this passage:

. . . then 4 miles in North Twin—by moon light S twin inlet   laughing loon. lighthouse island—distant shores. Ghostly trees mountain waste—pausing to hear wolves & see moose   hear hooting owls—

alternate roaring—rock camp at head of N Twin at 20 to 9 o'clock—
probably a dozen moose looking on.

After the Maine excursion, back at his cabin on Walden
Pond, he began expanding these notes, still working in the
same notebook. Since there are other entries following this,
on other subjects, one of which is dated December 2, it is
clear that he worked on the expansion at Walden in the fall
of 1846.

This first draft of his essay reveals a fact which is eloquent
of his method. Although there is quite enough of a straight-
forward narration of the excursion to justify calling this a
first draft of his essay, it does not start at the beginning. On
pages 78 to 84 of the notebook, following the daily notes, is
the expanded account of one part of the bateau trip, the
crossing of North Twin Lake. Following that, on pages 85
and 86, is a description of a false sunrise on the boat from
Boston to Portland. On page 87 begins his account of the
trip upriver from Bangor, which then continues in a chronological account to the end of the excursion. It is as if he
did not know, at this point, where his essay should begin.
(His daily notes had begun with details of the train trip to
Boston from Concord.) Another impression is that he has
not yet settled on the proper tone or style of his narration,
and is experimentally writing up various sections to catch a
fitting tone, before settling into the narration of the whole.

Another aspect of the first draft, obvious at a glance,
would rid anyone of the notion that Thoreau wrote easily or
intuitively. There is hardly a sentence of the whole draft in
which he has not made deletions, insertions, inversions of
order, or substitutions, and in many places he has added
fairly long passages in the margins or between the lines (not
always clearly indicating their proper position in the essay).

The first draft is for the most part an expansion of the
daily notes. For example, the passage from the September
5th notes is rendered thus:

The loon laughed and dived as we held our way—the fir and spruce
and cedar, occasionally hanging with moss, stood like the ghosts of
trees on the distant shore—We sang, at least with enthusiasm such

boat songs as we could remember—and listened to hear if any wolf responded—aware that we had perchance disturbed many a deer or moose quietly feeding on the shore—and even then [*two words un-decipherable*]—but we heard only the hooting of owls. On entering the lake, we steered for a little dot of an island hardly visible in the dark— where we amused ourselves with planning where the light house should be—and how we should like to live and be the light-house man. At length we drew up our batteau upon a smooth white sandy shore at the head of the lake—gliding in between some large dark rocks and proceeded to make our camp.

If we were to number consecutively the items listed in the selection from the daily notes, they would now appear in this order: 1, 4, 3, 6, 13, 8, 2, 10. Item 2 has been greatly expanded, items 5, 7, 9, 11, and 12 left out, and a detail about singing added after item 3. The impression, so far, is that the order has been changed to make the notes into a smooth, graceful narration of the experience.

The first draft is, as has been noted, a work draft; Thoreau made many corrections in it. In this passage, for instance, he added *grey* before *moss,* deleted *at least,* changed *perchance* to *perhaps,* and added *future* before *light house,* and *there* after *to live.* Then, with sweeping lines, he crossed out the whole last part of the passage, from *On entering the lake* to the end.

There are many such deletions of whole passages in the first draft, and many places where he breaks a train of thought, even in the middle of a sentence, and starts again. There are several places where he digresses into generali-ties not related to the events, suspending the narration; for example, on page 175, he interrupts an account of poling in rapids to exclaim, "Think what a mean and wretched place this world is—that half the time we have to light a lamp that we may see to live in it," and on page 196 he interrupts the account of climbing Mount Katahdin to speculate on the nature of fables and myths.

The implication is strong that Thoreau has not yet found a unifying theme or central concept which would give him a strict principle of selection and a clear tone; he seems to be groping for that unifying theme, as a composer of music or a painter might grope for the central simplifying concept around which all will fall into place.

When we compare the first draft to the first published version, we note that the writer did find such a theme, and did organize everything around it (perhaps working in one or more drafts which we do not have, between the first draft and the published version). The theme around which everything falls into order is the idea of wilderness.

A number of details in the passage under consideration show how this theme guided Thoreau. In the first published version (which appeared in the *Union Magazine* in 1848), the passage runs thus:

While Uncle George steered for a small island near the head of the lake, now just visible, like a speck on the water, we rowed by turns swiftly over its surface, singing such boat-songs as we could remember. The shores seemed at an indefinite distance in the moonlight. Occasionally we paused in our singing and rested on our oars, while we listened to hear if the wolves howled, for this is a common serenade, and my companions affirmed that it was the most dismal and unearthly of sounds; but we heard none this time. If we did not *hear,* however, we did *listen,* not without a reasonable expectation; that at least I have to tell,—only some utterly uncivilized, big-throated owl hooted loud and dismally in the drear and boughy wilderness, plainly not nervous about his solitary life, nor afraid to hear the echoes of his voice there. We remembered also that possibly moose were silently watching us from the distant coves, or some surly bear or timid red deer or caribou had been startled by our singing. It was with new emphasis that we sang there the Canadian boat-song,—

"Row, brothers, row, the stream runs fast,
The Rapids are near and the daylight's past!"
which described precisely our own adventure, and was inspired by the description of exactly this kind of life,—for the rapids were ever near, and the daylight long past; the woods on shore looked dim, and many an Utawas' tide here emptied into the lake.

"Why should we yet our sail unfurl?
There is not a breath the blue wave to curl!
But, when the wind blows off the shore,
Oh, sweetly we'll rest our laboring oar."
"Utawas' tide! this trembling moon

Shall see us float o'er thy surges soon."

At last we glided past the "green isle," which had been our landmark, all joining in the chorus; as if by the watery links of rivers and
of lakes we were about to float over unmeasured zones of earth,
bound on unimaginable adventures,—

"Saint of this green isle! hear our prayers,
Oh, grant us cool days and favoring airs!"

About nine o'clock we reached the river, and ran our boat into a
natural haven between some rocks, and drew her out on the sand.

If, again, we number the items in the first passage, from
the daily notes, they now run 2, 3, 6, 8, 13, 12, 10, with
passages about songs added after 3 and 13. The order has
been shuffled again, in short, and the passage in that sense
re-worked. But much more important changes have been
made. Although this passage is longer than the corresponding passage in the first draft, the material from the first
draft has actually been condensed and stated more concisely. The passage has been expanded by several additions
which stress the wildness of the setting. The wolves no
longer *respond,* but *howl,* and an added clause describes their
dismal sound. *The hooting of owls* becomes a clause about the
big-throated owl, uncivilized but unafraid, at home in the
wilderness. Not only moose may be watching, but bears,
deer, and caribou.

Above all, the changes in statements not about wild nature, but about civilized humans, show what is happening.
At first, the island which acts as a landmark suggests that in
time a light-house will be needed there, and a keeper of the
light—thoughts of the beginnings of civilization in that
area. This idea is completely suppressed, and the island is
left only as a wild landmark. Instead of the light-house
keeper, the rivermen take the stage. Their songs are fit for
the wild setting, songs such as the *voyageurs* had sung along
far-flung wilderness rivers.

In the same way, Thoreau suppresses other passages from
his notes and his first draft, which are interesting in themselves but do not fit his theme. He does not use his note
about the sailors he saw in the Boston station, who had run
out of money, nor a whole section of the first draft about the

boat trip to Portland, nor a passage about a Negro foreman in charge of a group of white loggers, nor a humorous passage about a tin-ware peddler, nor the description of an amusement-park device operated by a Canadian, which swung his customers in a sixty-foot vertical circle. None of these had a place in an essay the central idea of which was *wilderness*.

Into the account, on the other hand, go interesting additions: descriptions of debased human types on the edge of civilization, such as the Indians near Oldtown, and the politicians at Passadumkeag; a description of a sawmill devouring the wilderness; one of a bateau factory, making boats for wilderness rivers. He added a description of a typical frontier log cabin home, and one of a typical logging camp, also descriptions of the rivermen and their lives in the wilderness.

He deleted a digression about the nature of fable and myth, but added passages describing the feelings of a civilized man confronted with savage nature on Katahdin. He deleted a conclusion in which he quoted Thomas Heywood to excuse the informality of his personal references, replacing it with a conclusion summarizing the wilderness experience.

The theme of wilderness thus helped Thoreau give his essay point and unity. In keeping with this, he emphasized the drama of the quick dash into the wilderness and out again, building on the suspense of the approach to the wilderness mountain and the ascent. While his reader could be counted on to be held by the suspense, he inserted skillfully into his account all the generalized and typical descriptions; then, after describing the climactic ascent of Katahdin, he closed quickly, leaving out many details of the return trip which he had recorded in the notes and in the first draft, coming quickly, since the most dramatic part of the trip was over, to his conclusion.

There are other changes in the first published version, most of them stylistic, but some suppressions of personal details (such as the comment that the guide McCauslin was hired out by his wife). But the striking change from the first draft to the first published version is the achievement of a simple, dramatic, unified narrative and a fitting, consistent tone. What may seem an unstudied simplicity in the published version is, in short, a deliberately and painstakingly achieved simplicity.

Thoreau's account is drawn almost entirely from his own personal experience. There were books in print which would have told him about the area, and especially about the mountain he went to climb, but contrary to his usual practice he had not read any of them before making this trip. The first indication that he has been reading is in a note inserted into the first draft, in a different ink, giving the height of Katahdin "according to J." This is a reference to Charles Thomas Jackson, state geologist of Maine, who had climbed Katahdin in 1837. Since this first note from Jackson's book appears in the first draft, he may have been reading it in the fall of 1846, after his excursion, but the different ink suggests a still later date.

The use Thoreau makes of Jackson's book is slight. He derives from him statistics about the number of sawmills on the Penobscot, and the number of Indians in the tribe near Oldtown. He quotes him on the altitude of Katahdin, alludes to his route up the mountain, and notes that neither Jackson nor the preceding climber Jacob Whitman Bailey obtained a clear view from the top. He quotes from Jackson the report of Jackson's assistant, James T. Hodge, about the upper river and the route to Canada. Besides mentioning some ascents of Katahdin which had preceded his own, this is all the use Thoreau made of source books in the first published version of "Ktaadn" — just enough to fill in a few details he could not get at first hand.

Although the essay "Ktaadn" was thus published in 1848, Thoreau was still not finished with it. He made several changes between this and the final version which appeared in the posthumous book *The Maine Woods* (Boston 1864). Some of the changes are stylistic, such as the deletion of many adverbs, the clarifying of descriptive or expository passages, and more precise statement of his meaning in various passages. Some of the changes corrected typographical errors of compositors working from Thoreau's manuscript. Some reflected his further reading about the Maine woods.

His continued interest in the subject after the excursion of 1846 is shown in a letter written in October 1847 to his sister Sophia, then visiting the Thatchers in Bangor. He thanks her for sending newspaper clippings about an ascent of Katahdin, and adds "I . . . hope you will save and send me the rest, and anything else you may meet with relating to the Maine woods." In 1848, as the sections of the essay appeared in the magazine, he sent copies to cousin George Thatcher in Bangor.

His Bangor relatives may have suggested some changes in statements of fact which appear in the final version. For instance, the weight of an average bateau, which Thoreau gave in the first published version as 500 to 800 pounds, he scaled down to 300 to 600 pounds (which makes a difference, as two men carried the bateau over the rough portages). The weight of a good-sized moose he likewise scaled down, from 1200 pounds to 1000. He first said that a bateau would wear out in two years, but now adds, "or often in a single trip." The first version identifies the Indians' "no-see-'ems" as black flies; the revised version as midges.

Two small but significant changes involve Thoreau's second thoughts about Indians. He had been quite disappointed by the Indians he met on this trip, saying that they "looked like the sinister and slouching fellows whom you meet picking up strings and paper in the streets of a city," and adding, "There is, in fact, a remarkable and unexpected resemblance between the degraded savage and the lowest classes in a great city." On later trips to Maine, he came to know some unspoiled Indians, whom he liked and respected. He did not, even then, go back and delete his disparaging remarks, but he did soften the blow a little.

In his first published version, he had said that as guides the Indians were "less to be relied on" than whites; in the final version, he adds, "for the most part." In the first version, commenting on the white guides they finally hired, he had said, "We were lucky to have exchanged our Indians for these men"; in the final version he makes it clear that he was not thinking of racial distinctions only, by adding after the word *Indians* the clause "whom we did not know." (The white guides *were* known to members of his group.)

In the years after the first publication of "Ktaadn," Thoreau was still adding to his essay details gathered from his reading, and though the additions are not great in total amount, they help emphasize the idea of wilderness. In 1849, he received from Bangor a newspaper clipping about the death of a logger; this became a footnote in the final version, supporting his point about the dangers of the logger's job.

In 1851 was published John S. Springer's *Forest Life and Forest Trees*. The author had been a lumberjack; he wrote with authority, and Thoreau used him to back up some of his own statements. He added to his essay a footnote quoting Springer on the construction of a lumber camp; one on the curved surface of a rising river, which throws logs off to the side; and one on how timber cruisers climb trees to look for pines. He also derived from Springer a footnote about bears destroying bateaux, though he does not attribute it to him. He also uses a list of various specialized jobs, and probably from the same source a list of the tools used by loggers.

(Thoreau does not, it is interesting to note, take over the other man's attitude towards the wilderness, which in Springer's view is savage and terrible, the scene of bloody accidents, awful suffering, and fierce attacks on loggers by wild beasts. In "Ktaadn" the wilderness is stern and sometimes frightening, but beautiful.)

Another book Thoreau used at some time after his trip to Maine is François André Michaux' *The North American Sylva*. (He read one of the English editions, of which there had been several since the first in 1819.) From it he drew a fairly long passage about lumbering on the Kennebec.

Also, he added to the essay two observations from the *Jesuit Relations,* which he read in French. (The English edition did not appear until after his death.) The first seems to be a Thoreauvian pun, in which he applies a phrase about the abundance of rocks in rivers, to rock-filled piers protecting a dam. The second is a quotation about the abundance of fish, noting that the French explorers, like Thoreau and his companions, first confidently put the pan on to heat, and then started fishing.

In sum, Thoreau's method in the writing of "Ktaadn" can be clearly seen. Starting with an account of his personal experience and observations, he discovers, in the process of writing, a tone and a unifying theme, and he then re-works almost every detail of the structure in keeping with that tone and that theme. Even after the first publication, he is still revising for clarity and force, and still adding details which emphasize the theme. In this process, we cannot possibly distinguish skill in constructing sentences from skill in organizing the essay. The sentences work for the specific tone and theme, and could not be finished in themselves, apart from the theme which orders the whole.

It is interesting that Thoreau wrote "Ktaadn" in the same year in which he finished *A Week on the Concord and Merrimack Rivers,* for in that book the account of a somewhat similar personal experience is told *not* simply and dramatically as in "Ktaadn," but with many golden digressions. The difference in structure suggests that at critical points in the construction of the two works he felt quite different purposes, and decided on quite different themes. One difference is that while writing "Ktaadn" he addressed himself more to his contemporaries; it is timely in a sense in which *A Week* is not. For instance, in "Ktaadn" he gives the names of specific frontier families whom his readers will find hospitable, in case they should pass along the same route themselves.

In each of his separate works, apparently—certainly in those the writing of which has been examined in detail, and presumably in the rest as well—Thoreau constructed a whole artistic unit. Like most artists, he started with a working of his materials, discovered during this working of materials a life-giving unifying purpose or concept, and shaped the whole work to that. Certainly this organic method of creating a literary work is the method he followed in the writing of "Ktaadn."